THE PATH TO FREEDOM

STARTING A BUSINESS FOR THE RELUCTANT
ENTREPRENEUR

STEPHEN HAUNTS

Copyright © 2021 by Stephen Haunts

All rights reserved. No part of this book may be reproduced or used in any manner without written permission of the copyright owner except for the use of quotations in a book review. For more information, address: stephen.haunts@hey.com

First paperback edition May 2021
First ebook edition May 2021

Edited by Mandy J Crook
SeeMeAfter Editing and Proofreading Services
www.seemeafter.com

ISBN 978-1-9169067-0-9 (paperback)
ISBN 978-1-9169067-1-6 (ebook)

www.thepathtofreedombook.com

CONTENTS

Visit us at YouTube — vii
Side Hustle Success Podcast — ix
About This Book — xi
The Author's Story — xix

1. The Problem with Working for Someone Else — 1
2. Starting Out with a Side-Hustle — 21
3. Setting an Income Strategy — 41
4. Preparing to Dive In — 58
5. When Not to Go Self-Employed — 68
6. What Does Success Look Like for You? — 82
7. Keeping an Eye on Costs — 96
8. The Dangers of Building a Product While Still Employed — 106
9. What to Charge for Products or Services? — 121
10. Working with a Co-founder — 133
11. Product-Launching Strategies — 152
12. The Working Environment — 177
13. Being a Digital Nomad and Location-Independent Worker — 195
14. Getting Support from a Mastermind Group or a Mentor — 214
15. Staying Mentally and Physically Fit — 230
16. Beating Procrastination and Staying Focused — 243
17. The Benefits of Staying Small as an Entrepreneur — 263
18. Hiring Employees vs Freelancers — 276
19. Product Branding — 295
20. Personal Branding — 315
21. Marketing Basics — 335
22. Email Marketing — 363
23. Search Engine Optimisation and Content Marketing — 379

Final Thoughts	393
Visit us at YouTube	397
Side Hustle Success Podcast	399
Thank You!	401

This book is dedicated to my wife Amanda, and my children, Amy and Daniel.

VISIT US AT YOUTUBE

If you like the contents of this book, then please visit me over at YouTube where I talk about running small businesses and give updates on my own business.

http://bit.ly/PathToFreedomBook

SIDE HUSTLE SUCCESS PODCAST

Alongside this book, I also run a podcast called the Side Hustle Success Podcast, where I talk about various aspects of running small businesses.

The show is available on most podcast platforms such as iTunes, Spotify, Stitcher and many more.

https://www.sidehustlesuccesspodcast.com

ABOUT THIS BOOK

Some people are born to start up and run businesses. These people have a great idea one day, and then in a short space of time, they have an office and a team of people working to execute that idea. The idea of being worried about the risk of failure never seems to occur to these people. If for any reason, these businesses fail, they dust themselves down and immediately start thinking about their next venture. I have a friend called Steve who is like this. I always found it very impressive that the risk of failure never seemed to faze him.

Other people, and I include myself in this number, like the idea of running a business, but ultimately are terrified of the prospect of getting started, and even more scared of the risk of failure. I have spoken to many people over the years about business, and I have found that people who like the idea of starting a business but are apprehensive about making a move far outnumber people who, like my friend Steve, can jump headfirst into starting a small company. We all have our reasons for being worried about making a start; I will talk about mine in some detail in the next section of this book. Still, I have found that the main reasons for being reluctant about starting a business can be summarised into the following concerns.

You are worried about the state of the economy. The state of the economy in your home country can be a source of worry. Living through a recession can, quite rightly, make you think that there is never a good time to start a business. However, economic downturns can work to your advantage. Suppose you are considering starting up as a creative professional freelancer. As companies scale back with expensive full-time staff, more work tends to be outsourced as the overall cost of getting the job completed by a freelancer is much lower than the overhead of a full-time employee.

It is quite common for companies to use their full-time staff to work on the company's core product and then outsource all other work that relates to that product to freelancers. Because of this, freelancers can do well in an economic downturn. The transaction of working with a freelancer is incredibly easy for a company. They pitch the work; you agree a price. They pay 50% upfront, you do the work, and they settle the bill. There is no income tax for them to worry about, no pension contributions, no overtime, no healthcare plans or company cars to deal with. They pay for the work they want done, and that is the end of the transaction.

I believe now that a recession or fragile economy is nothing to be feared. At the time of writing this book, we have had to deal with a year of COVID-19 lockdowns, and the resultant economic disruption. The state of the world's economies was something that initially worried me. Still, as I work in a market sector that doesn't focus on people being physically in the same room, from a business point of view the year turned out okay. Don't let the economy drive your decisions too much. The state of an economy can be just as much an opportunity as a risk.

You are worried about uncertainty in the future. As well as worrying about the economy, it is also common to be concerned about your immediate future. With a full-time job on a salary, you have the safety net of a predictable income and benefits, which makes us feel safe and secure. I enjoyed that safety net for many years. But that supposed safety can lead to inaction when it comes to starting a business. Why risk a good, secure salary and benefits for a venture that may never bear an income to support you? Who needs that stress, right? If you are reluctant to start a business and are risk-averse by nature, it would be almost impossible for anyone to tell you any different. When you read my story in the next section, you will see that it would have been very difficult to change my mind.

However, starting a business does not have to be an all-or-nothing venture. There are no rules specifying that when you have an idea, you have to give up everything that makes you safe and secure to pursue that idea. We sometimes get blinded by the whole Silicon Valley expectation that starting a business means you need HUGE amounts of funding and personal risk to make your vision a reality, but that is not the case. A lot of people start a business as a side venture, or a side-hustle, to use the fashionable term. With a side-hustle, you work on an idea for a business as a side-line while remaining employed. If the idea takes hold, you always have the option of taking it full time in the future, but there are no written rules on when, or even if, you should.

You are worried about feeling like an imposter. Whenever you have an idea or work on those ideas, it is common to feel like an imposter compared to everyone else; primarily through the lens of social media where everyone comes across as perfect. By continuously comparing ourselves to other people, it is easy to start thinking that you are not good enough, or that you are going to be found out as a fraud. This feeling is known as imposter syndrome, and it is quite common, especially for people who are considering setting up a business. Imposter syndrome is something that can start as a little thought, and if left unresolved, it can build up to be very debilitating to moving forward with an idea.

The best way to beat imposter syndrome is to recognise the issue and train your brain to accept your part in it and take credit for your own past successes. Remind yourself that failing or making mistakes isn't the end of the world, but an opportunity that shows you how to do better on your next attempt. Sit down and think about your idea and write down all the reasons that you think you're not good enough or a fraud, then go over the list objectively and counter those reasons with reality; separate your feelings from the facts. Be aware of negative self-talk and when you catch yourself doing it, rewrite the narrative to frame the thought positively or even objectively. Accepting that you are just as deserving of success as anyone else is the first step to getting started on your business and turning your idea for a product or service into your next success.

You are worried about personal and business debt. Another debilitating issue that stops people starting a business is worrying about debt. You may have a lot of personal debt, and you feel that you need to maintain your day job and the security that it brings to cover your debt payments. I can certainly empathise with this concern, but there is no rule that you must resign from your current position and work on starting your business full time. You can quite quickly build a business on the side while still doing the nine-to-five job.

Depending on what type of business you are running, you might need different levels of funding to get yourself started. If financial debt is a worry that is putting you off, you don't need to take any forms of credit to get started. If you are building an information project, phone app, course or anything else that you can do with your computer, then the largest investment you are likely to need is your time. You can take as little or as much time as you need to get started when you build the business on the side. Suppose you are making a physical product that you sell, such as jewellery. In that case, you can start small and run with reduced inventory to begin with, and direct any profits from sales back into increasing the materials you can purchase.

Having already high levels of personal debt doesn't have to be something that stops you from realising your dream of starting a business. If you don't want to borrow any money to get started, then that is fine. All it means is that you will begin at a smaller and slower pace to get your fledgling business off the ground, and that is ok. Take all the time that you need and start small while focusing on reducing your debts via your day job.

You are worried about existing company benefits. At some point, when creating a small business, you may decide to take your venture full time and resign from your job. If and when that happens, you are not only giving up a salary; you could also be walking away from some attractive company benefits, like a pension scheme, or personal or family healthcare plans. If those plans are generous, it can be hard to justify walking away from them. When deciding to leave my full-time job and start working for myself, this was also something that I had to consider.

Having pre-existing company benefits should not be something that stops you in your tracks when planning to eventually take your business full time; you simply need to plan how you will fill the gap from losing these benefits. Of course, if you love your full-time job and want to keep your business as a side-hustle, that is fine—and makes the decision about company benefits even easier to decide on. Still, chances are good that you may want to go full time eventually if you can make a success of the business part time.

I had a similar dilemma, but I wasn't prepared to leave my job until I had saved up a financial runway and was earning a set amount per month, which I will talk about more in a moment. The decision was easier for me because the company I left to go and work for myself was a reasonably small start-up in its own right, so they hadn't yet set up a pension or healthcare plan for their staff. My wife had a pretty comprehensive family healthcare plan through her employer, so we were already covered for medical insurance. This made the decision more comfortable for me, as working for a reasonably small start-up, I was already used to the drop in benefits. I eventually did set up pension payments through my own company, but certainly not for at least a year; I wanted to get used to running the company before organising my pension.

You are worried about family obligations. Following on from some of the worries listed earlier—if you have a partner and/or children who are all dependent on your income, this can also be a source of worry when it comes to starting a business. As I have stated, though, there are no rules that you have to start a business and work on it full time straight away. Starting something slowly, or even classing it as a hobby, are equally valid choices. By starting slow, you let the business grow at the rate you choose, and you don't have to make any risky decisions early on that could affect your ability to provide for the other people in your life.

You are worried about the fear of failure. The final worry to mention, and the one that affected me the most, is a fear of failure. What happens if you build what you believe is the greatest product on the market, but no-one wants to buy it? What does this say about you as a person? This is a pervasive fear when doing anything new, no matter if it is starting a business, or tackling new skills in the workplace. We all have an inbuilt worry about what will happen if we fail. I will talk about my own fear of failure in the next section, as this was what I found quite debilitating for many years. Looking back on this, I can see I was worrying unnecessarily, but that doesn't make the fear go away. When thinking of starting a business, fear of failure is very common. If you tread carefully, manage your risk tolerance, and take small steps to succeed, you can hopefully alleviate that fear, as you start to have many small successes leading up to a larger win.

As you read this book, I want you to keep your appetite for risk in your mind. Everything I discuss in this book can work for you either as a side-hustle, where you build a business while still employed, or if you jump straight in and start your business full time. The amount of risk you choose to accept, and your decision whether or not to operate as a side-hustle for some time, is your decision and yours alone. What I can say, though, is that no matter what route you take, running a small business can be incredibly rewarding. However, I also understand that you may be scared about doing so. I know this because I was in that exact position. I was terrified of working for myself. I genuinely didn't know if I could do it.

My aim with this book is to help you think through the process of running a business and, I hope, help you weigh up the risks versus the possible rewards. At the time of me completing the writing of this book, we are in the second year of the COVID-19 pandemic. The economies across the world look very different from the time I started writing this book to the time I completed it. A large part of the world is in an economic recession, and many companies have collapsed, creating a massive surge in unemployment. You may be thinking that now is not a good time to start a business, but I urge you to work through this book and complete the workshop questions to help you rationalise your decision. Recessions can be a good time to start a business, especially if you are offering a service that is valuable to companies.

Recruiting and having full-time staff is a considerable expense for organisations, and during a global recession such as the one we're currently experiencing, many companies are having to downsize. They may be keeping their core product development in-house, but there could be many pieces of work for which they can't justify the overhead of keeping full-time staff. Graphic design is a good example of this. Being a freelancer or consultancy business could work in your favour, as this is a much more cost-effective way for companies to get work done without having to pay for a full-time member of staff. So, just because we are in a recession, don't think that you can't create a business.

This book isn't designed to be the only business book you will ever need. No book can claim that. My purpose in writing this book is to help you decide if starting and running a small business is right for you. I do this by demystifying a lot of the process and sharing what I have learnt myself through my own experiences, so that you have everything out in front of you when considering your plan.

Each chapter has a series of workshop questions at the end. These questions are not to test how much you remember, but to give you a series of exercises you can go through to help you decide and plan for the future. You can either do all the exercises as you go, or you can read the book first and then go back to complete them. I do urge you to work through the workshop questions, as they are designed to guide you through the thought process about what your business aims to create, and how you wish to run that business. A lot of these workshop questions replicate the thought process I went through myself to help alleviate my own fears of starting a business. You don't need any fancy equipment or software to complete these questions; all you need is a pen and paper.

I also want to say a big thank you for buying this book. If you are reluctant to start a business for any reason, I am very grateful for your trust in me to help you through this process. Running a business can be a lot of fun and very rewarding, and I hope I can help you succeed.

THE AUTHOR'S STORY

For most of my adult life, I have been scared of the prospect of starting a business. I look at some of my friends who run companies and have always been in awe of their ability to cope with the responsibility and the risk—especially those who were more than willing to take on a lot of personal debt to pay staff and bills when times were lean. I thought they were crazy, but I greatly admired the guts it took to do it.

My fear stemmed from when I was a teenager. At school, me and my friend Chris were obsessed with making computer games. I was the programmer, and Chris was the artist and animator. We had been making many game demos, trying to get publishers interested in publishing the games. We created a new demo for a game called *Terraformer*, which we developed for the Amiga 1200 home computer. The game was a cross between a graphic adventure and a real-time strategy game like "Command and Conquer", where you build up bases on planets to defend from hostile aliens. When you created your base on the planet's surface, you could click on the buildings with the mouse and enter the building, then walk around and interact with other people. This unlocked a story-based puzzle-solving element to the game.

We showed the game to one publisher and they loved it; they offered us—just a couple of teenagers—a contract to produce the game.

We thought we had struck the big time. We had "made it". Looking back, of course, we were young and naive, but what do you know when you are that age? I thought we would release the game, earn lots of money, build a studio, hire a team, and make more games.

We were two-thirds of the way through the production of the game; we had left school, and we were both at college. Our parents had convinced us that we should keep our education going. In hindsight, this was wise, as the company who manufactured the computer we were developing for, Commodore, went bust in 1994. Unfortunately, I didn't have the skills to build for any other platform at that time, I only knew how to make games for the Commodore Amiga line of computers, and that was a big problem. Because Commodore went bust, the publisher pulled the plug on any projects that were not almost complete. That meant us.

In the blink of an eye, it was all over. We were crushed; even grief-stricken. We went from a project that could have shaped the rest of our lives to nothing. I had been so sure this would work that I wasn't even planning on going to university; I now found myself applying to go. This single event was probably one of the most devastating things that had ever happened to me.

It was this one experience that gave me a fear of running a business. I never wanted to be in this situation again, where something that I loved could suddenly fail and be taken away from me due to events beyond my control. My dominant fear through the following years was a fear of failure.

In all honesty, I was too young and innocent to grapple with what was happening and deal with it in a mature manner. I was a teenage geek trying to make computer games with my best friend. What I needed was for someone to say to me, "It's ok, these things happen. Dust yourself off and try again later." I didn't have anyone tell me that, so I let this failure brew inside me over the years.

I went to university, and on my placement year, I got a position with a games company called Argonaut Software, beating a lot of competition for the role. I finished my placement year and had a fantastic time, but by the time I got to the final year of university, the courses I wanted to study were cancelled due to lack of subscription, so all that was left were business modules. I wasn't interested in these at the time, so instead I accepted an offer from my placement company to go full time and pulled out of university.

Even though the game I was making with Chris had failed years before, in the end, it did help me get an excellent job in the games industry. I spent many years making games and having a fantastic time, but my initial failure still scarred me; or more to the point, my immaturity prevented me from dealing with it properly. For now, I was happy being an employee, and I had no intention of ever trying to work for myself. The thought of it made me feel sick.

I worked in London for three years and then moved up to Derby, a city in the middle of England, for another games company. I met my future wife, and eventually settled down. In 2005, I left the games industry because of all the crazy work hours and got a job at an online bank as a software developer. It was this change of industry that started a sequence of events that over the next few years would lead to what I am currently doing for a living—and to the writing of this book.

When I was a child, I used to play a lot of music. I had lessons every week, learning to play the piano and the electric organ. Apart from making computer games, electronic music was another passion of mine, but it was purely something I did as a hobby. While working for the online bank, I rekindled my love for music production and started making music and sound libraries. These consisted of DVD libraries of sounds that I created that could be sold to other musicians to use as samples in their music productions.

I enjoyed making sound libraries with some quite whacky noises. One technique I particularly enjoyed was circuit bending, where you take old children's electronic toys, and rewire the insides. This, in turn, made the sounds entirely new and extraordinary. I would then record these and manipulate them on the computer to create even stranger sounds. My first library of these peculiar noises was called Electronic Critters. Initially, I just made this for fun, as I was using some of the sounds on my music compositions. After talking about these libraries on some electronic music online forums, an online retailer contacted me about listing my libraries with them, and I began making a small amount of money from my hobby.

After a few years, this hobby of mine was earning up to £18,000 per year, so I spoke to my accountant who had been sorting out my tax liabilities, and he suggested I form a limited liability (LTD) business. I was initially horrified at the prospect, but he explained the whole process to me and provided I kept good accounts through the year, it was not that complicated. He suggested that keeping the business money away from personal finances was a good idea, especially as I was selling goods over the internet. I went through the legal process to form a small company where I was the sole shareholder, and it was not as bad as I feared; I now had a side-hustle business, although I had never heard the term "side-hustle" before.

I was running a small business that earned a small amount of money, yet I was still employed full time, making a good salary with good benefits. The amount of time I spent on my business could be easily adapted to fit in with my life; this whole process was starting to resolve my fear of running a business. I had found a way to run it, while still under the comfort blanket of a full-time job, and with low risk.

After the birth of my first child, Amy, the music production and sound design took a bit of a back seat, due to the increased noise and tiredness levels. I focused on trying to do my day job well while tired from being up during the night with a baby and realised that even though I wasn't actively working on this project, it was still earning passive income. This was my first experience with the idea of passive income, although I wasn't familiar with the term at the time. The idea that you could make something and then continue to earn recurring revenue from it was very appealing. Up to that point, I had only known about earning a salary, which is selling your time for money. Now I knew about the alternative, my interest was piqued.

My full-time career was going well. I had moved companies a few times and had worked my way up the ranks, taking on leadership positions. My job was going well, and I still enjoyed what I was doing.

In 2014, I was approached by a training company called Pluralsight about building courses for their platform, which can be described as "Netflix for software development and professional development training". An individual or company can take out subscriptions for their team. Then the subscriber has access to the entire training platform, much like with Netflix, where you pay a subscription fee and can then watch whatever you want. I released my first course towards the end of 2014, which was a course about software developers transitioning into management. The course was called 'Developer to Manager'. The whole process of constructing a course was a tremendous amount of work, as it was like scripting and recording a documentary. It was very time-consuming as a project to work on in the evenings, but on the release of my first course, I could see its potential. While the amount of money generated from one course was relatively small, it was easy to see the potential growth as I created more courses.

I discussed this opportunity with my wife, as it took a lot of personal time in the evenings to make the courses, and we both agreed that it was a worthy investment, so I promptly signed up to create my second course, then the third, then the fourth, and so on. I worked on courses like this for three years, developing content in my spare time. It was exhausting, but I saw a notable financial return for all this hard work. I started to consider if this was something that I could do full time.

I was still very nervous about the whole idea of working for myself, but I was not as scared of the idea as I had been when I was younger. I now had the benefit of maturity and experience on my side, which I didn't have at sixteen. I was at a point where my little side venture creating training courses was earning me roughly two-thirds of what I was making in my full-time job. I started the conversation with my wife about what to do. On the one hand, I was earning great money as a software development leader, and a great side income from creating courses. Still, the amount of work it took to make these courses was massive, and I didn't relish the idea of effectively working two careers for too long. Staying employed with this side income was the easy option, but it didn't feel sustainable. The other option was to trust the level of growth I was seeing in the financial return from the courses and leave my full-time job. This effectively meant I was buying back my time. However, I would be temporarily at an economic disadvantage, as I would be dropping a decent and reliable salary and paying myself from the course earnings. This was the risky option.

Making a move to working on my courses full time worried both my wife and I, as we are both quite risk averse. Financially, we were doing well as a family. We had no debts apart from our mortgage, as we had cleared all our debt from our younger days by making a conscious effort to be more financially savvy and reduce unnecessary spending.

The thought of giving up a good salary was terrifying, though. It felt like a comfort blanket protecting us. In the end, we came up with a plan. I would carry on working full time and making the courses, but I would save as much money in my business as I could. The trigger for me quitting my job was to have an amount equal to nine months' worth of my salary saved up as a cushion. With this trigger in mind, I carried on as usual and waited to save up the safety cushion. I fully realise that a lot of people would be happy to start a business full time with less money saved up behind them, but for us, this was the amount that alleviated the worries enough to make it a reality.

To make the transition seamless, I agreed that when I went full time, I would pay myself the same salary and pension benefits that I was earning in my job. This would mean that each month, I would make a salary payment from the business account, just the same as my employer. From our personal joint account's perspective, a month would look no different, apart from the name of the company making the payment. By doing it this way, my wife would be more comfortable with the whole situation. She knew I had money saved up in the business, and our finances looked the same as before I quit my job. Based on how much I was managing to save, minus any expenses for running the business, I set a date in the calendar, which was July 2017.

When it came to that date, I had saved up the runway upon which my wife and I had agreed. I walked into my manager's office, and I handed in my resignation. I felt both elated and terrified. The plan to leave my job and work for myself had been kept quiet; only my wife and I knew of it. We told no-one. A few of my friends expressed concern, as the previous September I had turned 40 years old—they thought I was having a midlife crisis and were worried until we explained that we had made this plan some time ago. A lot of people, when they have a midlife crisis, buy a boat or a motorcycle; I was starting a business.

I had to work a four-week notice period once I handed in my resignation, but after that, I was free. The business that started as selling sound libraries and then morphed into creating online courses was no longer a side-hustle. It was now what I did for a living. I was finally self-employed, but instead of jumping straight in and taking on a huge amount of personal risk, I had started slowly by running my business as a hobby on the side, and I made the transition to going full time only when I was ready to do so, on my terms.

The fear that had begun twenty-four years earlier with my first business setback had finally been resolved: I was self-employed. The first three months felt very strange. I was waking up in the morning, sorting out the kids for school and then commuting across the hallway to my desk to work on my projects. It was a level of freedom that I was not used to. It didn't feel real.

Over time, my new work arrangement started to feel like my new normal, and now I honestly couldn't see myself going back into full-time employment. I often joke with my wife that I am probably unemployable at this point, as I am so used to doing things my way. Let's hope I never have to find out.

A lot of people have reasons for being nervous about starting up a business, and I hope both my story and the rest of this book help you to feel more comfortable about the idea of working for yourself.

You don't have to make significant steps to quit your job. Like me, you could spend several years running your business from the sidelines while you stay employed. There is no rush to leave the nine-to-five routine. You can run a small side business for as long as you want. Heck, you may never go full time and be happy with a little business on the side, and that is fine. I hope that by sharing my experiences in this book, that I can help you take a dream of running a business and help turn it into a reality, while keeping your anxiety levels in check and reducing the amount of risk you need to take. It is okay for a business to start small and stay small. There are no rules about having to grow, take on staff and in turn, more stress.

1

THE PROBLEM WITH WORKING FOR SOMEONE ELSE

In this chapter we are going to explore why you might want to consider working for yourself either in the short term, or in your future. There are many advantages and disadvantages to running your own business, just as there are to remaining a full-time employee.

It feels great to be productive and self-sufficient; it feels even better when you're doing the work you love and living the life you want. Working for someone else helps you achieve the former, but it may not fulfil the latter. As long as you have a means to earn a living, it doesn't matter whether you achieve your dream life or not, does it? Well, if you want to make the most out of your life, pursuing what you want does matter.

When you go after your dreams, you may have to choose between traditional employment or becoming your own boss. By selecting the right path for you, you will find more satisfaction and may avoid regrets later in life. You also won't be wasting your time and skills on something you don't like. Most importantly, you will find value in your life, which will make you happier and more fulfilled.

Sadly, it's not always easy to have clarity about what you want to pursue. More often than not, it takes a bad experience in the wrong path to realise that you should be somewhere else. Many self-employed individuals spent years as employees before the realisation hit them. Others had it easier; it only took a book, a seminar or an encounter with a successful person for them to know that, instead of being employees, they should be setting up businesses, scoring freelancing gigs or travelling the world.

Self-employment is on the rise, and according to a US Bureau of Labour Statistics report published in 2018, the rate at which people move into self-employment is steadily on the rise for people both with and without degree-level education. As well as this data from the US Bureau of Labour Statistics, another article in the New York Post from 2018 states that climbing the corporate ladder is no longer the American dream, with numbers of non-traditional and self-employed workers expected to reach as much as 33% of the workforce in the coming years—meaning a further 27 million Americans will leave their full-time positions leading up to 2021 and beyond. These numbers are quite significant and although they are US-based statistics, they also serve as a good barometer for the rest of the world.

I live and work in the United Kingdom, and although we are a much smaller country than the United States, we also have a good level of growth. A report from the Office of National Statistics quotes the number of self-employed people in 2001 as 3.3 million, which is around 12% of the population. By 2017, this number had risen to 4.8 million—15.1%—and this same pattern can be seen all around the world.

The subtitle of this book refers to the "reluctant entrepreneur", and by this, I mean someone who doesn't have the constant drive to build companies. I class myself in this category. Earlier in my career, I had no ambition to work for myself. I was initially content with the nine-to-five grind, but it was due to a change in circumstances that I embraced self-employment.

As I mentioned in the introduction to this book, I started producing online training courses for a company in the United States, mainly as a bit of fun; but once this started taking off, it opened up the opportunity to work for myself. So, in my case, I was introduced to self-employment through serendipity. Another common entry point to being your own boss is being made redundant from your full-time position. I have a few friends who started working for themselves this way. They were made redundant from good jobs and received severance packages equivalent to around six months of their full-time salary. This gave them a financial buffer to pursue their own self-employed careers. In one case, a friend of mine turned to self-employment because he was struggling to find a new job during a time of economic struggle after the 2008 global financial crisis. Instead of registering himself as unemployed and claiming welfare benefits, he decided to turn an interest of his into a small business, and he has never looked back.

Signs that You're Not Meant to Be an Employee

Should you be an employee until you're in your sixties or should you become self-employed now? To help you decide, consider the following signs that you're not meant to work for someone else.

You love to lead and make rules. When it's in your nature to take the lead and set the rules, it may not be feasible for you to stay as an employee for too long, unless it is your job to take the lead and set the rules. Signs of your character will inevitably slip, which may come across as bossiness to your co-workers. Moreover, you may clash with your superiors at one point or another. I have been in this situation many times, and even though I did have a successful career as an employee, there were often times when I would get frustrated with the general approach to a project or other people not pulling their weight. This meant I would want to implement something from my vision, but that was not always possible. Fortunately, I have always had personal pet projects on the go in the background that allowed me to scratch that itch. If this situation seems familiar to you, that could be a great sign that you would flourish running a business on your own.

Your desire to be a leader and rule-maker isn't necessarily a bad thing. Sometimes, it's more about being the first to test an idea or create a solution to a problem. It's also about liberating yourself from limits that aren't beneficial to you, and setting the rules that will drive you to happiness and success.

. . .

You're restless about your limitations as an employee. As an employee, what you do in the workplace is determined by your employer. To keep your job, you're supposed to perform your assigned tasks and abide by a set of rules.

Many of these tasks and rules are designed, intentionally or not, in a way that gives you limitations. For five days a week, you have to be at work from nine in the morning until five in the afternoon. During those working hours, you're not supposed to be running your own business or liaising with your clients as a freelancer. You're expected to help your employer accomplish their goals, not yours.

Limits are fine as long as you're content with what you're doing and what you're getting in return. But if these only intensify your hunger to explore other ventures or trades, the boundaries set by your employer can make you feel restless or even bored. As long as you are within the confines of your employer's limitations, you will need to suppress your desire for autonomy, and this can lead to a sense of futility and dissatisfaction.

About 18 months after I began my side-hustle, this fledgling business had started to bring in a respectable second salary. It wasn't enough to leave my job, but it was a useful amount of money. I started thinking about this new passion of mine all the time, even when I was at work for my employer. I couldn't help it. I was enthusiastic about what I was doing, and my day job had become unfulfilling to me. There was nothing wrong with my employer, they were a good company—but once I get fixated on something, I can't stop thinking about it, to the detriment of all else. If you feel like this, then perhaps self-employment could be on your radar in the future.

You're too creative and talented for your current job. Creativity is a must-have skill for a lot of jobs; however, in most professions, there aren't many opportunities to showcase much of your creative side. You have to be innovative, but you must also stay within limits, which may not sit well with you if you're a highly creative person.

As a creative person, you will always have that itch to create. You find joy in every chance you get to make something; it's even more satisfying when your creation is helpful to you and other people. Commendations are merely a bonus. But because of time constraints or work-related stress, you may be unable to focus on bringing your ideas to life.

Aside from your creativity, you may have many other talents which aren't honed and maximised in your job. Talents are often indicators of what you're passionate about, so if you're wasting them, you're also making it harder to know and pursue what's right for you. When you continue doing it, you're living your life for your employer, not for yourself.

Job satisfaction from creativity is something I struggled with for years. I started my career working in the videogames industry in the UK, which is probably one of the most creative technical industries one can work in. It was fantastic. After eight years in that industry, I decided to leave and get a "proper" job in banking. The reason for this was that in the games industry, the expectation was that you worked all the hours you could to get a game released. When I was young and single, it was fun. Once I got married and we wanted to settle down, buy a house and start a family, this lifestyle, while I enjoyed it, was not compatible in my view with a stable family life. Although I enjoyed my second career in banking and finance, it wasn't very creative. In essence, no matter what technology we were using, we were just creating, reading, updating or deleting data from a database. After ten years of writing these soulless web applications, I was really starting to miss more creative endeavours.

Jobs that fail to satisfy the creative urge can be a big problem for people who are creative. It's why a lot of people start freelancing on the side of their main jobs in something unrelated to their career; it's a way to both satisfy their creative urges and build up valuable experience.

You're passionate about facing different challenges. Challenges don't exist to make you feel terrible; they are there to give you opportunities to learn and to grow. Being an employee presents challenges. You may need to complete a report within a deadline. You may have to deal with unhelpful co-workers or annoyed customers. Nonetheless, these aren't that exciting to tackle compared to the ones you'll encounter while working for yourself.

Self-employment is a dare in itself. There are plenty of risks and difficulties involved. However, it exposes you to a wider variety of challenges in your trade, business, and lifestyle, which in turn enable you to acquire more skills.

Many of the rewards you'll enjoy as someone who is self-employed are usually challenges at first. For example, the idea of being your own boss is enjoyable, but in your first few days as such, it can be a huge test of whether you can motivate yourself to work or not. It can be tough, yet fun at the same time.

By the time I dove into running my side-hustle full time, I was already very good at my core skills for the business, which were writing scripts, recording courses and video editing. Going full time opened up lots of different challenges, such as incorporating a business, dealing with accountants, learning about tax law and regulations, and self-motivation, to name just a few. These were all new challenges; the sort of thing that you take for granted working for another employer, as they are all taken care of for you. As someone planning to go self-employed, there is nowhere to hide—you need to address these challenges head-on.

You want to become financially well-off. To be clear, not every self-employed individual is financially wealthy. Some are earning less compared to their salaried counterparts.

You can gain financial stability by working for 40 hours a week in a regular job. Your salary can cover your daily needs and monthly bills. You can also save a little each month. However, your monthly salary won't likely make you rich, especially if it's your only source of income.

If you want to achieve more than financial stability sooner, you ideally need various sources of income. Compared to a regular job, self-employment presents more opportunities to earn, both in the short and long terms. If you plan your income strategy well, you can be assured that you will have means for your usual expenses, and that you will also have more to save for future emergencies and to spend for wants.

The problem with a full-time job is that you are constrained by time. You earn a fixed salary for a specified number of hours per week. This becomes very hard to scale, as to earn more you are dependent on performance-based bonuses (which are always promised and rarely delivered), and small incremental pay rises that barely cover inflation and cost of living increases. This type of income is called *active income*, and we will be covering it more later in the book. Unless you have managed to negotiate an excellent salary with an employer, that not only covers your needs but allows you to save, you are going to be perpetually stuck in a cycle of just getting by—and you won't have the extra time to devote to creating a new income stream without giving up your precious and valuable free time.

You value your time more than other resources. Out of all your available resources—your time, money, skills and social capital—nothing is as irreplaceable as time.

You can lose your money and earn it back. You can also save it for future use and invest it so it will grow. You can gain and improve skills through training and practice. You may lose some of your abilities due to old age, accidents, or misuse, but some of them will remain with you.

Your social capital is made up of your relationships with people who can help you in your work. With the help of this resource, you can get career advice, land jobs and find business partners, among other things. When you cut ties with such people, part of your social capital is also lessened. Nevertheless, you can make new connections to make up for the lost ones and even expand your social capital.

However, when it comes to your time, you can spend it, but you can never get it back. You can't earn, save or expand it. You can only maximise its use by doing something you love and spending it with the people who are dear to you. If you consider time as more valuable than other resources, you won't enjoy spending much of it on a job that offers more benefits to your employer than to you.

It is this idea of time being irreplaceable that prompted me to name this book *The Path to Freedom*. At its core, what is freedom? In this context, it is getting your valuable time back to do with as you want. In my case, building up a training business as a side-hustle allowed me to earn enough to buy back my time from my employer—which is a fancy way of saying that I quit my job to pursue my business full time. While I was building that small business, I had to sacrifice my free time, as the only chance I had to build these training courses was in the evenings.

This was a sacrifice that I discussed in detail with my wife so we could make a joint decision on whether it was worth it. We decided that it was, as we could see the opportunity that lay before me; and that early sacrifice in personal time resulted in me quitting my full-time job, working the hours that *I* wanted, and being able to be more flexible with time off to spend with my family. No longer am I shackled to the idea of 20 days paid vacation leave from an employer. If I want to take some time out for a family event, then I can make that decision myself.

Since running my business full time, I have frequently volunteered to help out at my kids' school as a supervisor on school trips. For me, this is great as I get to see my kids in their school environment, which is a precious experience as they are growing up so quickly. Were I still working for an employer, this is something I would be unlikely to be able to do.

Ten years ago, if you were to ask me to define what wealth means, I would have probably said that it was having lots of money which you could use to pay for experiences. My answer now is that while money is important to living a good life, having control of your time is far more valuable, and to be in control of your time is to be wealthy.

Advantages of Being an Employee

It may seem as though I am being quite hard on the idea of being a full-time employee, but to be fair, being an employee isn't all disadvantageous. In fact, many employees prefer to remain as such because they love their jobs and hate taking on risk, and self-employment *is* risky. If you can't decide whether to stay in a regular position or to pursue self-employment, you need to weigh up the advantages of working for yourself against the following benefits of being someone else's employee.

The first advantage is that you have a dependable pay cheque each month. As a salaried employee, you're assured of the amount of money you'll be receiving every month. The predictability makes it easier for you to decide and stick to a monthly budget. You can immediately know how much of your salary will go to expenses and savings. Furthermore, you can determine the amount you can freely spend.

. . .

As an employee you don't have to manage your own taxes. Unless you're the one in charge of accounting in your organisation, you likely won't have to deal with the daunting task of managing taxes. Aside from filing, someone else will determine the deductibles and learn about new tax updates on your behalf. Another tax-related benefit of being an employee is that your employer may cover a portion of your Social Security taxes, or equivalent for the country you reside in.

An important part of any job, is keeping your skills relevant, and with being an employee, you get free training. During your first few weeks as an employee, you will receive training to help get you started. In addition to in-house training, you're exposed to various business processes, which gives you some insight on how to manage them properly.

Your employer may offer training and workshops from third parties, too—much like the ones I originally began my business creating. Another advantage is being picked to attend conventions in other cities or even overseas. Aside from advancing your skills and promoting your company, one of the best things about these opportunities is that your employer pays for them.

Friendships that bloom in the workplace are some of the most long-lasting relationships you can ever have. You spend so much time working with your co-workers that you understand each other's struggles and celebrate milestones together. They listen when you want to vent. They extend help when you need it. Thanks to them, brainstorming ideas is made more fun and more efficient. Does the idea of missing out on the above advantages scare you? If it does, you may be better off working for an employer.

Also, as an employee, you don't have to plan networking opportunities by yourself. By simply being hired, you have gained instant connections made up of your co-workers. Depending on your work, you may also have to interact with clients, contractors and suppliers. Through constant deals, they may come to form part of your network. You can also meet people through training, workshops, and conventions.

You can learn and make mistakes without risking and losing as much as you would if you were working for yourself. Thanks to your employer, you get to learn new software and systems without spending your own money on them. As one of the users, you're given a chance to learn how to operate the software correctly. If you unintentionally cause one of them to malfunction, you may not have to pay for the repair. Additionally, you're not required to contribute to any ongoing maintenance. Through practice and observation, you'll also learn what not to do.

Just like your pay cheque, your working hours are predetermined, making it easier for you to plan and follow a schedule. You can also do things more quickly out of routine. Being in your workplace for several hours a day may be stressful and boring at times, but once you go home, you can relax. You don't have to worry about tasks all the time. I know we only just discussed about the importance of having control of your own time, but in reality, not everyone wants to be in control of their time like that. Some people are just as happy doing the nine-to-five routine and then going home.

To help them achieve their business goals, employers have to attract and retain talent. They do this by offering their employees benefits such as paid vacation and sick days, performance-related bonuses, retirement plans and health insurance. If your employer provides free meals and mobile phone plans, you can reduce your monthly expenses significantly. Other enticing benefits your employer may offer include free health check-ups, life coaching services, tuition reimbursements, and gym memberships.

Advantages of Working for Yourself

Choosing self-employment involves losing all the perks of being an employee and risking your own resources on a venture that may fail, and as a business owner, this is always something that rests on your mind. It certainly did with me when I started out. Despite these risks, there are plenty of things that make it a more worthwhile option than traditional employment.

As your own boss, you're in charge of choosing which ventures to take on from day to day. You can explore different fields and bring your ideas to life. You also decide how much of your time and money you're going to invest in each venture. No one's going to set limits on you except yourself. You are responsible for your successes as well as your failures – the buck stops with you and you alone, unless you are also working with a co-founder, which is something we will be covering later in the book.

You determine your workplace and working hours as well. This privilege enables you to prioritise your loved ones over other things. You can work at home, especially in the early stages of self-employment. At home, you can wear and do whatever you want but still work. The only few occasions which may require you to don business attire are meetings with clients.

You're free to choose who you do and don't want to work with. When you're an employee, you may not be allowed to make deals with some individuals and organisations as ordered by your employer. However, working with someone of whom your employer disapproves isn't as bad as working with someone *you* dislike, be it on a personal or professional level. Unless you're ready to lose your job, you can't really say no; but this isn't the case with self-employment. While there are no assurances that your preferred clients and collaborators will accept your offers, at least you're not forced to work with people you dislike.

Increased ability to save money. If your sources of income are limited, saving is likely a part of your monthly budgeting. It's always wise to save and to minimise your expenses. However, it may take some time before you can achieve your target amount. As self-employment gives more opportunities to make money, you can also save more. Once you're able to meet your target amount, you can then pay attention to additional income streams. You can take risks without worrying about not having enough money to save.

Avoiding the daily stressful commute. The day-to-day trip to work is bearable, and can even be enjoyable at times, when your home and workplace are both situated in the same small town. But if you're working in the city and living in the suburbs, words won't be enough to describe the hassles of your daily commute. You may have to run, queue and squeeze yourself into a crowded bus or train, or be stuck in traffic if you drive to work. And you have to go through it all while ensuring your business attire remains neat-looking and stressing about whether you will make your next meeting.

When you decide to work at home, you can spare yourself the stress and cost of commuting. You may also opt to rent an office that's quite distant from jam-packed roads and sidewalks. We will be covering working locations later on in this book, but having the flexibility to work where you like is truly liberating.

You don't have to make reports for other people. You don't have to relay information to co-workers as ordered by your employer. You don't have to be the one dealing with your employer's business partners, clients, and suppliers. In my business, I work with clients all over the world. I have spent years building up those relationships, and over time I have come to genuinely enjoy talking to my clients. I would even say that some of them have become good personal friends as well.

Saying goodbye to office politics. Stress and personality differences are the basic ingredients to potential misunderstandings in a typical workplace. If you perform well, some of your co-workers may feel threatened. When you're praised, some may feel envious, prompting them to gossip about you. There's also the possibility that you're the least favourite of your employer; as horrible as that sounds, it does happen.

Avoiding a toxic environment. Rather than risking your mental and emotional health, you are sometimes better resigning and finding a job elsewhere. If you don't care to risk experiencing it all over again somewhere else, being self-employed is your best option.

I have worked in some very high-pressure environments in the finance sector, and the one thing I do not miss at all is the office politics. Even in some places where I was actually enjoying the work itself, over time I would start to disengage with the company and the people I worked with due to the level of politics, gossip and backstabbing that went on. Once that starts, you are on the road to leaving that company, either by your own doing, or the company managing you out. Who needs that level of stress in their lives?

You can also save on childcare and other services. If you are a parent, you know that childcare services aren't cheap. Imagine the money you can save by caring for your kids yourself, or being available to pick the children up from school because you have the flexibility in your working hours. While in some countries, employers will provide a fixed term of paid parental leave for their staff, it still remains to be considered who will guide their children in their early years. This prompts some employees to quit their jobs, letting the other parent earn for the family while they bring up the children. Others hire nannies so that they can return to their jobs.

When you're self-employed, you can avoid many of these childcare costs, or significantly reduce them, and still earn while at home spending more time with your children. You can be there to comfort your kids when they need it the most. You can have peace of mind that they aren't being mistreated in the care of others. Most importantly, you can teach them the values that are important to you yourself.

. . .

When you are a master of your own destiny, you can feel the successes of your venture. If you're working for a corporation, you won't likely feel the benefits of winning deals with particular clients. You may get a performance bonus if you're among those who helped get those deals; you may also be promoted or receive salary increases. Sadly, such benefits are infrequent and uncertain. Your employer and outsiders may rave about the growth of the company. However, you may not personally feel the excitement, especially if you don't get anything in return.

Once you become an entrepreneur yourself, you can be as excited about your successes as your former employer was about theirs. You can feel the growth of your business yourself because you're the one receiving the benefit. Exerting your efforts on a venture is much more rewarding when you get to see the results first-hand.

Before you hit milestones as someone who is self-employed, you're going to face rejections and other difficulties. Some people will question your decisions; others will look down on you. Lenders and landlords may not accept you because you don't have a stable income. You may encounter scammers along the way. Some clients may be too demanding. Your pay may be delayed or worse, denied. While these are all troublesome, these experiences will only make you stronger and wiser.

You can build a more long-lasting legacy when you are in control of your own business and customers. No matter how hard-working an employee you are, tales of legendary employees are still rare. If you want to be known or to be remembered for a long time, you need to do something remarkable. As an employee, regardless of how impressive your output is, every success you make will be partially or fully credited to your employer; and this can make your job feel less rewarding.

On the other hand, if you work for yourself, you have a greater chance of being personally involved in the development of a product or service that could benefit a lot of people. You can also manage your business until it grows into a multimillion-dollar empire, enabling you to inspire and create jobs for hundreds or even thousands of people. Remember the world-renowned corporations that had humble beginnings such as Apple Computers being started by Steve Jobs and Steve Wozniak in a garage?

Disadvantages of Working for Yourself

Realistically, working for yourself has disadvantages that you may or may not handle easily. Before you go full time, you have to prepare for the following potential disadvantages.

You lose boundaries between home and workplace, and between free time and work time. Working at home can both be a blessing and a curse. At first, you think it's stress-free. You can work while wearing pyjamas and sitting on your couch. You can eat whenever you want. However, you're likely to procrastinate when you're around sources of comfort. The worst part isn't the procrastination, though; it's the loss of your boundaries. Home is supposed to be relaxing, but it may cease to feel that way when it also serves as your workplace. Sometimes, it's too bothersome when family members interrupt or meddle with your work, making it harder for you to concentrate.

Unless you're following a schedule, being an entrepreneur or a freelancer can make you forget about the difference between personal time and work time. When there's a problem with your business, you can hardly sleep at all because you have to fix it; otherwise, you're going to worry about it all night long. Even when you go on a family holiday, you still have to update your clients and handle their requests.

When I first quit my full-time job to work for myself, my intention was to work from home. I did this for about nine months, and it was great at first, but after a while I started noticing some problems. That line between work and home had become blurred. For example, I would work all day, then pick up the kids from school; but instead of spending time with them, I would say, "I just need to finish something off on my laptop, I will be ten minutes", then before I knew it, an hour had gone by. It's very common, and this will affect most people who work from home, even if you have a dedicated workspace in your house.

In the end, I realised that I needed to address this issue, so I found a local co-working space and took out a full-time desk lease. This meant I had a desk assigned to me that was permanently mine, so I could set up my own kit on it. I then used the co-working space three days a week and worked from home for the other two days. I really enjoyed this balance, and something I quickly realised was that, even though I didn't miss working for an employer, I did actually miss the routine of going to work where you have to get up, shower and dress, and then go out.

After six months, the opportunity for a private office came up and I jumped at it with open arms. I now had my own fairly large room, that I could set up how I wanted, and it was private and quiet. I am the only person who uses this room, apart from once a month, when my podcast co-host Kevin comes in to record show episodes. Having this space has made me more productive than I have ever been. It's where I am writing the majority of this very book.

You have to complete most tasks all by yourself unless you can afford to hire people. Being an entrepreneur or a freelancer isn't just about creating products or content. Self-employed people have to wear many different hats at once. It doesn't matter how good you are at creating your products—if you don't know how to network and promote, you probably won't win many clients. Therefore, if you want to make self-employment work in your favour, you have to prepare for various tasks such as networking, marketing, negotiating with clients, and managing your website.

Then there are those mundane but critical tasks you have to do, both when you're starting out, and during your entire time as a self-employed individual. You have to apply for the necessary licences and certifications before you operate a business. You have to prepare your business and income taxes as well. You need to make sure all your equipment is in good condition, and potentially also clean your own office.

In my own circumstance, I am good at creating courses, recording, video editing, writing etc., but there are also tasks that I am not very good at. Every now and again I need graphic design work done. My podcast, the *Side-Hustle Success Podcast*, is a good example. It needed a logo, intro and outro theme tunes, and sound stings for each section of the show. I could have attempted to do these myself, but I know the results wouldn't have been great, so I hired some freelancers to do the work for me. I have no intention of ever having full-time employees, but I do hire freelancers when I need something done which I know I am not good at myself.

You have to pay for work-related expenses. Initially, you may not spend much money because you're working at home and using your own personal computer and equipment. You'll shoulder the costs of licensing software etc. yourself. However, you'll soon have to pay for electricity, internet and telephone bills, and insurance. You may also have to shell out money for meals with clients. If you want to avoid some of the more mundane tasks, you will have to pay for services such as accounting, marketing, and website and social media management. Other expenses you have to cover include taxes, repairs, and maintenance.

All businesses have costs, and as the owner of the business you are responsible for them. In your previous employed life, all these costs were taken care of already by the company so you may not think to factor them into your budget.

You may feel lonely. While it's great to stay away from office drama and politics, part of you may miss the company of co-workers. No one's going to lend you a hand right away. No one's going to brainstorm with you. If you're living and working alone, you may have no one to talk to unless you call someone or go out. Loneliness can make it hard to remain productive and motivated all the time. When you're always away from people, how are you supposed to know what your potential clients really need and want?

I consider myself to be very introverted—I recharge my mental batteries by spending time by myself. Still, there are times when I crave some human company. If you are an extrovert, recharging your mental batteries by being around people, you may find this solitude even tougher to deal with. When I was working from home, I was starting to feel a little isolated. Renting a desk at a co-working space really helped alleviate that isolation as there were lots of other like-minded people working there who I could talk to. The co-working space had the social benefits of working for a company, but with none of the office politics, as everyone there was working on their own businesses or freelancing gigs. Even though I now work in my own private office, I do still occasionally walk over to the co-working building and chat to people, and once a month, we all go for lunch together.

If you are considering making the jump in your future to start a small business, don't forget to factor in potential isolation. You need to consider how you are going to get the level of in-person human contact that you need for your mental well-being. I am fortunate in that I get to travel to a lot of other countries to speak at conferences. When I am there, I normally extend the visit to at least a week so I can experience the location. When I am in a different city, I normally plan to spend at least one or two days in a local co-working space so I can get work done, but also so I can have the opportunity to speak to local entrepreneurs. It's amazing the interesting people you meet when you put yourself into the correct environment.

The Author's Approach

Everyone has their reasons for wanting to create a business. For some, it may be a hobby, something to do on the side. For others, it could be an escape from a company or a career that they no longer enjoy. You could be driven into creating a business out of necessity, such as redundancy in a stagnant jobs market. Everyone is different. I explained my reason for starting a business and the fears I had to overcome in the introduction to this book, so I won't cover that ground again.

For me, when I finally decided that it was time to go full time after running my online training business for a few years, it wasn't because I didn't like my day job. I enjoyed the company I was working for; there was no animosity with upper management, and I liked the team I had working for me. My decision to go full time with my business came after many years of working in the evenings and trying to save up enough of a financial safety net to cover me if anything went wrong. Other people may take that jump a lot sooner than I did, but as someone who is risk averse, I wanted to make sure I waited until a time that was right for me.

When I finally left my last employer after working my notice period, it was a strange feeling. I had a sense of freedom, but I also felt exposed without the comfort of a company looking after me. I was no longer operating in a single role, I was now in a position where I had to do everything, even though I had been working on tasks like marketing and accounting when I was running the business part time.

I have found the most significant benefit for me, apart from working on my projects, is having family freedom—especially with the 2020 coronavirus pandemic. Working for myself gives me more time for my family, particularly with the before- and after-school routine for my children. When I was employed, I used to commute on the train to a city called Nottingham, which took about an hour. This commute meant I had to leave early in the morning, usually before the kids had woken up, and I would get home after the children were back from school. My wife, who works from home, had to get the children ready for school every day and do the school run because I had to be at the office in Nottingham before 9am. Since working for myself, I am no longer constrained by regular office hours and working routines. When working from home, I would help my wife get the kids ready for school, and we would take it in turns to drop them off. This made my wife's life more comfortable, and it also allowed me to enjoy spending more time with the kids in the morning.

During the coronavirus pandemic, we had a five-month period here in the UK where we were in complete lockdown, and both kids were off school. In this time, my wife and I had to home-school our children. My wife works a nine-to-five job from home, so she still had to be present for meetings and getting her tasks done, even though her company was very accommodating with home-schooling needs. For my part, I was lucky in that I could be very flexible. I had just signed a contract to produce a new course for Pluralsight, so that had to be delivered; but all other projects, including the writing of this book, went on hold for five months. While I didn't want to delay these projects, I was very thankful to be in a position where I could slow projects and then focus more of my time on my children's education. For me, this whole lockdown situation highlighted the positive benefits of working for myself, as I could be adaptable with my work to allow me to help at home. That has been the single most significant benefit of working for myself so far—the flexibility to be present for my family.

Summary

In this chapter I have tried to set the stage about working for yourself and seeking that path to freedom. Self-employment is on the rise around the world as people are seeking more freedom and flexibility, both in the type of work they do, and when and where they choose to do it.

We have talked at length about the benefits of working for yourself, but you should keep in mind that it is not for everyone—in fact, some people may still prefer to work for an employer, and that's okay too.

You may be ready to start a business now, or you may be thinking that this could be something you do in the future. This book is here to help make this decision and transition easier for you. At the end of each chapter there are a set of workshop questions. These questions are not there to test your comprehension of the chapter. They are self-reflection questions to help you decide both if this lifestyle is for you, and if so, how best to plan your new career.

You can either work through the questions as you read each chapter, or wait until you have read the entire book and then work through them all at once. This is up to you, but I do recommend you tackle the questions, as they are a helpful tool in planning your path to freedom.

Workshop Questions

(1) Split a piece of paper into two columns titled "Advantages" and "Disadvantages". Then in each column, write down the advantages and disadvantages of your current workplace. You should have entries in each column, but be honest—no one needs to see these except you.

(2) Write down how you currently feel about quitting your job and starting a business. Is there anything stopping you? This question is to help you identify any barriers to you becoming self-employed.

2

STARTING OUT WITH A SIDE-HUSTLE

In this book we will talk a lot about side-hustles, as well as working full time as a self-employed person. In this chapter we will discuss what a side-hustle actually is and why it is a good thing.

If you are not completely happy with where you are in life, whether in your career or your personal life, it is time to make a change. The change that you are looking for might be in adopting what is known as a side-hustle. Let's start out by defining what exactly that is.

We can define a side-hustle as a product or service that you offer or sell on the side of your current full-time job to earn extra income. You also need to know that side-hustles are a little different to side jobs. When you take on a second job, or a side job, you are trying to increase your income. When you incorporate a side-hustle into your life, you are trying to increase your well-being, happiness, and overall improve your life. Your side-hustle isn't necessarily going to increase your wealth straight away. It can increase your income, but it could take time, as side-hustles don't always offer a steady pay cheque like a regular job.

In terms of starting a business, a side-hustle offers a much lower-risk way to become an entrepreneur, as you are not sacrificing your main income while trying to establish your business. You may work on a side-hustle alongside your full-time job for many years before you decide to make your side-hustle your full-time venture, or you may decide to never take it full time and keep it as a side business. Both of these are perfectly fine. In my case, I waited a few years before I decided to leave my job and work on developing training courses full time.

Another way a side-hustle differs from a part-time or full-time job is that *you* set your schedule. The amount of work you have to put into your side-hustle depends on how much time you are willing to dedicate to it. You don't have someone telling you what you need to do or when you need to do it. You don't even have someone telling you how to do it. In this case, you are your own boss.

When you decide that you want to venture out into a new side-hustle, you first need to know that the ideal side-hustle for you will depend on your personality, your ambitions and goals, and what you like to do. When you decide on a side-hustle, you want to do what is best for yourself.

Typically, you will be working for another employer when you first establish your side-hustle. Therefore, you'll need to prioritise your side-hustle on the weekends or evenings. This can create a pretty chaotic and stressful life for some people. However, if you are determined to make your side-hustle work, some of the daily stress will be eliminated.

In general, a side-hustle allows you to build your own business while still employed. This means that no matter what happens with your side-hustle, you will continue to receive a steady pay cheque from your current job. You are able to do this until you decide that it is time to turn your side-hustle into your career. There are some exceptions to this, which we will talk about later in this book.

In this book we will talk about starting a business as a side-hustle, with the dream of taking this fledgling business full time as your new career. It is also important to mention that although we are discussing the path to freedom to eventually become self-employed, some people may be happier building a business and keeping it as a side-hustle while remaining employed. This is absolutely fine, there is no rule that says you have to leave your full-time job and work for yourself. The majority of what we discuss in this book is just as relevant if you intend to keep your business as a side-hustle.

But How Do You Do It?

The first section of this book is about preparing yourself to run a business with the plan of eventually taking it full time, but let's first take a high-level look at how you get started. When you are already working a full-time job, thinking about starting a side-hustle can be worrisome, especially if you have a family to take care of or other commitments. If you have a significant other in your life, you need to make sure they are on board as well. You should also ensure that you have a schedule in place, so that you can make time to take care of your family and yourself. However, you will find that with a few tips and tricks, establishing a business, working your full-time job, and taking care of your family is all manageable.

Preparation. The key to being able to manage everything is to be prepared. You should also make sure you are prepared for the future; in fact, imagine that you will have this side-hustle for several years. While a lot of people find they are able to make their business a full-time commitment within a shorter time, it is important to get yourself into the mindset that this could take years. It will help you prepare mentally and emotionally for the added employment. The more you want to succeed, the harder you will work, and the easier it will be to set aside a portion of your precious spare hours with friends, family, and "alone time" to work on your side-hustle.

Find your passion and build your skills. The more passionate you are about your business, the more easily you will be able to get yourself into the right mindset and prepare for the long haul. Furthermore, if it's work that you love, it will feel less like a job and more like a potential career that you can enjoy.

Once you have selected your passion, you will need to build on your skills. Even your favourite musicians build their skills through practice; you should do the same. If you want to draw, then make time in your day to draw. If you want to write, build a habit of writing every day. If you want to be a photographer, invest in a good camera and start taking pictures regularly.

Your first customer. You will feel a huge sense of pride once you have helped your first customer. While most will pay for your services, there will also be times when you might wish to offer your services as a volunteer to build up a portfolio. If this happens, you need to be mentally and emotionally ready. Remember, every step will lead you toward your ultimate goal.

I had a friend who was a great photographer, but he needed to build up a portfolio in order to promote his business. He had four different sets of friends who were getting married over an 18-month period, so he offered up his time to shoot their weddings for free, on the condition that they agreed to allow him to use shots from their weddings as a part of his promotion. When he built their wedding albums, he only charged them cost price to print the images and made separate copies that he could use to show potential clients. This approach worked well for him and made it easier to book paying clients in the future.

Some people will find their first customer even before they establish their side-hustle as a part-time business. This allows them to validate their idea and ensure that the path they are on will work in the long run.

Also, remember to always ask for feedback from your customers. You can do this by sending an email and simply asking them for feedback on how you can improve, or what they feel you are doing well. Honest feedback and constructive criticism can feel a little frightening when you are starting out, but if you train yourself into the mindset that you can use this feedback to improve your service, then you can start seeing it as a positive part of running a business.

. . .

Know your goals. What do you want to gain from your side-hustle? Are you looking to build your business, do you want to increase your income to pay off debt, or are you looking for something that you want to do for the rest of your life? Whatever your goals are, you need to define them and write them down. Start by typing them out or writing them down by hand and hanging them on your wall so you can see them daily. When you are establishing your side-hustle, all of your actions will be guided by these goals; they will help you make decisions and keep you on track.

Create a milestone action plan. On top of your goals, you will want to create milestones. These are steps that you will work toward in order to reach your goals. At first, you may have an idea of a milestone, but be unsure when you are going to reach it. You might even struggle with an idea of *how* to reach it. If you find yourself struggling, you shouldn't worry too much. Creating milestones is just another way to set you on the right track and keep you there. You don't need to set deadlines for your milestones. Instead, write down a milestone and give yourself ideas on how you can accomplish it.

When I was building my first training course, I took a similar approach. I had a final delivery date set, and I knew how many modules were contained in the course, but I couldn't really accurately predict how long each module was going to take to script, design, record and edit, as I had never done it before. Instead, I put my focus on the first module, where I wrote the script and recorded all the content for that script. Once I had completed that module and submitted it, I then had the experience to roughly predict how long the rest of the course would take to create.

The main lesson there is that if you are overwhelmed by the scope of some work, break it down into manageable chunks and just focus on completing the first part. This is a great technique to reduce the anxiety of a large project.

Hang on to your full-time job as long as you can. When you start out a side-hustle, you need to be careful that you will not do anything to jeopardise your current full-time job. You should understand where your boundaries are without having to ask anyone. You might have a job where you can't talk about your business at all, but you might also have one where they support it. A lot of how you handle your business will depend on your full-time job environment. If you have a job that prohibits working on side businesses, or claims ownership on anything you produce, then you need to be especially careful.

The best way to make sure your full-time job and side-hustle don't collide is to keep them completely separate. Don't work on one while you are on the other job, and don't use resources from one job for the other.

Once you find that you are unable to manage your full-time job any longer, because your side-hustle has turned into a full-time commitment and is earning enough income to at least buy back your time from your employer, it might be time to put in your resignation notice. You will also know it is time if you start to feel burnt out because you are working too much, feel too stressed, and find your job performance is lacking in one or both areas.

Later in the book we will talk in more detail about the potential dangers of building a product or service while still employed. The aim isn't to put you off, but to help you avoid any trouble.

Examples of a Side-Hustle

A side-hustle cannot exist without you first having an idea for a product or service. I can't tell you what you should build, only you can do that; but in this section, I will show you a few ideas to hopefully get you inspired. There are many examples of side-hustles. In fact, there are hundreds of great ideas that could become your next business. Let's focus on a few of the more well-known side-hustles of today.

Freelance work. It doesn't matter whether you are an artist, woodcarver, writer, or film producer; you can pretty much do any type of freelance work if you have the skills. When you take on a job as a freelancer, you are working independently for a person or a business. For example, as a content writer, you might be hired to write blog posts for a company. If you are an artist, you might be asked to paint a family portrait. If you are interested in video filming and editing, you might search for opportunities to film someone's wedding, a family reunion, or a school play. While the work might start off small and will probably offer very little pay, you will continue to build your resume with each job you acquire. This will help you establish yourself in the freelance industry.

Finding freelance work is quite easy with sites like Fiverr and Upwork, as they give you access to a global market, although prices can be forced down with so many people competing on those platforms. If you are looking at a market in your area, you will need to investigate the best ways to reach local companies to offer your services.

Graphic design. Graphic design is another popular form of freelance work available if you have experience. If you have very little experience in graphic design, you can always purchase a software program, such as Adobe Illustrator or Photoshop, which can help you learn and expand your skills. Another way to get your foot in the door is to ask non-profit organisations or businesses that may need help with digital material. While you might not get paid, especially if you're offered an internship or volunteer opportunity at a non-profit organisation, you will receive professional experience, which is great when building your resume and portfolio.

Online coaching. One of the great advantages of the internet is that you can pretty much do everything online. For example, if you want to help people become motivated to succeed, you can look into creating an online coaching business. You can become certified as a life coach this way. With this, you will also want to create a website, an email, or direct messaging service so people can reach you if they need someone to talk to. I know several people that have started up coaching businesses on the internet, and they charge hourly fees to meet with people either in person or over Zoom calls to help mentor or coach them in different areas such as success, motivation, and business.

. . .

Reselling on Amazon or eBay. Selling items on Amazon or eBay is no longer just considered a way to make a few extra dollars every month. There are a lot of people that build their reselling business up, so they are able to make this their full-time job. It doesn't matter if you find yourself purchasing items at garage sales, second-hand stores, or purchasing on Amazon and then reselling the items for a profit. This is a great side-hustle that you can work on in the evenings, or a few days out of the week.

Remote tutoring. There are always going to be people looking for a little extra help for their child's homework or their own schoolwork, or wanting to learn a second language. Thanks to the online world, people are now able to become tutors right from the comfort of their home. However, this type of side-hustle will often depend on both your schedule and that of the person you are tutoring. If you are looking for a side-hustle where you don't have to worry about anyone else's time, this might not be the best venture for you. It still does allow flexibility with your schedule, however, and gives you the added benefit of helping someone expand their education.

Real estate investing. While channel-surfing, you might have come across a television show about buying, renovating, and selling houses. Real estate investment, or "house-flipping", is becoming a well-known side-hustle that can quickly turn into a full-time career for some. When you flip a home, you will purchase it, update the house, and then sell it for a profit. Many people will also live in the home as they fix it up.

Another real estate investment strategy is to purchase a multi-family unit, such as an apartment building. You can manage the building yourself, collect the rent, and make this a second source of income. If an apartment building isn't what you're looking for, but you are interested in renting to other people, you could purchase a house and turn this into a two-family home or rent it out to university students. Many college students would rather rent out a bedroom in a home and share a house with other students than live in a dormitory on campus.

Catering company. If your passion is cooking or baking, but you don't have the time or capital to focus on opening a restaurant, you might want to consider starting a catering company. Most parties, business meetings, or events that require catering are in the evenings or during the weekend. Therefore, this may allow you to keep your full-time job until you are able to make your catering business full time. Furthermore, you can potentially prepare any food in a kitchen provided by the client. When I turned 40, my wife booked a catering company to prepare a meal in a large house we had hired for the weekend for me and all my friends and family. One factor you need to watch out for is any applicable hygiene laws. When it comes to preparing food for other people, you need to make sure you have all the required licensing and follow all regulations.

Develop a software application. The belief that there is an app for everything is true. In fact, scope for useful apps is practically limitless, and you might just have an idea that will work! Furthermore, many people are able to develop a more advanced app by looking at existing apps and building on those concepts. As long as you don't break any copyright laws, you can develop your own app.

Like with other side-hustles, you will need to prepare when planning to build an app. What will the app do? How will it work? What platform are you going to develop it for, etc.? You will also need to either have or learn the necessary software development skills to build your app. Fortunately, there are a lot of online courses that can help you learn the coding side of app development. You might also be able to get help by teaming up with someone else who has knowledge of creating apps and forming a partnership. Remember, a side-hustle is all about developing your skills.

Some Advantages of a Side-Hustle

One of the greatest benefits of a side-hustle is that you are able to do something you are passionate about during your free time. When you find your niche, meaning something you excel at and are passionate about, you are more likely to work harder, because you love doing what you do. Furthermore, you are working towards a dream which you created. There are a lot of mental and emotional benefits when you are working toward something you love to do, which adds to the list of benefits of a side-hustle.

Your mental and emotional health will improve. You will start to feel more confident in your work, which will have a direct impact on your self-esteem. You will start to feel happier and freer as you continue to work on your side-hustle. Furthermore, a more positive mindset is going to make you feel physically better.

The flexibility of your workplace and schedule are other benefits. You are able to set your own hours. This means if you only want to work on Saturdays from 10am to 4pm, or Monday and Wednesday evenings from 6pm to 8pm, it's entirely your decision. You don't have anyone else telling you when you should and shouldn't work. At the same time, you have the freedom to either work in your home, or you can rent out an office space for when you need it.

You also don't have to provide a lot of money upfront, unless you are getting into real estate investment or want to build your physical products and need investment for materials. Most side-hustles are services where you spend the time to do the work and get paid once the work is completed.

Another benefit is that you are able to increase your income with a side-hustle. While you might need patience before you really start seeing an increase in your income, eventually you will be able to pay off any debt, build your savings, or invest your money. This will give you more financial security and make you feel financially free.

Some Disadvantages of a Side-Hustle

By now, you might feel like there are no downsides to a side-hustle. Unfortunately, whenever there are advantages, there are also some disadvantages.

First of all, side-hustles can add more stress to your life. There is no doubt about it. If you are going to add a business into your already busy schedule, you are going to possibly create more stress for yourself.

While your business might be something you love to do, it will still take time away from relaxing and unwinding.

When I was building my online course business, I gave up evenings and a lot of time at weekends for a few years before I went full time. Granted, I wasn't spending every evening working on courses, but I spent at least three or four evenings a week either writing scripts on my laptop on the couch, or upstairs in the spare room recording and editing the courses. Luckily, I have a very supportive wife who could see that there was potential in what I was doing, and that support helped a great deal.

Another disadvantage is that you can find yourself with no downtime or alone time. Psychological research has proven that having alone time is important; this may be more important for some people than others. When you decide to establish your side-hustle and make it a full-time commitment, you can go through months where you have very little to no downtime. This can negatively affect you mentally, emotionally, and physically. I find I have this problem myself. Although I am a classic introvert who enjoys my own company, I do still have a limit to that, and I occasionally need the company of others. Thankfully I made a lot of friends at my local co-working space that I frequently go for coffee with, and I still travel to a lot of conferences to speak. I have met so many people on the speaking circuit that it is rare for me to go to a conference and not know at least two or three people to hang around with.

It is important to think ahead of time about how you are going to interact with people if you eventually leave your job and take your side-hustle full time. You need to understand how you handle isolation and have a plan for dealing with it.

The final disadvantage I want to look at is the possibility that you could start to neglect your full-time job. At first, it might seem that everything is going great. This might be because you have very little work to do with your side-hustle. However, once you start to get more customers, you will start to notice that more and more work will come your way. While this is great and can get your adrenaline going, you might find that you are starting to put your full-time job to the side. You might be taking too many vacations to work on your business; you might be trying to sneak side-hustle work into your full-time job, or you may find you can't concentrate on your full-time job. This can negatively reflect the type of employee you are and, worse, you could be fired from your full-time job. We will talk more about the dangers of working on a side-hustle while still employed later in this book.

Skills You Will Develop When Running a Side-Hustle

Because they have experience in the workforce and are still spending most of their time working for someone else, a small business owner can approach starting a side-hustle in a different way to someone who doesn't have a lot of experience in the workforce already. Being an employee for one company while starting up their own puts them in a unique position to excel.

Small business owners need a specific set of skills to run their business effectively—some skills you already have, either through college or your career experience, and some you will learn while running your business. People who want to start their own company as a side-hustle most likely have already acquired these skills while working for other people. Having a general knowledge of these skills means you can adapt them for your specific field of business.

Leadership Skills. Leadership doesn't just mean leading others. When starting a small business, you as the owner need to have leadership skills, even if you're the only employee with no one else to lead! When you deal with suppliers or freelancers, for example, you need to demonstrate good leadership even though they are not employees of your business. When you are negotiating prices for supplies, good leadership skills will give you the advantage in the negotiations, and you will be better placed to reach an agreement that is favourable to you. When you negotiate work with a freelancer, you need to be a good leader in order to set out what you expect from their work, direct their efforts and produce good results. You need to be able to demonstrate your vision for what you are building.

If your small business grows enough to hire more employees, then you will need good people leadership skills. Leaders are the ones who set the tone of the business, keep staff morale up, and make sure the bottom line is being met.

Project Management. Having solid project management skills means you can effectively manage resources like time, money, and staffing (either your staff or freelancers). You need to see the big picture of how each project fits into the scope of the overall business plan. Project management often means defining the goal, then working backwards and setting milestones along the way. Once you have established the goal and the route you intend to take to get there, you can identify the specific steps you'll take to reach each milestone, and ultimately, your goal.

Delegation. As a business owner, you won't do everything on your own; good leaders know how to delegate. If you take on every task alone to keep the business afloat, you'll be overworked and burnt out in no time. Delegation means you know who will do the best job on each task, and assigning those tasks accordingly. Workforce management tools help small teams work collaboratively—they can see everything that needs to be done and pick and choose the duties they can accomplish.

If you are the sole employee at your company, you should have a good grasp on what tasks you are well positioned to work on. Anything for which you do not have the skills, you should delegate to someone else, such as a freelancer. A good example of this might be logo design; outsourcing this to a graphic design freelancer makes sense if you are not a good designer.

Financial Management. If you are not good with money and are prone to overspending when you shouldn't, then starting a side-hustle might be a risky move for you, but you don't need to be a financial expert with a degree in accountancy to start a business. While a financial education can help you out with legal regulations, bookkeeping and accountancy, some of these skills can be learnt on the job while you are establishing your business.

Budgeting. Budgeting for your small business includes all the expenses needed for its daily operations, like a website, phone line, office supplies, and the myriad other expenses that can occur. It also includes any cost of production if your business sells products that need physical assembly.

Accounting. Accounting is more than just knowing if your business is operating at a profit or loss. Accounting relates to all of the finances needed to run your small business effectively, including paying salaries and expenses, matching Social Security (or national insurance in the UK), medical insurance funds, and filing business taxes.

Communication. An effective leader knows that communication is not limited to the spoken word, but also includes body language and written language; in a formal letter, in emails, and even you put on your business' website and social media accounts. Good communication is an exchange between people, so a good communicator also needs to be a good listener. You also need to pay attention not just to what's being said, but to how it's being said, and tailor how you need to reply accordingly. Communication skills are vital for interacting with employees, co-workers, and customers, as well as for networking in the business field.

Customer Service. Good customer service is vital to keeping a business afloat. This isn't limited to just interacting with customers in person and online during the sale. This includes the refund process, dealing with an irate customer, and following up with them after the transaction is finished.

Human Resources. Until your business has more than one employee, you won't have to concern yourself much with Human Resources (HR), but it's an important skill to have. HR departments in larger companies deal with the hiring and firing of employees, but also manage any interpersonal disputes that arise between co-workers. Working with a small team may make it easier to handle these situations, but taking a course in HR management is a good way for a leader to reinforce these skills.

Sales. Sales is something at which people either excel or fail. The sales tactics you use will depend on the field you're in; whether you need to really push a sale, or if keeping it casual will have a better success rate.

This is one skill you may be naturally geared towards, or it may require a lot of effort and a steep learning curve.

Marketing. Marketing is one of the most valuable skills you need, and there are plenty of ways to learn online if it's not something that comes naturally. Marketing a side-hustle includes promoting social media outlets, sending engaging emails and newsletters, and having an eye-catching website that employs SEO (Search Engine Optimisation). We will be spending a lot of time looking at marketing and branding later in this book.

Public Speaking. Even if you conduct all your side-hustle business online, you ideally need to be a skilled public speaker. When you give presentations, you need to sound confident and sure of both yourself and your business. Stumbling over words or not being able to come up with something off-the-cuff can make people doubt the strength of your business. Public speaking is a skill, like sales, which can be practiced and improved upon over time.

Flexibility. Being flexible means that, while you may not be aware of what twists and turns may come your way, you're prepared to adapt the best you can. Whether having to find another supplier at the last minute, or attempting to follow the trends of the industry, the most successful business owners are able to roll with the punches instead of getting stuck on how they expected things to be.

Determination. Determination goes hand-in-hand with flexibility. Good business owners need to be able to adapt to changing circumstances and be determined to do so. Don't see change as a negative, but rather as a positive step and a personal challenge. It's easy to give up when the going gets tough, but that means giving up on your business. Industry is hard, and owning a business is stressful most of the time; being determined to make it work means your side-hustle will flourish.

Resilience. Resilience comes naturally with flexibility and determination. The ability to get back up after something gets in the way of your business is crucial, even if it means getting back to a business that's slightly different than it was before. Being resilient means that if someone else is marketing the same product as you at a lower cost, you will step up to show why your product is superior. If the market is oversaturated, you will pivot and come back with something the knock-off companies haven't thought of yet, without missing a beat.

Resourcefulness. Resourcefulness is something most business owners have in spades because it's what pushed them to start a business themselves. Resourcefulness means seeing the problem and figuring out how to solve it with what is available. It might mean creating your own business to help everyone else solve the same problem. It might mean knowing who to call when your website is hacked. It might mean knowing what to research to solve something on your own. Resourcefulness means taking advantage of every second and every opportunity to be a problem solver.

Strategy. Business owners use strategy to plan their business while also being ready to change any future moves in a flash. You will need to think strategically about the long-term impact of the immediate business decisions you make. You could see that investing in one option now, even if it's more than you can afford, could pay off in the long run and be worth it. Strategy also means being able to predict possible problems and prepare for them now. That doesn't mean worrying about everything to come; it just means having a contingency plan for anything that might jeopardise your business.

Time Management. Time management is a skill you will need to develop quickly. It's one thing to work full-time for someone else and know that an eight-hour day will be dedicated to set tasks. Managing a side-hustle is quite another, and means you will need to handle your time in more specific ways.

Having lists of what tasks need to be done can help you manage your time. Ranking duties not just by order of importance but also by how long the tasks will take can help prioritise things that need to be done in the little time you will have to dedicate to your side-hustle.

Time management is especially important when considered that you will be working beyond your full-time job, juggling a side-hustle with family and other obligations. Time is money, and getting lost in one project for hours might cost you big bucks in the long run.

Creativity. Many think creativity is a skill people are either born with or lack. In reality, operating a business for a while will help you develop creativity. Even if you start a business by hiring copywriters and designers, you'll see the finished project on your website, take it in, and learn from it. Creativity doesn't specifically apply to only artistic tasks. A lot of the soft skills previously mentioned, like resilience and flexibility, require creativity in different ways. Being a creative thinker means you can think outside of the box and come up with innovative solutions to keep your business relevant.

How You'll Learn

Whether you already have all the skills you need, or you're learning as you go along, as a small business owner you will learn the ropes in a couple of different ways.

Trial and Error. Trial and error is the easiest way to learn. If you took time to take courses about everything you needed to know, you might never get around to feeling prepared enough to start a small business. Jumping in and getting started might seem anxiety-inducing, but sometimes the best thing to do is just try and learn from any mistakes you might make.

It's easy to worry about problems that may never arise or, conversely, assume that things will run smoothly. Once you are in the thick of it, you'll have more invested and will be more determined to figure out a solution. That solution might not be right, but you're involved and will figure it out with time. Sometimes it's more important to learn what works for you rather than what someone else might suggest as an answer.

Learning from Others. You can pay attention to how other businesses are run and learn from their failures and successes. What you notice from customer service when you visit a store or restaurant may convince you to change something in your own operations. Getting a follow-up email might inspire you to integrate that feature into your customer service.

Owners can also learn from others by taking courses. Some cities have small business collaboratives that sponsor practical workshops. Many colleges offer human resource, finance, and management courses for audit. After getting the business up and running, you will know what you need to learn more about and can find a course that focuses specifically on that.

Starting a business is a massive undertaking, but having a well-rounded skill set will help you with challenges you'll face while getting everything off the ground.

The Author's Approach

When I started dabbling with forming a business creating sound design libraries, I had no intention of doing it full time. I loved my day job, and the major reason I sold my sound libraries was to earn a little money that funded the hobby. I had never heard of the term side-hustle, but this was what I was running. When I started moving into online training, I again had no intention of doing this full time. It wasn't until the business showed reliable growth and I was earning near to my day-job salary that I even entertained the idea.

I could have gone two ways with my business. I could have kept the training business as a side-hustle; this way, I would have been earning a fantastic side salary along with my dependable salary from my job. It was a very tough decision to make to take my business full time. I am a very creative person by nature; I love building things, whether that's software, courses, books or videos. My career had taken me more into a management-based leadership role. I enjoyed this role, but it lacked the creative element that I love; it was this thought that helped tip the scales for me in my decision to go full time. Once we were sure the business was making enough money and would continue to do so, the decision was much easier to make.

I now spend my days creating. I still build courses for Pluralsight. I develop short courses for Skillshare. I teach in-person classroom workshops around the world, speak at conferences, and write books (like this one), and produce for YouTube. The term content creator gets bandied around a lot on platforms like YouTube, but that is precisely what I am now, a content creator. I cannot see myself doing anything else.

I feel as though I have come full circle. For most of my adult life, I was scared to start a business for myself; now, my biggest fear is that my business fails, and I have to get a regular job again. The irony is not lost on me.

The whole concept of a side-hustle is fantastic as it ultimately lowers the barrier to entry and lowers the risks involved with creating a business. I am forever grateful that I eased myself into the idea. For the reluctant entrepreneur or someone who is very risk-averse, starting a small side business (or hobby business) is a great way to get started. You will know if you hit the point that you could take your side business full time, but as I have already stated, there are no rules that you ever have to do that. A side-hustle can stay a side-hustle; you don't need to take it full time if you are still uncomfortable with the idea.

Summary

Before you begin to establish your side-hustle, you need to make sure you go through the correct steps in order to be successful and not jeopardise your full-time job. This means you need to find something you are truly passionate about, create an action plan, write down your goals, and establish a timeline for your side-hustle that will leave you with both family and alone time. You also want to make sure that you keep your side-hustle and full-time job separate. Even when you find yourself with too much work, do everything you can to keep them separate.

Once you start your side-hustle and you have picked up some work, reassess your action plan, goals, and how well you are handling everything. If you find that you are struggling to keep your full-time job and side-hustle separate, work on an action plan that will allow you to break free of this struggle. Once a month, re-analyse where you are mentally, emotionally, and physically, in order to decrease your chances of taking on too much and potentially burning out.

Thousands of people have turned their side-hustles into their full-time businesses, and you should be no exception to that possibility. As long as you have the passion, dedication, and drive, you will be able to balance the art of a side-hustle and your full-time job until it is time to focus on what you really want.

Workshop Questions

(1) What skills and interests do you have that you think could become a successful business?

(2) Is going self-employed a decision you can make yourself, or do you need to discuss this with other people, such as a partner, or parents? What do you think their reaction will be?

3

SETTING AN INCOME STRATEGY

Starting a small business requires lots of planning, and one area you need to decide on is setting an income strategy. What type of income are you going to generate? How frequently do you expect to be paid? We are going to explore income strategies in this chapter.

Financial security enables you to live the life you want. To achieve this, you have to be mindful of your income sources. It's not enough for you to take additional jobs, sell more products or make better investments. You should plan where your revenue will come from so that you don't have to focus on making money all the time. To start planning, you should first know the differences between the two main types of income: active and passive.

Passive vs. Active Income

Active income refers to the money you earn from offering your time. The monthly salary, commissions and performance bonuses you would receive as an employee are this type of income. Self-employed people can also earn an active income. These include freelancers or individual contractors who spend their time to work on projects requested by clients for a fixed fee. Providing services such as consulting, advertising, designing and editing are other sources of active income.

In contrast, passive income is the money you get without lending your time or service. Initially, you have to invest time and/or money to create these sources of income. You may not earn much to start with, either. But what makes this attractive is that you keep on earning for a long time, practically without doing anything. These days, one of the prime examples of getting passive income is writing and selling an e-book, or an online training course. The training courses I produce fall into the passive income category. I have to do a lot of work upfront to create the course that I am not paid for, apart from a small completion fee when it's published; but once it is published, the course will constantly be generating income. Even when I am asleep or on holiday, people are watching the course.

Both types of income have their fair share of advantages. While passive income is more beneficial in the long run, it doesn't mean that you have to disregard active income. After all, your first income was likely an active income when working a full-time job. Additionally, the money you'll use to get passive income is mostly from your earnings when you're rendering services (active income). To gain a better understanding of the importance of each type of income, below are the key differences between the two in the context of self-employment.

Short-term benefits. The best thing about active income is the assurance that you'll get compensated for trading your time, provided that you're not dealing with problematic customers, and that nothing happens to deplete your client base. The pay is also generally better, compared to your initial payment from a passive income stream. Active income helps ensure that you have something to spend on daily and monthly expenses.

Long-term benefits. If you don't wish to keep offering your time for the rest of your life, you'll need sources of passive income, along with a retirement plan. You never know when your services will become obsolete, so it's better to prepare for the lack of demand by setting up passive income streams.

Flexibility. When you're self-employed and reliant on active income, the one in control of your time isn't you; it's your client. Therefore, you're not truly working for yourself; you're still working for someone else. If you want flexible working hours (and the freedom that's often associated with self-employment), you need to work on generating a passive income. Once you have products or services set up that generate passive income, they require less ongoing maintenance, which is a big benefit. Once you release your product, you just let the money flow in, and you focus on the marketing and awareness of your brand.

Involvement. As its name suggests, active income requires your involvement in a task over a period of time. Thanks to video calling, emailing and Skype calling services, you may not need to be physically present to provide your service. Selling is also made more accessible due to global shipping services. Still, sources of active income do require your constant attention throughout the life of that engagement with the client. Passive income streams, on the other hand, may not demand as much involvement. More often than not, you have to take a few steps before you can generate passive income. As I mentioned with the courses that I produce, I could be spending anything from two to four months creating a course, depending on its complexity, for which I am not being paid. I only start to get paid once that initial time investment is completed, and the course is released.

Availability. As long as the machines haven't taken over all the jobs, there'll always be a demand for people who offer services. Compared to passive income, it's easier to find opportunities to earn an active income. However, passive income streams are readily available as well, as you're the one who's going to create opportunities yourself. It is sensible to think about combining both active and passive income streams. This is exactly what I do. The courses I release and the books that I write generate my passive income streams, but I also do small active income engagements that bring in money in the short term, which offsets the time I spend creating products and services for passive income. The active income jobs I take on tend to be speaking engagements for privately run seminars, or in-person classroom training. The combination of both active and passive income helps to give me a more stable and predictable income stream.

How active may turn passive. Something that you might want to consider is turning your active income streams into a passive income stream. Let's assume you are a software developer working for a company as a full-time employee. Your salary is active income as you are trading your time for money. How could you get more control over your career and also generate a passive income? In our scenario, let's assume you have decided to resign from your job and start your own small business. Once you have worked your notice period, you start part-time contracting for three days a week, where you write software for clients on a day-rate basis. These three days are generating your active income, and it is not uncommon that as a contractor, you are most likely earning a very good rate that makes those three days at least equivalent to your five days as a full-time employee.

On the remaining two days of the week, you decide to create some training courses about software development using your skills. Your first course takes you a couple of months to create in which you are not being compensated, but that's okay, as you are earning a good rate from your three days of contracting. You release the course, and you start earning some passive income from it. This income may start out small, but it's consistent. Over the next two years you create a further eight courses, and your passive income starts to equal what your original salary was as a full-time employee. In this position, you are earning a good steady active income that compensates for the time you spend building courses, and the courses earn a growing rate of passive income.

It sounds too good to be true, doesn't it—but this is becoming quite a common way to run a small content-based business. Using your skills that have traditionally been part of an active income activity, you can also build products to generate passive income. In this example, you may decide after three years that you want to stop contracting for a year and go travelling and build your courses while seeing the world. With a steady and growing passive income stream, it is perfectly possible for you to both travel and earn a good steady income. People who choose this lifestyle are referred to as "digital nomads" or "location-independent workers". It is very popular and is a subject we are going to explore later in the book.

Additional types of income. Multimillionaires don't tend to rely as much on either active or product-based passive income. More often than not, they're into the least-known type of income: portfolios. Portfolio income covers the interests and dividends you get from having securities such as mutual funds, bonds, and stocks. This type is sometimes categorised under passive income because they may or may not require your involvement, and they offer long-term earning opportunities. The problem with portfolios, though, is that the value of the securities may depreciate; which means that you can lose money instead of earning more. Nevertheless, if you're adept with investments, having portfolios can give you profits that are way higher than the amount of your active and passive income combined.

Experienced entrepreneurs who have large passive income streams will often move spare money from their business into portfolio investments; this could also be something like a stocks-based pension fund. This is something I do, by moving money each month from my business as a contribution to a pension fund which I can see grow over time. While I am not intending to rely on a pension income, retirement planning of this kind is still a good idea as you never know what will happen in the future. I will state, though, that if you are planning to invest money into a pension or portfolio fund, please take advice from a financial advisor first, don't just take my word for it.

Basic Financial Planning

Nowadays, plenty of finance-oriented blogs, podcasts, seminars, live streams, TV shows, and other media offer free or low-cost financial advice. While many of the financial tips are indeed helpful, they are written with regular employees in mind. Therefore, self-employed individuals, especially freelancers, have to look harder and go as far as hiring a financial advisor to get more suitable guidance.

Let's look at the basics of handling your finances as a self-employed person. The road to financial security doesn't just involve improving your sources of income; it's also about managing your expenses. Aside from diversifying your income sources, you should also carry out the following strategies on maximising the use of your income.

Save an emergency fund. The early stages of self-employment are devoted to building a client base and generating passive or active income streams. During this period, you may earn less than the amount of your previous monthly income.

As a remedy, you should make a list of your personal expenses and categorise each as either fixed or variable. Fixed costs are those whose amount is unchanging, while variable costs are those whose amount changes from month to month. Monthly savings, health insurance, and house rent/mortgages are examples of fixed expenses. Variable expenses cover groceries, fuel, repairs, and maintenance. Once you're done with your list, determine which costs you can reduce (typically, these will be made up of variable expenses).

As much as possible, however, you should already have an emergency fund set in place before you fully dive into self-employment. It doesn't hurt to stay in your job for a few more months to save for an emergency fund, does it? Such funds should enable you to pay for personal expenses in your first six to twelve months of self-employment, in case you're unable to earn significantly in the early stages of freelancing and managing your business. As a guide, I would recommend saving a minimum of three months of your net (after tax) salary; ideally six months if you can manage it. Having money set aside like this will help to reduce the stress of starting a business, if you have to seek out freelance gigs or build passive income-based products. Starting a business can be stressful in its own right, so don't add to the stress with the fear of running out of money.

List down all your sources of income and the amount you've earned from each. Like your expenses, you should also know where your income will come from. Don't just try to memorise everything. Make a spreadsheet about your potential income sources and the amount you want to try and earn from each. This will give you an idea of how much you're likely to gain every month, provided that there aren't significant crises affecting your income streams. When you're well-informed about your earnings, you can adjust your budget and plan for additional investments accordingly. I recommend planning on the side of caution. It is easy to just put numbers onto a spreadsheet that look attractive, but you need to be realistic. If you are planning on being a freelancer, you should start by taking on freelancing jobs that you can work on in the evenings while you are still employed. When you have done this for a while, you will have a good idea of the earning potential from each job that you can then scale up to form your full-time predictions. If you go into freelancing without experiencing some of that type of work, it is very hard to plan what your income can be.

Trying to guess potential from passive income streams is even harder unless you have some money coming in from this in the first place. In my case, I had a few years' experience of earning passive income from my courses already, which helped me plan and build up future projections to make an informed decision about quitting my job. If you don't want to wait as long as I did, then taking the gradual approach, like the example we discussed earlier, might be a better idea, where you freelance or consult three days a week for a stable active income, and then build your passive income projects on the other two days. The key thing is that you need to plan ahead by understanding your outgoings and bills and being realistic about what you can earn to start with, and having a saved financial buffer makes this much less stressful.

Separate personal and business finances. When running a small business, you may lose the physical boundary between your home and the workplace, but you must never let personal and business finances get mixed. You should have a separate bank account for personal funds and another one for company funds. In a world where many clients are wary of getting scammed, owning a business account also helps boost your reliability online. It's not that easy to open a bank account for a business, and you need to provide a lot of documentation to the bank, but if you don't have a business bank account, some clients may not take you as seriously as you would hope.

Clarity is another benefit of having separate personal and business bank accounts, provided that you don't use them interchangeably. If you have to pay for workplace maintenance, office equipment or even meals with clients, you have to use your business account. By using your accounts appropriately and responsibly, you can learn more about your spending habits and identify your possible tax deductibles.

When creating a business account, one thing that you will need to consider is whether you stay as an independent sole trader, where any money you earn belongs to you; or whether you will incorporate as a limited liability company, where any money you earn belongs to the company and you have to pay yourself from the business. The main benefit of the latter is that if anyone takes any legal action against you, they will be suing the company and not you personally. We will talk more about company incorporation in the next chapter.

For my own business, I incorporated as a limited liability company and set up a specific bank account linked to the company, not myself. I liked the comfort in knowing the business was a separate legal entity from me personally. Using a business account and some online accountancy software, I can easily track my income and expenses so that I can plan how much to pay myself each month, and how much needs to stay in the business to pay expenses and tax.

Get suitable insurance. Emergencies can ruin your financial health in an instant. Don't let that happen by getting the right insurance policy for your needs. If you already had medical insurance offered by your previous employer, it's a good idea to continue that. If this isn't possible, you should consider getting another policy. Make sure your family is also covered. Having life insurance is also advisable in case anything happens to you which limits your ability to work; you don't want to be stuck in a position where you can't work, and you have no way to earn an income. You should apply for coverage as soon as you can, because premiums tend to become more expensive as you grow older.

Your business must also be insured to protect you and your work from liabilities. In terms of coverage, nothing can beat a comprehensive insurance policy. However, the price tends to be unattractive, especially for small-time entrepreneurs and freelancers. When shopping insurance for your business, go to a provider that specialises in insuring small businesses. Moreover, take into consideration the areas that you can skip to cut down on the total costs. For example, if you're working at home and already paying home insurance, you may not have to get another insurance policy for your home office.

Automate your savings and other monthly deductions. Do you find it hard to resist spending money before setting it aside for expenses? If so, you should automate your monthly deductions, particularly on fixed costs such as rent, subscription fees, debt repayments, and insurance. Aside from instilling discipline, this practice also saves you time and effort. The last thing you need as a new business owner is to realise you have misjudged your expenditure and spent more money than you have. Where possible, try to set up automatic payments for your outgoings, that all go out of your account at a specified time. I personally have most of my bills leave my account in the first week of the month, meaning I can plan additional expenditure in the remaining weeks of the month, knowing that my business account balance is going to be stable.

Familiarise yourself with the tax deductibles you're entitled to. As long as you're earning money, paying tax is part of your responsibilities. To make it more bearable, you can reduce the amount you have to pay by declaring your deductible expenses. If you only have one source of income from a full-time job, you may only need to file personal income tax returns. Otherwise, you may have to pay business taxes. You're entitled to different deductibles for each type of tax. Your location is also a factor. In some countries, expenses which are deemed deductibles on personal income tax include educational expenses, medical expenses and contributions to government-initiated retirement plans.

Each country has their own rules on what you can or cannot deduct from tax, but generally the most common deductibles are as follows:

Workplace expenses. Rent is the top workplace expense, but this may not be applicable if you're working in your own home. You may still claim other workplace-related deductibles, such as renovation and maintenance expenses. This was a consideration I had to take into account when I started renting a private office; the outlay each month was costing me a lot of money, but the amount is a valid tax deduction.

Operational costs. You need services such as electricity, internet, and telephone, and other business operational expenses. Your expenses for office supplies such as pens, paper, folders, and printer ink fall under this category as well. If you have a website with your own domain name that you use to promote or sell, your payment for this is considered another operational cost.

Asset expenses. All of your office equipment and furniture form part of your assets. These include your computer, phone, printer, external drive, chair, and desk. While you may not recoup the entire expense for these at once, you can claim them as deductibles based on their depreciating value. When you buy assets such as computers, laptops or other expensive hardware, their value starts to depreciate over several years until they are technically not worth much to the business. This depreciation affects the amount of tax relief you can claim on them through your accountant. The amount you can claim depends on what country you are in, but there is a better option, where instead of laying out the initial cash to buy the hardware, you can lease it instead.

When I was introduced to the idea of leasing my equipment, it was a revelation to me. Instead of owning an asset that steadily depreciates over time, you instead take out a lease over a few years. This has a number of benefits. First, the lease payments are classed as a service that you pay, which means you get tax relief on them. Paying a lease is no different to paying a plumber to fix a broken sink. The next benefit is that you do not have to lay out all the money in one go to buy your equipment. This is very helpful when you are starting out. Instead of paying $4000 for a high-end desktop computer, you can split the payments over the lease term which helps with your cashflow. The other benefit is that after the lease term, say two years, you give the equipment back, sign a new lease and they send you brand new kit—and who doesn't like new computer equipment?

The equipment that you lease will also be covered by your business insurance, which means if anything goes wrong with the equipment, the leasing company will handle the replacements.

Leasing may not be for everyone, but if you want to maximise tax relief, lower your initial outlay for equipment and have the equipment replaced routinely, then this is definitely worth looking at.

Subcontracting expenses. Aside from saving you time, subcontracting is also cost-effective. The expenses you incur for these services are deductible, so you can claim tax relief on them. I use a lot of freelancers to help me with my business, and I tend to use websites like Fiverr or Upwork. While I do have to pay out the money to cover these freelancing expenses, I know that if I provide the receipts from these sites to my accountant, they will factor them into my final yearly tax calculation.

When you are starting out in your own business, there is nothing more time-wasting than struggling to implement something that is not your core skill set. If you try to calculate how much your time is worth per hour with your income, the cost of getting a freelancer to do that work is definitely worth it, and you will end up with a higher-quality result.

My skill sets are software development, writing books and scripts, recording courses and video editing. My skills are not in graphic design or anything artistic, so I tend to outsource these to freelancers. I have had logos and book covers designed by people all over the world, for not a lot of money, and they always do a much better job than I could ever hope to achieve.

The dreaded tax office. Out of all the expenses you will have to pay as a business owner, your tax bill is the least exciting, but also one of the most important. If you do not have your tax calculated correctly and you fail to pay your business taxes on time, then you run the risk of getting into a lot of trouble. If you do not do effective tax planning, you could easily overspend in your business and then be left short of available funds when you have to pay your tax bill.

My own personal solution to this problem is to have a separate business savings account set up, and whenever I have an invoice paid, I automatically move 15% into that savings account. At the time of writing this book, our corporation tax rate in the United Kingdom is currently 19%, but I move 15% into the savings account. Once that money is in the savings account, I do not touch it until my accountant has filed my tax return and told me how much to pay to Her Majesties Revenue and Customs (HMRC), which is the UK equivalent to the United States' IRS.

Even though I provision 15% of my income, my tax bill always ends up being much less than that total calculated amount, this because my accountant will have taken into account my expenses and deductibles, which means every year I have a little bonus money left in the tax account, which is nice.

If you take one thing away from this book, it should be, "Don't take risks with your tax liabilities." Failing to pay your taxes can land you in a lot of trouble, with large fines, your business potentially being struck off, or even worse, you going to prison. The risk just isn't worth it, so save a portion of all your paid invoices into a savings account that you can't easily access.

Other expenses. The fees you pay for legal, accounting, advertising, and other professional services can form part of your deductibles, too. You may also claim tax deductions based on your costs for insurance, business software and membership in professional organisations. If you're meeting clients, your meals and other expenses are reasonable deductibles as well.

Again, the types and amounts of deductibles differ between countries. If you're not familiar with the tax laws in your area, you should consult a tax expert instead of trying to figure it all out on your own. Also, don't forget to charge all these above-mentioned expenses to your business account–and remember to always keep your invoices and receipts.

Take advantage of tools for managing finances. In addition to professional services, managing your finances is made easier thanks to various software applications and packages. You can now automatically send, receive and schedule payments. Other tasks you can automate include accounting, budgeting, invoicing, tracking expenses, scanning receipts, and even investing.

During your tool selection, don't focus on the fees; the main factor you should consider is the aspects of financial management that you want to automate. In the US, some tools you may wish to consider include *IRS2Go*, *FreshBooks*, *Moonlighting*, *Expensify*, *Xero*, and *Acorns*. If you're worried about the possible costs, read user reviews and try those that come with free trials, but keep in mind that tools advertised as free may not be reliable.

Personally, I use Xero to manage my accounting (this is not an official endorsement). I like the fact that I can hook the system up to my bank account, so any transactions appear in Xero. Then I can set up rules for those transactions so around 80% of them automatically get filed into the correct categories. This means the amount of time I have to spend on bookkeeping is reduced to about half an hour a week. At the end of my financial year, I can generate profit and loss statements, general ledgers and balance sheets, which my accountant uses to file my taxes. My accountant also has read-only access to Xero, so he can log in and see how I am doing, and if I have any questions, he just logs into Xero to see what is going on. I highly recommend a tool like this or one of their many competitors. They all seem to be pretty evenly matched on features, so you just need to pick a platform that fits your needs, but they will save you a lot of time and stress.

The Author's Approach

When setting an income strategy for my business, I always strive to aim for a passive income wherever possible. All of my publicly available training courses are passive-income based. That means when I create the training courses, I don't get compensated for the time I spend making them; I get paid afterwards as people watch them. That could be seen as a risk, as you never know how many people will watch the courses, but at the start of my journey, I created the courses while still employed, which lowered the risk.

I don't focus solely on passive income; I still do some work that garners active income (selling my time for money). I do some occasional consulting jobs, in-person training and bespoke training for companies that are all billed based on how much time I spend on that piece of work. I try not to do too much active-income work, but it can be a great way to supplement my main income.

I have always been cautious with financial planning. When I first resigned from my full-time job to work for myself, I already had eight courses released and was earning a decent passive income. My wife and I discussed the right time to leave my job and work for myself, and we both agreed on an amount of money equivalent to nine months of net salary that I had to save up as a buffer while I grew the business. Reaching this target wasn't too hard to do, as I was already earning a good passive income which I had been saving over the previous two years. When I hit my target, I wrote a letter to my manager and resigned. The amount of money my courses brought in was not at the same level as my full-time salary at the time. Still, I could see that over the previous two years of working on these courses, there was a growing trend, and I estimated it would take a further six to nine months to hit my previous salary level if I were making courses full time. It was a risk, for sure, but it was a calculated risk made less stressful by having a financial buffer saved up.

I had already formed a limited liability company, which meant money for the business was in a business bank account, separate from my personal finances. To make the business accounting more manageable, I run two bank accounts. One account is from a large and more traditional bank. This bank account already supported sending and receiving payments from European and United States businesses. When I give out any bank details for payments, it is always these account details I give to people. I also use a more modern internet bank for my daily running of the business. Each month I make sure that account has enough money in for running the business.

Most bills come out of this internet bank, and I administer it from an app. One feature I like with this account is that you can create sub-accounts for savings goals, which you can move money into as and when you need. The money is still in the main account when you move it into one of these goals, but it is not included in the principal balance. Every time I clear an invoice into the primary bank account, I move a percentage of it into the internet bank account and into a savings goal to keep any business tax separate. What this means is that no matter what happens, I have the money for my tax bill saved away. Every year I deliberately overestimate the amount I need to save, as company expenses deductions always lower the tax bill, so each year there is a little bonus left over.

I am always strict about saving away tax money, as a friend of mine once ran a small business but was not very careful with his money. One year he overspent by a large margin, and when his company tax bill (corporation tax in the UK) came through, he didn't have the funds to pay it. He owed over £17,000. You can imagine how much stress he was under trying to pay the tax bill. One of my golden rules since then is, "Never mess with the tax office." They will always get the money owed to them, even if it requires legal action and penalties against you.

Twice a year (January and July), I perform a spending review where I go through expenses for the previous six months and look at any recurring payments. I do this to make sure they are still relevant. Some regular costs are contractual, so they have to come out, such as office rent or some subscription contracts, but I note in my calendar when they are due to expire so that I can review that expense then in case I want to cancel it before it renews. Performing this simple review twice a year helps me to optimise any payments I make and have a good handle on where the company money goes. Having this level of awareness of your finances is a very sensible idea, and I recommend going through the exercise, which typically takes me only about half a day.

Having an income strategy is essential when you are starting. Passive income typically requires you to do work at risk to build the product or piece of content, and then you hope people will pay for that product. Passive income is riskier because it is hard to predict at first. Active income is more predictable as you know what you are getting for the time involved. Active income is hard to scale, though, as there are only 24 hours in a day, and you can only charge so much before you become uncompetitive. A balance of active and passive income is the key to success—and this balance may change over time, where you start with more active-based income and then switch to passive—but it is essential to consider when starting out. I began as primarily passive-income based, but this was because I was earning an active income for the time I spent at my original day job.

Summary

When you are planning to go self-employed, it is a good idea to plan out your income strategy before you dive into leaving your current job. Are you intending to earn an active income where you trade your time for money? Are you building a product to generate a passive income? Passive incomes can take a while to build up to a good level, so if you do not have that income already flowing in when you are running your business as a side-hustle, then you would be best planning in some active income work to keep money coming in.

It is very possible to build a business that solely lives off a passive income stream, but you need to plan for this to potentially take a while to get to the level that you need, so be realistic about where your company revenues are going to come from.

You also need to be very mindful of your expenses, both personally and from a business standpoint. It is a good idea to list out your fixed and variable expenses, so you have a good idea of what money comes out of your business and when. If you are planning to leave a full-time job to work on your business, I recommend that you try to save up at least three months of your net salary first to help bridge the gap for any lean times. This will drastically reduce the amount of stress you face when starting out.

Workshop Questions

In this series of workshop questions, you are going to think about the type of skills you have, and how you could turn those into active or passive income streams.

(1) Write down your main skills that you want to leverage in your business. Then for each skill, spend some time thinking about how you could earn either an active or passive income from them? For example, if you are a software developer, you could earn an active income by contracting for other companies on a day rate. For a passive income, you could build software development online training courses or build

a cloud-based software as a service product that generates revenue from recurring monthly subscription fees.

(2) Identify what skills you are not very good at and would need the help of a freelancer to perform.

(3) Now you need to make a rough financial plan to determine how much money you need to make to earn a profit after paying yourself.

1. If you are operating as a sole trader, list all of your personal fixed and variable expenditures. This covers everything from groceries, loans or credit card debt, mortgage/rent payments, and any other bills. This becomes the minimum amount you need to stay afloat.
2. If you are a limited business, do the same personal income calculation, but also perform the same exercise for your company's expenses. This will help you think about how much you need to earn as a minimum.

4

PREPARING TO DIVE IN

Moving from a side-hustle to full self-employment is a significant life event. It's reasonable to have fears before and during your transition into self-employment. More often than not, your concerns will be a result of your confusion and unfamiliarity with the many aspects of self-employment. If this is the case with you, you can find the courage to take the plunge by making the necessary preparations. In this chapter we will look at some considerations you may want to think about if you are planning on leaving your full-time employment.

The current economic climate is beyond your control, but unfortunately, it can affect you in many ways. These days, the stability of the economy isn't guaranteed. Due to economic unpredictability, the company you're working for may employ drastic means to remain in business. One of the measures your employer may use is a reduction of the workforce. So, if you think your job is secure, think again because it may not be the case.

To combat this, you might consider taking freelancing or other part-time jobs as additional sources of income while you are still working for your employer and planning a side-hustle business. You can find plenty of stories online about full-time freelancers and entrepreneurs who were able to survive and even thrive during economic recessions. Consider them as proof that the current economic climate may or may not work in your favour, which is also the case when you're relying solely on your income as an employee. I have several friends who started freelancing as a reaction to potential layoffs at their full-time jobs. They initially intended their freelancing opportunity as a temporary measure; but ten years on, it doesn't seem so temporary and they have done very well for themselves.

The good thing about self-employment during economic crises is that, as businesses attempt to minimise their losses and expenses, they often downsize and turn to independent contractors to get work done at a much lower cost. Such practice is known as outsourcing, and outsourcing is cost-effective to businesses regardless of size, as it doesn't require providing employee benefits or setting up an additional workspace to accommodate the independent contractors.

Saving and Cutting Down Expenses

It's good to hope for better days ahead, but it's always better to be optimistic but still prepared for what could go wrong in the future. As you probably appreciate, emergencies and failed ventures can entail financial burdens, especially if you're not insured. So, as you prepare to change careers in the future as an entrepreneur, learn to start saving money and reduce your expenses. It is better to get into this mindset earlier and turn it into a habit before you make drastic changes to your employment.

In the last chapter, I talked about the importance of saving an emergency fund of at least three months net salary, but you should also save for your business venture, too. You could choose to apply for a loan, but what if you barely make a profit during your initial year as a full-time entrepreneur? Don't add another potential stressor to your upcoming transition by financing your venture using borrowed money; it is much better to use the money you saved in advance.

While saving money aside, you should also try and reduce your expenses. You're not going to be relying on a steady pay cheque soon, so you may not be able to spend as generously as you previously have.

Therefore, you should get into the habit of spending your money more wisely. Learn to prepare your favourite meals to cut down your trips to restaurants. Rent instead of buying an item you're just going to use a couple of times. Find out which expenses aren't offering you value and eliminate them. It also pays to shop around for utility providers like electricity, gas, internet and water, as companies will be very keen for your custom and can offer you good deals, which means you lower your monthly costs.

Choosing Employee Benefits to Continue

If you are planning on leaving your job, examine the benefits you're already getting. There's a great chance that you can't continue getting some of them after you leave; examples include catered meals, transportation allowance, and employee discounts. However, you may be able to privately continue current benefits such as retirement plans, health insurance, and gym memberships. Doing so lets you reap the compounding rewards from having held those plans, policies and memberships for a long time.

You should talk to your HR department to ask if an employee benefit could be continued if you resign or get terminated. You should also check with the third-party provider of those benefits. Keep in mind that you don't have to continue all the benefits that you can. Focus on those that give you financial protection like insurance and retirement plans.

Naming and Registering Your Business

You don't have to wait until your product is complete and ready to sell before you spread the word that you have something to offer. Begin by giving your business a name. Make sure it's not registered already by another company in a similar area to you. You can do this by checking the databases of government agencies that handle business registrations. Once you're sure that your business doesn't share the same name as others out there, prepare the necessary documents and fees to have your company registered. You can typically register companies on the internet or via an accountant.

Don't obsess about your branding colours and logos at the very start unless this is a core part of your product. You should put more attention on the development and quality of your products, and possibly look to hire a freelancer to produce the graphics.

You might be wondering whether you should register as a legal business entity. The main benefit of registering as a limited liability company is that you are personally separated from the company itself. This means any money the company earns belongs to the company and you have to pay yourself from that company. In this set-up it is recommended to also hire an accountant, as they can deal with the formal filing and calculation of taxes. The other benefit is that in the case that someone wants to take legal action against your company, they are suing the company and not you personally, which means none of your personal assets like your house are at risk.

You could, of course, stay as an independent sole trader until such time as you launch your product or service, or when you leave your full-time employment, but registering as a limited company is a good idea eventually. I have had some occasions where the company I was pitching for work insisted that I was a registered legal entity and had all the necessary business liability insurances before they would work with me; this is something to bear in mind.

Building a Client Base

Having a client base is crucial for the success of every business venture. It ensures that you have sources of active income as you work on generating passive income streams. Gather as many clients as you can while still working for someone else. Having a stable client base before you leave full-time employment means you will be able to hit the ground running when you start your new self-employed life, which will significantly reduce the level of stress you will encounter when starting out.

If you intend to be a freelancer, Fiverr, Upwork, Craigslist, LinkedIn, and Twitter are good bets at finding your first few clients. However, freelancing sites may not be ideal options if you're offering consultation, which often requires face-to-face meetings. You will have to make use of other networking tactics, such as requesting meetings and attending local meetup events.

Scheduling

Flexible schedules, when running your own business, seem like a blessing at first. However, it can turn into a curse when you spend more time relaxing or procrastinating than working. You can do so when you've established various income streams, but while you're still starting out, you have to grind way longer than you used to. If you've only worked eight hours a day before, you may find that you now have to work ten or more hours, juggling production, promotion, and administrative tasks. You shouldn't worry, though, as some tasks become more instinctive after some time, or can be automated. For now, determine your working hours and days. Don't forget to add a day off for you to run some errands and to relax.

I must admit I struggled here when I started out after leaving my job. I was working from home and the lines between work and home life became blurred, especially when I was really busy. Luckily, after not too long I decided to start working from a co-working space to help give me that separation between work and home life. Although I still did work in the evenings, I made sure it was after the kids had gone to bed. Coincidentally, I am writing this very chapter with my laptop from the sofa!

Making Improvements

It's never too early to think about business expansion plans for the future. As early as now, have a vision of what you want your career, business, and life to be like in five, ten or twenty years. Define your business strategies and lifestyle changes based on such. Consider the skills you need to learn and improve. Think about the kind of clients you aspire to work with.

Your life and business ventures may not turn out as perfectly as you envision them to be. However, having an idea of what and where you want to be will help you tread through life and business with a purpose. It's way better than navigating aimlessly. In the future, when you want to stop working and just settle down, you can comfortably do so because you know you've achieved your purpose in life.

Preparing to Dive In

Finally, when you're financially, mentally and physically ready, it's time to keep your emotions in check. Becoming self-employed can drive you crazy at times. The positive lifestyle changes it brings can excite you. However, the stress from your workload and adjustment can make you irritable. Anxiety is another emotion you're bound to feel.

It's going to be uncomfortable and it's okay. You're neither the first nor last person to go through the transition period. Others were able to survive and thrive afterward. Emulate them. Brave the fall because you're also capable.

The Author's Approach

As I have already mentioned, my trigger for diving in was to save up a sufficient financial safety cushion to help buffer any potentially tough months. Leaving a comfortable salary and committing to an income that was passive and hard to predict was terrifying and a potential risk —and when you are risk-averse, it's a hard decision to make.

Another consideration was leaving behind any company benefits. When I left my full-time job to work on building online training courses, I didn't have health insurance, as at the time I was working for a small start-up. Fortunately, my wife had a flexible health insurance plan through the company that she worked for, so she added me onto that plan. I felt that this was important because as a self-employed individual, I needed to make sure we had a good health plan in place in order to get speedy treatment in case of illness.

The other consideration was a pension. My last job hadn't set up a pension scheme as they were still a small start-up themselves, but I had been concerned that I was now out of the pension loop. I spoke to a local pension advisor, and in the end, I set up with an online pension provider and merged all my existing pensions from all my previous employers into one place. If you are considering doing something similar, I recommend speaking to a pension advisor first and taking their advice. With my new pension scheme set up, I could easily make company pension contributions, which not only tops up my retirement fund but gives me a corporation tax advantage in the UK.

I had already set up and registered a business many years prior to going full time when I was selling sound libraries, so I didn't have to deal with the learning curve of the physical mechanics of running a registered legal entity. Registering a limited liability company had posed one problem for me, though. At the time, I was working for a bank which is a government-regulated company. Part of my employment contract stated that I couldn't have a controlling interest in any other company without express permission of the bank. There were quite strict rules around conflicts of interest, so I had to go through a formal approval process, which took about six weeks to complete. In the end, they gave me permission to create the company, provided I didn't change the focus of the business, which at the time was selling sound libraries and music. Before creating a registered company, you should always check that this will not be an issue with your current employer, and we will talk about this in more detail in Chapter Eight, "The Dangers of Building a Product While Still Employed".

Summary

In this chapter we looked at some areas you need to think about before you finally quit your job, or if you have an end date in the future. It is always a good idea to make sure you are as prepared as you can be, so that when you do finally leave your job, there are no nasty surprises waiting for you. One of the areas we looked at was identifying the local economic climate to see if leaving your job to go it alone is a good idea. Only you can make this decision, but it pays to be well-researched, and remember, freelancers and small entrepreneurs can thrive in times of economic trouble as companies look to reduce costs; and one way they do this is by using more freelancers, as they are more cost-effective than a full-time member of staff.

Another area we discussed was to really scrutinise your expenses. Can you make cutbacks to lower your outgoings? Can you move utility bills over to other providers as a way to get a better deal? There is a lot of financial planning you can do ahead of time that can really increase your chances of success.

Another important area is to look at the current benefits your employer provides. If you take no action, these benefits will stop once you leave your employer. Do you rely on any of these benefits? If so, which ones do you need to restart, or can you continue with some of the benefits privately? It is always a good idea to have medical insurance if you are living in a country that doesn't have a national health service like the UK does. In countries like the US, health insurance can be a large monthly cost, so you need to factor this into your monthly expenses.

If you are operating your business as a side-hustle, where you run the business while still employed, you need to put a lot of emphasis on growing your customer base. If you have some consistent customers who frequently give you work as an active income stream, then you will be in a much better place than if you leave your job and then start hunting for customers.

The key to thinking about becoming a self-employed business owner is planning. The more you plan and mitigate any potential problems you can identify, the higher the chances of your success going forward.

Workshop Questions

(1) Take a good look at the economic climate in the country you are operating from. Based on what you can see, do you feel now is a good time to start working for yourself?

1. How stable is the company you are working for? Could redundancy be on the short-term horizon? If so, would it be worth you hanging on for a severance package that can give you a financial buffer?

(2) Make a list of all the company benefits you currently receive and how much those benefits cost you. This will include items such health and dental insurance, pensions, gym memberships, cycle-to-work schemes, etc.

1. Decide which of these benefits are most important to you

and whether you want to either take out a new version of the benefit or continue the existing benefit, if you can.
2. If you need to take out a new version of the benefit, add this to the fixed expenses list you made from the last chapter and adjust your revenue targets accordingly.

(3) If you haven't already, think of a name for your business.

1. Do you need a logo upfront? If so, can you build this yourself or do you need some help? Can you ask an artistic friend for a favour, or will you need a freelancer? If you need a freelancer, research how much this will cost you.

(4) Start thinking about where you can work once you finally leave your full-time employment. Will you work from home, or will you want to use a co-working space?

1. Research local co-working spaces in your area. Look at costs for hiring a flexible desk per day as well as booking a fixed desk?
2. If you feel that a co-working space is a good idea so you are not working from home all the time, add the projected costs to your fixed or variable expenses from the last chapter and adjust your revenue goals accordingly.

(5) Take a deep inward look at your personality and write down the types of distraction that will prevent you from working.

1. Does your home office area have a TV and/or games console nearby? Would you be prepared to move these out of the way, so they don't distract you?

(6) Start identifying some short-term business goals, even if you are not planning on leaving your full-time job yet. Write a set of goals for one month, three months, six months, and one year.

   1. Make sure the goals are realistic. They will help you with strategic planning to plan how to best use your time.

(7) Take a critical look at whether you currently have all the skills you need for your new venture.

   1. Do you need any technical training on particular technologies?
   2. Do you need to read up on marketing and advertising?
   3. Do you need to research how to form companies in your country?

5

WHEN NOT TO GO SELF-EMPLOYED

We all love the dream of working for ourselves, but we have to also be realistic about our goals. We have talked in previous chapters about quitting the daily nine-to-five grind and working on our own terms, but there are some circumstances that you should consider when going self-employed maybe isn't such a great idea.

Commitment and determination can take you far when you are planning to go self-employed; however, timing still plays a role in how and when you're going to make that commitment. You can't game timing, but there are ways to find out if the odds are in your favour. When you are deciding whether to go self-employed, make sure you're not dealing with the following problems.

Lack of Plans

Setting goals is easy, but you need plans to make those goals achievable. You may still accomplish your goals even if you don't have plans, but the probability is low; and it will take time and a lot of mistakes.

Diving into freelancing or self-employment without a plan is bound to be wasteful of your resources. Don't do it just because your boss reprimanded you, and you want to quit and work for yourself. There's a great chance you'll do your new self-employed job badly, as you would be acting on an emotional impulse instead of a well-planned and carefully executed decision.

In contrast, when you lay down your plans, you'll be able to know how far you are from accomplishing your goals. You'll also get better, but not mainly because of mistakes; you'll improve over time because you *intend* to. And you'll save time because you can eliminate steps that aren't crucial to your success.

Debt Problems

If you're still far from paying off your debts and the compounding interest generated by them, and your financial commitments are already causing you stress, it's probably not the best time for you to make the move to self-employment. The stress from your debt issues can affect your work. Your debt repayments can eat up much of your initial profits and your limited budget during the transition. Additionally, you're bound to encounter a client who's going to pay late or won't pay at all. You can't afford to sacrifice your emergency fund to cover for those debts along with your daily needs.

It is very easy to say you should pay off your debts before going self-employed, but that is easier said than done. A lot of people are just not in a position to get rid of any debts quickly. If you can't wait to pay off your debts before going self-employed, negotiate with your lenders with a view to decreasing the amount of your repayments or consolidating debts together to make the repayment more manageable; this will require you to reassess your budget. You may have to reduce the amount you save for your emergency fund each month. As a result, it will take a longer time to have such a fund that's fit for your expenses, depending on how big a fund you wish to save. To avoid this happening, perhaps consider applying for another job that you can do during the weekends or at night as a potential short-term solution. Working a part-time job while trying to establish a business is perfectly fine and quite common. A good friend of mine, and my podcast host partner at the *Side-Hustle Success Podcast*, Kevin Taylor, did just this. Kevin is the founder of *Steel Beam Calculator* and *Timber Beam Calculator*, a Software-as-a-Service application for the building and structural engineering industry. When he quit his full-time job, he worked a part-time consulting job for two days a week, and the other three days he would work on his fledgling company. If you are in a position where you need to manage debts, then this is a great way to start off without putting yourself in financial harm's way.

Not Researching Enough

When you have senior and more experienced colleagues at a regular full-time job, you can ask them about how to do certain tasks in your workplace. But as a self-employed person, you no longer have such a luxury. Thankfully, you can find most of the basics of freelancing and self-employment online and in books like the one you are reading now. The problem, though, is when you're having a low motivation day—or when you think you know more than you do. You won't have an extensive network of people around you to help you out as you did in your full-time job. Reduce your chances of failure by practicing humility and asking for help. You can do so by admitting you don't know much yet about your new profession, so you need to learn as much as you can first before jumping into self-employment. You should also make an effort to be more dynamic about mixing and networking with like-minded people doing the same kind of work as you. Reaching out to this network for help from time to time can be invaluable.

Being a New Graduate

College or university will have taught you many life and career skills, and successfully graduating will have boosted your confidence that you can make it in the real world; that you can be your own boss soon. You'll certainly need that quality, but you need to test it out and improve it first by experiencing what having someone else as a boss feels like.

Having an employer brings many benefits to new graduates, as the former is often the one who enrols the latter in their initial retirement plans and health insurance. You can also hone your work ethic much faster and more efficiently if you opt for a regular job rather than self-employment immediately after you graduate. While this is not always the case for everyone, getting a few years' commercial experience in regular employment will still be beneficial before starting on your journey. Use the time working for another employer as a learning exercise in both working with other people, and working within real-world deadlines and constraints.

Too Much Self-Doubt

Self-doubt when starting a new business can either be a problem that might hold you back, or one that prompts you to prepare excessively. If the latter is the case, such a quality can be an advantage. But when it hinders you from doing the actual work, it's undoubtedly a drawback.

Too much self-doubt prompts you to avoid risks because you think you can't handle them. You think you're going to fail, so why should you try? You fear failure, and that's not a good thing—every successful freelancer will experience both sunny and rainy days. One failure may feel unbearable when you are dominated by self-doubt.

If your self-doubts are brought about by an anxiety disorder, you should seek advice from a qualified counsellor or therapist about the best ways to control these doubts. However, if it's just the kind of doubt that makes you think of alternative plans all the time instead of pushing forward on your main plan, the best remedy is to take a holistic view over what you are doing, and then focus on taking small steps forward, one at a time. No matter how insignificant or small you think the step is, the move forward in your work can curtail your doubt and give your confidence a boost.

If you suffer a lot from self-doubt, I suggest focusing on trying to get to the bottom of it first before you consider working for yourself, as that doubt will be amplified when you are your own boss.

Lack of Self-Discipline

When I originally quit my full-time job, I already had a flourishing business. I waited until I had hit my savings goal that I had discussed with my wife, and then handed in my resignation, with a new training course contract signed and ready to go. On my first official day of working for myself, slightly nervous that I was now in the big bad world of self-employment, I sat there at 9am and thought, *now what*? I felt strange that I had no one telling me what to do, even though I knew what I had to do, and this kind of made me hesitant. In the end, I went out for an hour-long walk to think things through. When I got back, I sat down and finally managed to start working.

Without the need to clock in or having someone watching you work, can you really will yourself to finish your tasks without any supervision? Sometimes, the pressures you experience in a typical workplace are the very reasons you get things done. So, when you're free from any pressure, you may end up doing nothing at all, and spend too much time on Twitter or YouTube, convincing yourself that you are working, when in fact you are just procrastinating.

Self-discipline isn't innate; it's a trait you need to develop for yourself. You showcase it when you face temptations. At home, things like staying in bed, watching TV and eating comfort foods are your common temptations. These make you want to avoid work. When you're disciplined, you get up from your bed, ignore temptations and proceed to your work tasks. If you can't resist these temptations, you possibly shouldn't start freelancing just yet; otherwise, you'll run into problems reaching your output levels and hitting your deadlines. We will be talking more about beating procrastination and getting focused later in this book.

I would advise that you take a long look at your level of self-discipline in your current job. Even though you potentially want to leave and start your own business, how you behave in your current job will be an excellent barometer for how you would behave in your own company. Are you disciplined in completing your work? If not, I would focus on solving that problem first; if an employer is paying you do to a job, you should be disciplined enough to get that work done to a high standard, even if you do want to leave.

Inability to Motivate Yourself

This problem can sometimes be associated with your lack of self-discipline. There may be instances, though, where there are no temptations around, yet you're still unable to do anything productive. Your inability to motivate yourself will cause you to delay tasks. You'll also feel miserable when you think about the time you wasted.

If you don't have and can't find the drive to work by yourself, it could mean you don't want to be freelance enough. A lack of self-motivation could also be a key symptom of underlying depression; in this context, it could even be a depression brought on by the isolation of self-employment—a lot of people suffer from that lack of human contact without realising that that's the reason. You might want to be your own boss more than anything else in the world, but if you suffer from depression—or anxiety, for that matter—addressing those conditions first with a trained health professional until the symptoms are appropriately managed would be paramount before embarking upon self-employment.

Self-motivation can be a tricky beast to tame, and doubts in your motivation can strike at any point. For me, when I started out working from home, I was pretty well motivated for about nine months; but when I started to struggle separating home and work life, it also started to affect my motivation to actually do my work. One day, I had the realisation that I had just spent two weeks "working" from the sofa while watching seven seasons of Big Bang Theory on Netflix; and even though I was working at the same time, I wasn't focusing as well as I should have been, and I wasn't as motivated as I used to be. For me, that was a wake-up call, which is why I started seeking out a local co-working space to split my time between home and work. I wish I had done it sooner. I was now working in an environment with like-minded people. I made many new self-employed entrepreneurial friends, and I also met Kevin, my co-host for the *Side-Hustle Success Podcast*. Because I was mixing with like-minded people, I was super-motivated and a lot more productive.

As with self-discipline, if you struggle to motivate yourself before starting a business, it will be amplified when you do start working for yourself. You need to take a good long look at your motivation and see how you can get to the bottom of this problem to try and fix it.

Difficulty Learning and Multitasking

If you want to make progress sooner in your new career, you have to learn and do tasks as quickly as you can because time really does equal money. There are other factors to consider as well, but continually improving your skills and completing as many tasks as you can are among the few that you can control. More often than not, people find it hard to learn because they are unwilling to invest their time in self-development. You're going to be slow from the start, but you won't stay slow if you dedicate time and effort to improving yourself.

I personally put a lot of emphasis on continual learning. It's probably a side effect of building training courses, but the company for which I produce those courses gives me a free subscription to their platform, so I make sure to use it. I learn on there all the time. I like to designate Fridays as learning days, if I am not trying to meet a tight deadline. I listen to podcasts constantly when I am commuting or going for a walk, as I tend to absorb a lot from just hearing people chat. I also like to read business and productivity books. I have made it a habit to read for at least 30 minutes before going to bed. By putting this focus onto learning, I broaden my horizons and learn new skills, including how to run my business more efficiently. Just a small bit of learning each day or week quickly adds up over a year. You will be surprised what you can learn when you put your mind to it.

When you run a business, you have to wear lots of different hats. Productivity experts will tell you that multitasking is bad, but as a business owner, you will frequently find yourself having to switch tasks. You may be working on developing some software when a support request comes in from one of your customers. To provide good customer service, you will have to jump onto their request straight away. When it is tax season, you will have to organise your receipts and expenses and make sure your bookkeeping is up-to-date. These are all tasks that you probably didn't have to worry about when you were full-time employed; but now that you work for yourself, you will need to do these.

If you do not enjoy learning and you are not very good at multitasking before you start working for yourself, you are going to struggle when you have no choice, so it would be a good idea to start planning on improving these skills before you take the plunge.

Emotional Instability

While you can bump into good people along the way, the world of freelancing and self-employment can remain harsh to those who aren't ready for it. Prospects can reject you, some clients can be unbearable, or a sizeable project can overwhelm you, and your requests may get ignored. If you're faint-hearted, you may not be able to survive it. It's even riskier when you have issues managing anxiety, anger, or sadness. Once you've stabilised your emotions, working for yourself can be incredibly rewarding; otherwise, you may want to hold off for the moment, especially if you do not deal with rejection or criticism well.

I will happily admit that I was never someone who took criticism well, and it was something that worried me about working for myself, but I had to learn to let go and embrace it. This is especially true of doing public speaking; you will always get at least one person who didn't enjoy the talk and wants to make a big deal out of letting you know. In my previous working life, that criticism would have probably been enough to make me stop public speaking; but one thing that being self-employed has given me is a very thick skin. If someone gives me negative feedback that is not constructive or useful, I just ignore them. It is very liberating. Of course, if the feedback is constructive and helpful, then I am thankful and embrace their comments.

I highly recommend taking an introspective look at your emotional state. Be honest with yourself—how do you take rejection, negativity, criticism, and being ignored? These are all to be expected as a self-employed individual, so you need to be honest with yourself about how you deal with them. If you find those things hard—and I am sure most people do—it doesn't mean you can't be self-employed, far from it; but you need to know that these things do happen, and you should be prepared for them.

Too Much Stress

It may not be a good time to dive into freelancing or self-employment if many stressful things are happening in your life, such as buying a house, getting married, or any other major life event. Even if these are seen as positive activities, it remains disadvantageous as these are still potentially stressful. It can be even worse if you're dealing with a loss.

You don't have to wait until you're free from any problem before you freelance or start another business, but it is always easier to make the switch when your stress levels are low. If you're the kind of person who easily bounces back after a problem, working right away can even help you get back to your usual self sooner.

Not Being Able to Say No

Being a people-pleaser can make others like you. In the long run, however, they'll hang out with you to ask favours because they know you can't say no. This trait brings additional disadvantages when you're working as self-employed, as many people assume you have more free time.

If this is your problem, you should master the art of prioritising. Are people who make incessant requests more important than your work? Learn to draw the line somewhere, as those people often don't know how to stop themselves.

I can guarantee that when you first start out running a business, whether you are a freelancer, or building a product—whenever anyone comes to you with an idea or some extra work, you will not be able to say no. You will be in the mindset that if you don't say yes now, then other future opportunities may not arise, so you feel as though you have to do everything. This is a normal feeling, and extremely common. I was exactly the same. I said yes to additional training course production requests; I spoke at as many events as I could. I just never said no. After a while, this starts to burn you out as you can't do everything, and the work you should be focusing on starts to suffer.

It took me about a year to start getting comfortable with saying no. I have reduced the number of conferences I speak at, but I still do enough to feel satisfied. I raised my prices for in-person training to weed out smaller gigs, and I put my main focus on the online training courses that I develop and my other important projects—like this book. Did the wheels fall off my business for saying no more often? No, they didn't. I am just as busy with meaningful work as I ever was, but I feel much more in control of what I work on day-to-day.

The Author's Approach

I didn't approach going into self-employment lightly. It was terrifying and not something I could jump into straight away. I have always been someone that plans everything meticulously, especially around my finances. My wife and I have worked hard to reduce our debts by reducing our spending and being thrifty. We cut back on going out drinking, going out for meals, and buying stuff we did not need.

When we first got together in 2001, we were like many young people starting in our careers. We had student debt, car loans and credit cards. I strongly feel that if we hadn't been careful with our finances and got rid of all of our debts, I would never have gone full time on a business. The pressure of making enough money to cover life and debts would have been too much for me. Our decision to get rid of any debt was something we did long before I ever had any ideas for creating a business; if anything, we wanted to reduce our debt before having children. Even though our debt reduction had nothing to do with starting a business, I am glad we did it. Reducing our debt removed a considerable amount of stress from running the business each month, as the amount I need to guarantee earning is lower than it is with a whole bunch of loans and credit cards.

I am not suggesting that everyone who starts a business needs to clear away any debt first. While it is ideal, it is not a rule. Reducing or even consolidating debts (definitely seek financial advice before doing this) into lower monthly payments makes your life easier. I appreciate that not everyone is in a position to do that. Still, I recommend going through an exercise to assess personal finances and understand what debts you have and where your money is going, and work out what you can cut down on as much as you can. This way, you can more easily calculate how much you need to earn in your business to survive. You also need to factor in what you need to set aside for business and personal tax payments in your estimates. You can't forget about tax responsibilities as that will cause you a lot of pain and heartache further down the line when the tax bill comes in.

When I first went from a small side-hustle business and made the jump to going full time, I was already confident that the business was going to work. The confidence came from many years of building up a portfolio of online training courses and learning how to promote them. The only actual difference between a side-hustle and a full-time business is the time you can spend on it per day. I had already established my business, and it was running smoothly; going full time just meant I could spend more time on it.

With self-discipline and motivation, I had already been good at motivating myself to get work done. Even after a hard day at my day job, I frequently looked forward to the time I could spend making my training courses, even if it was only for an hour in the evening. I didn't work every spare hour that I could; I paced myself, but this was time I enjoyed. While I looked forward to the time I could spend on my side project, I still enjoyed doing my day job. I didn't aspire to work for myself because I hated my job. I have been fortunate in that I have worked for some great organisations, and it is my experience over 20 years that gave me a lot of stories to write about and include in my training courses.

Even though I enjoyed my day job, after having early success with my training courses, I had the seeds of resentment form in my mind about working eight hours a day only to make money for someone else. For some people, this is a significant factor in wanting to work for themselves. It wasn't a substantial factor in my decision, but I was having those thoughts. What if instead of investing those eight hours a day in making money for someone else, I give them back to myself and invest that time in making money for myself and my family? It was that word, investment, that started sticking in my mind. You only have limited resources in life; time is one of them. Where do you want to invest your resources—in someone else's venture, or your own future? The groundswell of this thought, my wife and I reducing most of our debts, and a few years' track record of successfully selling my courses all giving me a head start, was what helped push me to act and go full time.

Summary

The main theme for this chapter was about whether you are prepared to be self-employed from multiple different angles. First of all, do you actually have a plan? What are you going to build? What are your goals? These plans, along with the income strategies that we discussed earlier in the book, are a crucial part of your future success. How can you succeed if you don't know at what you are supposed to be succeeding?

Debt is another area that you need to focus on. If you have a huge amount of personal debt that you are struggling to pay each month, then now might not be the right time to go self-employed. If you do have a lot of debt but also have a burning ambition to become self-employed, then you could always look at restructuring your debts into a consolidated plan over a longer time, which will give you lower monthly payments. I recommend you speak with a financial advisor first before doing anything like this.

The next main area we focused on was around mental preparedness, and this covered many topics such as dealing with self-doubt, discipline, and motivation; followed by struggling with multitasking, pre-existing emotional issues, and stress. If you suffer from any of these issues, then I recommend that you try to work through them before starting a business, as some of these problems can be amplified when you are working for yourself. The assistance of trained health professionals, as well as ensuring you have the support of family and close friends, can really help you out here.

Workshop Questions

The following questions are more self-reflective and introspective. They are there to help you assess yourself both mentally and physically before embarking on the path to self-employment. Some people may feel uncomfortable writing such details down but remember that no-one else has to read any of this. These are simply a tool to help you reflect on your own current state.

(1) Spend some time creating a plan for your new venture.

1. Split the plan into two sections: "Side-Hustle", and "Self-Employed"
2. In the Side-Hustle section, write out a list of everything you need to do while you are working on the company in your spare time. How many clients do you need to have to make a good profit? How much of a product do you need to build before launching? What do you need to do to prepare yourself for leaving your job (i.e. savings, reducing outgoings, or restructuring debt?)
3. In the self-employed section of the plan, write down what you feel you need to grow your business in the first six months. How many extra clients do you need now that you are full time? What product features do you need to release? How are you going to market your product or services? What revenue growth would you realistically like to see in the first six months?

(2) Make a list of all the debts that you have (if any), such as loans, credit cards, student debt, etc.

1. Write down the monthly interest and repayments for each debt.
2. Add up the monthly amounts to see what your outlay is.
3. Look up how long you have left on each debt to repay.
4. Circle any debts that are less than six months away from completion. You may want to clear these off sooner if you can.
5. For everything else, research loan companies that allow debt consolidation and see how much you can lower your

monthly repayments by refinancing your debt. Please seek financial advice before taking out any new loan, but for now this is research.

(2) Take a long, critical look at your personality traits and write down any times over the last year that you have suffered with self-doubt, or lack of self-discipline and self-motivation.

1. Is there a common pattern emerging with any of these problems?
2. Look at the causes. Are any of them within your control?
3. If any were in your control to address, what could you do differently?

6
WHAT DOES SUCCESS LOOK LIKE FOR YOU?

Everyone who starts a small business, whether it's a product, service or freelancing business, has a different idea of what success is to them. It might be that they want to free up more time to spend with family. Some might want the flexibility to travel more while working, and for others, it could be the ability to scale their income to more than they earned as a full-time employee. In this chapter, we are going to look at what success means for you.

In the regular office world, you are assigned work by a manager, you are expected to meet a deadline, and then you start on the next task, repeating this cycle every day. When you are a freelancer or working on your own product or service, you get to work on a variety of different tasks, giving you a lot of variation in your daily routine. Once you get paid, you become your own accountant and HR employee, adding up every single expense and reaping all the benefits of your work.

Self-employment is a flexible work discipline that recognises agility and adaptability. This is a field in which you can build up your community for far more than just professional reasons—a community that shares resources, knowledge, and motivations. Self-employment or freelancing can be described as working by yourself, but the successful freelancers know that it is not about working alone. The key to success lies in how well you keep yourself connected. Before leaping into this lifestyle, you might have certain doubts and fears that need to be addressed, and we acknowledged some of these in the previous chapter. You might be wondering whether you need to quit your full-time job or not.

It is possible that you will need to make a lot of compromises, though this is not always the case. You have the option of keeping an office job and then moving on to build a business that will help maintain your lifestyle.

Down the Rabbit Hole

What is the difference between the people who decide to live well and embrace each day, and the ones who choose to save all their money for the end of their career, only to realise that life is short? It depends on how they approach their lives. Some people can be distinguished in a crowd based on their goal-setting principles, philosophies, and priorities. An organised person or someone who is engaged in a nine-to-five job might want to retire young and select the kind of work they want to do, acquiring more wealth and probably waiting around for a big payoff which will give them a little financial freedom. On the other hand, a freelancer or self-employed person is free to work according to their own convenience, having the ability to take vacations whenever they'd like, while saving for their future and automating their work to reduce stress. They basically undertake all the tasks that let them live their lives on their own terms.

After several years of doing the same job, it may take some deep soul-searching to realise what your passions are. This helps you understand your dreams, rebuild old hobbies, and learn what it is that you want from life. The goal is not to get rid of everything bad, as this will only leave a vacuum within you; rather, it is to strive to experience what is best for you in this world.

Being financially comfortable and having the ability to live life like a millionaire are two different things. Money can be measured based on how you control your life, such as when you want to do something, what time you do it, or with whom. For instance, if you work a 40-hour week and you make $250,000 per year, you may be earning a large amount of money, but you are confined to continue working those same 40 hours a week, and if you lose your job, that salary goes away, unless you can replace the job. Compare this to a freelancer who works as many hours as they wish, making on average $80,000 a year, but with complete control over how and when they work. The freedom to choose is where the real power lies. Although we talk about freelancers, I am also referring to anyone who strikes out on their own to be self-employed to work on their passions—this might not just be freelancers, but people who design and develop products and other services.

So, who are these freelancers? Freelancers are those who reorganise their schedule and propose a remote work agreement, accomplishing 90% of the results in less than half of the time. Essentially, this gives the freelancer the time to take a vacation and plan their work according to their needs. They can also be business owners who remove the least beneficial projects and customers, outsource operations, and travel the world while remotely managing a website for their business; these are referred to as "digital nomads", and we will be covering that topic later in the book.

There are plenty of options out there, and they all start with reshaping your assumptions about work culture. To begin this new life, you must first unlearn everything you know about the concept of "success", and change the rules.

Golden Rules for the Self-Employed

Making retirement an end goal is a slippery slope. It's similar to life insurance, and it should be approached as a worst-case scenario; that is, you should consider retirement when you are physically incapable of carrying out your duties due to old age or any other reason preventing you from earning a living. It is a flawed goal for a few real reasons. First, it is an approach based on the assumption that whatever you venture into during the prime of your life is something that you will not necessarily enjoy. So, in a way, you are setting yourself up for failure from the beginning.

The pitfalls of retirement planning. In today's world, traditional retirement planning can go on for 40+ years, and inflation lowers your purchasing power by 2% to 2% each year. So, if you take the financial atmosphere and the economy's health into account, even one million dollars may seem like chump change in your retirement fund. The math then says that your golden days would become more like your more frugal younger days again, which is probably not the ending you were hoping for. If the math works favourably, it means that the odds might be on your side, provided you work diligently on increasing your income throughout your life. However, chances are you will soon get bored and start to look for a new job, which is in stark contrast to the initial plan. This doesn't mean that you shouldn't have an emergency retirement fund; it just means that having retirement be your only goal isn't a good idea.

Consolidating pensions. When I started working for myself, I was quick to make sure I consolidated all my pensions (make sure you take financial advice before doing this), and then contributed to my private pension fund each month, even it if was only a small amount to start with. I consider this retirement fund an investment, but I am not planning on depending on it as a sole means of income when I am in my golden years. It is simply a worst-case scenario retirement fund in case anything goes wrong business-wise.

Why wait until old age? Switching up periods of rest and activity is an essential part of survival. Instead of making retirement the end goal, a freelancer is at liberty to take mini-retirements during the course of their life. Choosing to prioritise personal life over meaningless work does not indicate laziness or a lack of productivity, though current life conditions might make us believe otherwise. Your emphasis needs to be on being more productive instead of just keeping yourself busy.

· · ·

Seizing the opportunity. Are you waiting for an extraordinary sign to quit your current job? Those stars that you are wishing upon might never align. The universe doesn't owe you anything. If something is important to you, then you need to put in the necessary effort to *make* it happen and alter your course according to what works for you.

Go ahead and make the most of the opportunities that come your way. As a business owner, you will make good decisions and also plenty of bad decisions, and these will need dealing with as they happen. We all have our strengths and weaknesses. If you know that your strengths help you do your best at work, then continue to hone them. Downplay your weaknesses, and don't spend all your time trying to fix them.

A lot of the time, your desires will turn into something that you didn't expect, and this applies to both time and possessions. Your lifestyle should centre around utilising your free time productively, which means that you need to do something because you like it instead of doing it simply because you feel obligated.

Learn the value of money vs time. The power of money is undeniable, but it's never the solution to the core problems in life. Thinking that more money will solve all your problems is the laziest way to avoid self-criticism and decision making, which is pivotal to a life of enjoyment. You can become occupied in this race to earn money and pretend that it will fix everything, but it will only be a constant distraction that stops you from seeing the bigger picture. Since everyone around you is a part of this same cycle, you will hesitate to trust your instincts, which will most likely tell you that it is all an illusion.

Fixed income is measured by one variable, and that is the dollar (or the currency of the country you live and work in), while relative income is measured by time and the dollar. For example, if Jane makes $100,000 per year while working 80 hours per week, then she makes $25 per hour. Now, if John makes $50,000 per year working ten hours per week, he makes $100 per hour. What Jane makes is fixed income, while John's, on the other hand, is relative income. Relative income is much more important than fixed income for freelancers and small, single-person business owners alike.

. . .

Being aware of stress. Not all stresses are bad, and freelancers don't need to work towards eliminating them all. There are two types of stress. One type of stress makes you feel weak, less capable, and less confident. Self-destructive criticism, abusive mentors, impossible or very tight deadlines are examples of this type of stress. The other kind of stress involves role models who make you surpass your limits, training that removes unimportant goals, and calculated risks that will force you to step outside of your comfort zone. This type of stress is important for stimulating growth, provided the stress is kept to manageable limits.

What is Success?

You may have come across people who are retired and ultra-rich, but are still unfulfilled and unhappy at the same time. Too much free time could be one reason for this, but isn't that what we are all after? Not at all; well, I certainly am not. Plenty of free time comprises the building blocks of self-doubt. When you eliminate the bad things in your life and do not replace them with good things, then it creates a void within. Decreasing work based on income is not the target; rather, the goal is to get more out of your life. It is important that you stop repressing yourself and get away from the habit of procrastinating. Let's say you decide to ski in the Alps or go to the Caribbean. Well, you should certainly do it! However, there might come a time when you can't sip on piña coladas or go skiing. This is when the panic and doubt start to set in, along with the self-criticism.

You might wonder to yourself why you're bored even though this is all you've ever wanted. This is normal among goal-oriented high performers who downshift after a long time. The more goal-oriented you are, the tougher having downtime becomes. You must replace the concept of a lack of time with one where there is an abundance of it. Retirees can also become depressed due to social isolation.

Not to offend anyone with a nine-to-five job, but most of those employed in such jobs tend to become mere cogs in the corporate machinery. Not all of those employees are ambitious, and their laid-back attitude doesn't do them any favours. For such people, offices are good for free coffee, gossiping, sending cat or dog videos, attending meetings that accomplish nothing, and other idle work. The job might be a dead end, but it's the human interactions that keep it alive. Once you reach the stage of retirement, you will be cut off from the daily interactions you were used to, and the solitude will become increasingly overwhelming.

Once you get rid of the nine-to-five job, the big questions become harder to avoid. In a world of infinite options, decision making becomes far more difficult. Like every other person, you will also experience certain moments of doubt. While the rest of the world seems to get on with their nine-to-five jobs, you might feel like you are lost somewhere. You might even start questioning all your life decisions. Common doubts include the following:

- Does this help me lead a better life, or is laziness clouding my judgment?
- Did I quit the race because I couldn't handle it?
- Will this get better as it goes?
- Am I even successful, or is this all a joke?
- Did I lower my standards too much?
- Why isn't this making me happy?
- Do I even deserve to live the life I want?

These doubts can be surpassed once you realise that they are all outdated comparisons using the "money equals success" and "more is better" concepts that tend to distort your perceptions of what life must be. These thoughts can easily overpower you when you have nothing with which to replace them. Think of a time when you felt your best—when you focused on the moment without getting distracted. Once the mind loses external focus, it turns inward and looks for problems to solve, even though they may be unimportant or even imaginary. If you have a target or an ambitious goal that gives you no other option but to grow, these mind-numbing doubts will cease to exist. When you are in the pursuit of finding a new focus, the big questions will not distract you.

Life exists to be enjoyed, and it is important that you feel good about yourself. Everyone has different ways of getting there, and the paths taken will keep changing. Two elements are fundamental to everyone: to keep learning and developing as a person; and to fulfil a higher purpose in their lives. To live is to learn, and the higher purpose is all about doing something that improves other people's lives as well, rather than just your own. I'm not talking about philanthropy—you don't have to donate all your life savings to help starving children—but you should ideally be concerned with helping others. The services you can offer in life are not merely about saving lives or the environment. For instance, if you are a musician and put a smile on the faces of many, then that is also a service. It is an attitude. These are all good starting points for freelancers and self-employed people. If you really want to be service-oriented, then you need to be able to do things for others without expecting any appreciation in return.

When you are self-employed, you can take a short break from your work every now and again, and start regularly analysing your life. Concentrate on learning and self-development and doing your bit to contribute through your business, to humanity as well as your customers. Doing so will help increase the meaningful interactions you have with people and with your customers when you have virtuous goals as part of your measure of success.

Over time as a business owner, regularly make notes of all self-criticism that you inflict on yourself; start maintaining a journal to make a list of all your negative thoughts. Whenever you feel self-criticism creeping up, you need to make an effort to replace it with positive thoughts.

Redefine answers for questions like the following (we will come back to these in the workshop section of this chapter):

- What are you good at?
- What do you want to be the best at?
- What makes you feel content and happy?

- What are you most proud of accomplishing in the past?
- Can you repeat this or develop this further?
- What do you love sharing with people?

An Example of a Side-Hustle for Social Good

Good friends of mine and members of the Nottingham tech community in the UK, Jessica and Moreton, are a great example of running a side-hustle business where the focus isn't on turning a profit, but on raising enough money to run a free software development conference called DDD East Midlands. DDD stands for Developer Developer Developer and is an open-source template for running a technical conference, with multiple subject tracks for talks from new and experienced speakers. The speakers submit talks and the talks for the day are picked through a democratic voting mechanism by the attendees. The conference is free of charge to attendees, but the costs for running the event, including venue hire, insurance, and catering are raised through selling sponsorship packages to local companies, who get to advertise their wares at the conference, and even have a small exhibition stand on the day.

This is a great example of a company that was set up to benefit a local community of software developers. They have registered as a limited liability company and they are running it as anyone would run any other business. Raising money is important—it would be naïve to think that it is not when it is a community event, as the money is needed to fund the event and keep it free for attendees—but profit is not the goal; any money left over is reinvested into the following year's event.

While Jessica and Moreton are running DDD East Midlands as a limited liability company, this is very much a side-hustle. Both of them are full-time employed, and at the time of writing, this isn't likely to change in the near future; but you can quite easily imagine an interesting trajectory where they could scale up this event—or even multiple events—to the point where they could be paid for running conferences. They both serve as a great example of flexing the entrepreneurial muscle for the benefit of their local software developer community. The experience of running this business and conference has provided them both with some excellent new skills.

Mistakes to Avoid

When you are making a complete shift in your lifestyle, mistakes are unavoidable. It involves fighting impulse after impulse that you learned in your old employed life. This is all part of the process, so try not to get frustrated. You should also avoid aiming for endless perfection, rather than being great or good enough in your professional and personal life. Perfection is a nice ideal, but always try to see it for what it is—an unattainable destination.

A common mistake a lot of freelancers and entrepreneurs make is trying to do work that is better left automated. Learn to streamline all the tasks that are capable of being automated. By doing this, you can successfully reduce time wasted and improve your productivity. As a freelancer, your quality of work matters more than the number of hours you spend working.

Viewing one product, project, or job as the be-all and end-all of your entire life is not an ideal perspective to have. Life is too short to be a pessimist. Whatever work you're doing now is just another stepping stone to your next venture. When in doubt, take a break or sit back, and try to view things from the perspective of a third person. Be as impartial as you can while analysing your life, and over time, you will be able to change your perspective.

If you are failing to recognise the social rewards of life, you should surround yourself with positive people who are also not part of your work life. Happiness, when shared through friendships and relationships, is easily multiplied.

The Author's Approach

When I look at my journey into self-employment, I can say that my priorities and views of success have shifted. When I was building training courses as a side-hustle, my view of success was increasing monthly revenue and hitting a savings target so that I could leave my job. We have spoken about the fact that money isn't the be-all and end-all, and it certainly isn't, but it *is* a valuable tool to help you realise your vision.

Once I had hit those initial goals, the next goals were to increase revenues to surpass my required salary level and leave a surplus in the business, so that I could grow and invest in new projects. This very book is a project I am investing time and money into, to turn a goal into a reality. Even though a big goal was to initially raise revenues, I also wanted the management of my time to be a success measure. One of my passions is public speaking—I absolutely love it. When I was employed, I still got to attend some conferences to speak, but they were few and far between, and I had to ask permission from my employer to go, sometimes using some of my annual leave. Once I had command over my own time, I could take on as many public speaking events as I desired.

Travel and seeing the world had been a goal of mine for many years. When I was younger (in my twenties and thirties), I never travelled that much, apart from a yearly summer holiday with my wife. By accepting public speaking engagements, I could travel the world, which is normally paid for by the conference organiser, and experience countries, cities and cultures that I hadn't seen before. I would often extend my trip for a few days to a week so I could see the city and also work from local coffee shops and co-working spaces. I was living the digital nomad dream, except I wasn't a full-time traveller, more of an occasional nomad. Travel, and being able to carry on with my work while travelling, was one of my success measures. In reality, I can do my job from anywhere in the world as long as I have electricity and a good Wi-Fi connection; and to me, that is a successful achievement.

Another key success point for me was being able to take time out to volunteer at my children's schools by being a parent helper on day trips. Such a small thing is invaluable to me, because being able to see my kids in their school environment is not something I could do often when full-time employed.

The key point that I am illustrating is that although money is not the final success measure, it is a tool that, if handled properly in the running of your business, opens up more opportunities that you can enjoy and benefit from. So, instead of waiting until retirement to enjoy life, you can enjoy life as you work. I feel that this is a healthy way of looking at how financial success helps lead to other self-defined successes. My goal isn't to become a multi-millionaire, that's not what I am working towards. I am aiming to continue doing what I am doing in my business, while creating a comfortable lifestyle for me and my family; and achieving the dream of working on new projects, where not all the projects will make a lot of money, but they will allow me to scratch a creative itch.

Summary

Having a firm grasp on what success means to you is a vital step to trying to identify how you can start, run, and grow your new business. It is common for people to think that money is the ultimate success measure, with the mindset of, "If I earn a lot more money, I will be happy." That isn't always the case. As we stated earlier, a financially wealthy retiree may have a lot of money, but they are not necessarily happy once the novelty of free, unoccupied time wears off. Money and financial wealth are, of course, still important, but you should treat them as a tool to unlock future goals and dreams. At the start of running your business, you will be obsessing about making enough money to cover expenses and pay yourself—that is normal—but as you grow the business, start to think about other success measures that will drive your business, customers, yourself and hopefully humanity forward.

Workshop Questions

The workshop questions for this chapter are about understanding what you are good at, what your passion is, and how you can use these to set future success goals.

(1) On a piece of paper, write down what you are good at:

1. What are you good at in your current employment?
2. What hobbies / skills are you good at outside work?

(2) Write down what you want to be the best at:

>   1. This list is aspirational; do you want to be the best at something to do with your day job? Do you want to take a hobby or interest to the next level?

(3) Write down what makes you feel content and happy:

>   1. Just because you are very skilled at something, doesn't necessarily mean you are happy doing it. Highlight any correlations between what makes you happy and skills you are good at from either your job or personal hobbies and interests.

(4) Write down what you are most proud of accomplishing in the past, either professionally or personally:

>   1. Can you repeat this or develop this further?

(5) Write down what you love sharing with people

>   1. This might be something artistic, blog posts, or poetry. What do you want people to see that you are proud of the most?

(6) Take your list of skills, what makes you happy, and what you like sharing, and see how many items you can match up. For example, you

may be skilled at web development; long coding sessions make you happy; and you love sharing blog posts.

1. These associations should hopefully help you start to see patterns between skills and passions, that you could use to start producing goals that result in something you share. The sharing doesn't have to be for free, it could be a paid product.

7
KEEPING AN EYE ON COSTS

You have decided to create your first side-hustle business while still employed full-time; but just because this is a small business, doesn't mean that cost control and accurate record-keeping are any less important than in running a larger business. In this chapter, we will look at the basics of bookkeeping and record-keeping.

Many people get intimidated by the idea of bookkeeping. Unfortunately, it's an integral part of running a business. Even if you can afford to hire a bookkeeper or an accountant, you should still familiarise yourself with the process. After all, whoever you hire to keep your financial books won't have any power to decide which expenses to cut down or how you're going to increase your revenue. Successful entrepreneurs make their own financial decisions by considering and analysing previous transactions in their financial books.

If you're dreading the level of terminology and numbers involved, you should remind yourself that you're still starting out as a business owner, and therefore your financial records don't have to be too complicated. You can begin your bookkeeping with a single spreadsheet.

There are sample templates online that you can download. However, it will also help if you ask a professional accountant to look over your books before you file your tax return.

You can also use one of the many excellent online bookkeeping software packages that are available, such as Xero or FreshBooks, as they make keeping your finances in check very straightforward. I personally use Xero, which I have connected to my business bank accounts, so all transactions are sorted into the correct categories for me. When I get to tax time, Xero generates all the reports I need for my accountant to file the appropriate tax forms.

Each month, I load up my financial accounts and look at the total amount of revenue that came into the business, and my total expenditure. Each month should be in profit, where my outgoings are lower than the revenue coming in. If they are not, then I want to know why, and I can look at the different financial categories to see where spending may have increased over time. This level of insight, especially with online accounting systems, is a very powerful tool.

The Essence of Bookkeeping

Lots of small businesses fail because the people behind them didn't pay much attention to the financial health of their companies. If you don't want to be one of them, make bookkeeping one of your priorities. You can't identify and resolve a problem in your business's financial health if you don't have financial records in the first place.

What if the cost of your supplies or raw materials for your product were to increase significantly and wasn't likely to go down anytime soon? Unless you raise the prices of your products, this will lower your profit margins. Keeping accurate financial records lets you be aware of the specific impact of events like this on your business. You can see at a glance that your earnings are decreasing because of the increased expenditure, and know exactly how much your losses are.

Imagine that your side-hustle is creating wallets. If your raw materials cost $2.50 for each wallet and you sell them for $9.99 each, you are making a $7.49 profit; but if the cost of your raw materials increases over time to $3.50 per wallet, then your profit margin is reduced to $6.49. If you keep a constant eye on your finances, you can monitor these trends over time and then make a business decision. Do you absorb the raw materials price rise so that your customers don't have to pay extra, which reduces your profits? Or do you raise your prices, which may put your product at a higher cost than those of some competitors? You can only make these decisions if you are aware of your business's financial numbers.

Bookkeeping Tips

Budgeting your personal finances is one good way of preparing yourself for the bookkeeping tasks for your business. Nevertheless, it will help if you don't wait until you master the art of budgeting before keeping financial books for your business. As soon as you set up your side-hustle and start spending, you should start recording your expenses. Make this a daily, or at most, a weekly habit.

An easy mistake for a new side-hustler to make is to delay worrying about keeping financial records. Then, before you know it, months have elapsed, and you struggle to remember everything that needs to go into those records. No matter how much money you earn, even if it's only a small amount, those earnings will be subject to taxation, so not keeping accurate records straightaway will cause you lots of problems later down the line. You may only earn a few thousand dollars, but if you have correctly identified your expenses in your books, then the amount of tax you pay on that small amount can be significantly reduced. If you don't have those details recorded anywhere, then you will not get the tax relief you are entitled to. Effective bookkeeping will save you money in the long run.

Below are some additional bookkeeping tips you should keep in mind. There are no hard-and-fast rules, apart from the fact that bookkeeping is essential for any business, but these guidelines should help you get started.

Collect all bills, invoices and receipts. Tax authorities are thorough; they can potentially penalise you even when you're just missing one receipt upon an audit. Therefore, you should file your bills, invoices, and receipts properly. Scanning or photographing your invoices and receipts lets you have digital copies that you can back up in multiple places. It's vital that you do it while the printed receipt is still readable, as it can fade; I have had instances where the print on receipts has faded in my wallet, which makes them virtually useless. I collate all my receipts and then store them in folders for each month. Then, I routinely take photos of the receipts and store them digitally, along with any other files I need for my accountant. You need to be as thorough as you can when keeping records. If you lose a receipt for an expensive line item, then you cannot claim tax relief for that item, which can start to get costly for you around tax season.

Have a tax plan. Having a tax plan helps soften the blow of tax payments at the end of your financial year. This means that you should set aside around 10% to 30% of your profits for your tax payment, depending on the tax rate for the country within which you are operating. It seems high, but if there's a surplus remaining after you have paid your tax bill, you can roll it over for the next tax season—or pay yourself a little bonus.

Whenever I have an invoice paid, I automatically pay 15% of that invoice amount into a separate account. The current corporation tax rate for me, in the UK, is 19%, but I know I will never pay that much, so I provision 15% and set it aside. Then I feel comfortable in the knowledge that no matter what happens, I have the money set aside for the tax office. I have known people that have not followed this advice, and when it came to the tax payment at the end of their financial year, they had overspent and didn't have the funds to pay the tax bill. Can you imagine how stressful that would be? Paying tax isn't pleasant, but it is a legal necessity, so set the money aside each time your business gets paid and free yourself from that unwanted stress.

Unless you are an experienced bookkeeper or qualified accountant, there's a high possibility that you might make a mistake, such as an error in categorising expenses. If you're going to file your business taxes on your own, let an accountant go through your books first. I always say that even though you are paying for an accountant, their services should be thought of as free, because they should be able to save you more money in tax than they cost. I pay on average between £500 and

£650GBP a year for my accountant to file my tax forms and look over everything. While it sounds expensive, they always save me more than that in knowing how to apply various deductions and reliefs based on my claimed expenses.

Categorise your expenses. It's a simple trick, but it helps ensure your books look organised. You should make a list of expenses and categorise them into *fixed*, *variable* or *periodic*. Periodic expenses are those that you only incur in certain weeks, months or seasons. Variable expenses are those that can change each month; for example, a phone bill might be in this category as the bill could change each month according to usage. Fixed expenses are items like office rent that do not change each month.

Aside from classifying your expenses based on how much and how often you pay, you should also have another expense list that features some or all of the following example categories: *general expenses, travel, subscriptions, IT equipment, sales,* etc. Different expense categories will have different rules about the amount of tax relief you can claim. If you use an online accounting system, then they will be automatically set up with the appropriate categories for your country or state, that your accountant can make tax deduction calculations from.

Expense	Date	Amount	Frequency	Category	Balance
Hotel stay 3 nights	3rd Feb	-$400	One off	Travel	$4600
Restaurant meal for 4	3rd Feb	-$150	One off	Entert'	$4450
Office rent	5th Feb	-$500	Fixed	Rent	$3950
Invoice #01 paid	10th Feb	+$3000	One off	Sales	$6950
Phone bill	12th Feb	-$34	Variable	Phone	$6916
Apple MacBook Pro	20th Feb	-$3000	One off	IT	$3916
5k monitor	20th Feb	-$1100	One off	IT	$2816
Flight from LA to London	22nd Feb	-$1500	One off	Travel	$1316
Business insurance	23rd Feb	-$120	Fixed	Insurance	$1196
Invoice #02 paid	25th Feb	+$2500	One off	Sales	$3696
Invoice #03 paid	26th Feb	+$5000	One off	Sales	$8696
Tax Provision @ 15%	28th Feb	-$1425	Variable	Tax	$7271
Salary	28th Feb	-$2000	Fixed	Salary	$5271

Table 1: Example bookkeeping for one month, assuming a starting balance of $5000

If you look at the preceding table, this is an example from some financial books for a single month, that has a starting balance of $5000 at the beginning of the month. Here we can see a series of transactions that have been entered into the books. On the first column we have what the expense is, for example, a three-night hotel stay. Then we have the date of the transaction, i.e. when you made the payment. Then in the next column we have the actual amount of the transaction. Next is the frequency; in the case of our hotel stay, this is a periodic transaction, as it isn't necessarily a recurring event. Next, we have the category. For the hotel stay this is filed under *Travel*; the Apple laptop and 5k monitor are under *IT equipment*, etc. Depending on the country in which you are running your business, you may have different tax deduction rules for different categories of expenses, so the accurate classification of categories is important. Then in the final column, we have the running balance for the business bank account.

In this simple example of a month's transactions, you can see that our expenses were $6404. We can also see that in February we had three invoices totalling $10500 paid into the company, which are marked as *Sales*. At a glance, we can see what the outgoing expenses are, how much we have been paid into the company, and easily work out our profit for the month, which is $4096. We don't want to get caught out at the end of the year, so at the end of the month we calculate an amount, in this case 15%, that we want to save away into another account, which equals $1425. This covers the potential tax for the invoices that were paid in that month.

As we are storing away the tax money for safe keeping, this means that at the end of the month, our disposable money left over from the revenue generated during that month is $2671. Once all the other expenses have been accounted for, at the bottom of the table we finally pay the company owner $2000, which leaves $671.

However—this doesn't take into account the opening balance of $5000 of retained earnings from the previous month. That $671 doesn't feel like a lot, so what happened?

Well, this month was an expensive month and there were some periodic expenses that wouldn't normally occur; in this case, a hotel stay, a meal out, a new laptop and monitor, and a flight to London. These are all probably very valid expenses, but we can instantly see that the month was expensive, even though many of the costs wouldn't happen every month. The flight to London could be attending a conference in order to win more business. The laptop might be replacing an old laptop. The important thing is that you can look over your books and see what is going on. In this case, this was just an unusually expensive month; however, if you had lots of large fixed expenses that went out every month and you were just breaking even, then that highlights a larger problem with your income/expenses ratio, which might prompt you to cut back on fixed outgoings.

Bookkeeping at its simplest doesn't need to be much more complicated than this to start with. Keeping a spreadsheet was how I started. At the start of each month, I started a new tab in the spreadsheet and entered the starting balance for my business bank account at the top of the sheet. Then I would list all my transactions, which I manually reconciled from logging into my bank. I did this for a few years before I started to use an online cloud-based accounting system like Xero, but initially when my number of transactions were low, the spreadsheet did me just fine.

The Author's Approach

Apart from my general fear of starting a business, the other area that filled me full of dread was accounting and bookkeeping. From the outside, bookkeeping looked complicated. You need to keep track of lots of receipts, tie them to transactions, and then allocate those transactions into categories that the accountant can use to determine which deductibles can be applied to your tax bill.

My first attempt at bookkeeping started when I formed a limited liability company while creating sound libraries. I started with a spreadsheet, but my accountant recommended using a free software package called GNU Cash, a bookkeeping tool where you manually enter transactions and categorise them. At the end of the financial year, you generate a series of reports, a profit-and-loss statement, balance sheet, and general ledger. These reports go to the accountant who reconciles all that data with my bank statements and then he prepares the tax submission to the government.

I learnt very early on that bookkeeping is much easier if you keep it updated every day. I created a habit of spending fifteen minutes each morning updating. If I didn't, then it took significantly more time to keep them up to date.

The first year of implementing bookkeeping was the hardest, but once I had gone through my first end-of-year tax submission and understood the process better, the following years didn't feel as intimidating. The most significant bit of advice I can offer is to get an accountant and make sure you ask them any questions you have. My accountant was brilliant at showing me what to do with the bookkeeping and advising me on what I needed to submit at the end of the financial year so that he could prepare my tax documentation.

Of course, you can pay for someone to do your bookkeeping for you, but this is an expense that you will need to pay out. My co-host on the *Side-Hustle Success Podcast*, Kevin, uses a bookkeeper, and he is happy doing so. I went down the self-educated route for keeping my books. With my accountant's help and reading a book on basic bookkeeping, I worked it all out. Thankfully, it is not complicated, and if you keep on top of your records every day or every week, it doesn't become too much of a burden.

I used GNU Cash for a few years, and was reasonably happy with it, although entering transactions from a bank statement into GNU Cash and double-checking everything was a lot of work. While listening to some of my favourite podcasts, I heard about an online accounting system called Xero. Xero is a cloud-based accounting platform that integrates with your business bank account and synchronises transactions. Instead of entering all the transactions by hand, the bank sends them to Xero. You can then tag those transactions into different categories like general expenses, travel, hardware costs, software costs and entertainment, etc. You can even set up rules to recognise certain transactions and automatically tag them into the correct categories. All you need to do then is check the transactions and accept them or change the category they are applied to. Once I had Xero set up, it was a revelation. Xero saved me so much time; I could reduce my daily bookkeeping to just a few minutes a day.

Xero isn't the only platform that works this way. Another popular platform is FreshBooks, and no doubt there are many others, but Xero is the one I heard about and it is what I still use today. It's not perfect, but it works. It saves me time, making my end-of-year accounting process much easier as I can log in and generate the required reports to send to my accountant. I have granted my accountant read-only access onto the platform too, so he can log in and query any transactions. Being able to self-serve like this saves him time as he doesn't have to contact me each time; he can look himself. I am not officially endorsing Xero. It works for me, but there are alternatives you can use. I suggest doing some research, trying out the different options and pick the one you like. There is a monthly charge to use a tool like Xero or Fresh-Books, whereas GNU Cash was free to use, but that cost is tiny compared to the time it saves me.

I no longer fear bookkeeping. It has become part of my daily routine to check transactions and keep the accounts up to date. My financial end-of-year process is now as simple as generating a series of reports, downloading statements and sending it all over to my accountant to prepare the tax calculations.

My company's end-of-year is at the end of February. My tax bill has to be paid by the end of November. In March, I send everything over to my accountant. He works everything out and then tells me how much I have to pay to the UK's Revenues and Customs. Knowing in advance what my tax bill will be is very helpful.

Whenever I have an invoice paid into the business, I move some money into a separate bank account for tax provisioning. As soon as I have enough money saved up in that account, I pay the tax bill. I have made saving away tax money on each invoice payment a habit, as I never want to be in the position where I don't have enough money to pay the tax office. This is even more important at the start of your business journey when you have fewer funds in the business. Tax is the one bill you must always make sure is paid on time.

Summary

In this chapter, we explored the importance of keeping accurate financial records for your business. No matter how small your revenues are for your side-hustle, you need to accurately record your expenses and categorise them appropriately so that accurate tax calculations can be made. We also discussed the importance of provisioning a percentage of any revenue that comes into your company into a separate bank account so that when tax payment time comes around, you have the money set aside. Overspending and not having enough funds to pay the tax office is very stressful, so setting aside a percentage of your revenue will keep you out of trouble with the tax authorities.

Workshop Questions

(1) On a piece of paper, or a spreadsheet, copy the bookkeeping template discussed earlier and have a go at maintaining bookkeeping records for a single month of transactions. Make sure to apply your opening balance at the start of your record to maintain an accurate balance through the month.

1. If you haven't started a business yet, take a single month of personal expenditure and practice maintaining the spreadsheet.

(2) Perform a brainstorming session and try to plan what you think would be your costs for running your business.

1. Think of any fixed costs that have to be paid each month, such as a broadband internet charge or a repeating subscription charge.
2. Think of any variable costs that you may have to pay that are frequent, but different values, such as a mobile phone bill.
3. Think of any potential periodic costs that could come up, such as ad-hoc train or airfare tickets.

8

THE DANGERS OF BUILDING A PRODUCT WHILE STILL EMPLOYED

Building a side-hustle business while still employed is a great way to develop a business idea, and it also reduces a lot of the risks of setting up a business. However, you have to be careful that you don't fall afoul of your current full-time employer. In this chapter, we will explore what you need to consider so that you don't run into any problems.

You have always wanted to own your own business. You have worked with your current employer for a few years and understand a bit more about running a business and what you want to do. However, you are worried about the dangers of building a project while you are still working full time. Other than the obvious risk of reaching the burnout phase, you want to know what other dangers you need to watch out for.

It is hard to believe that an employer can own the rights to something you build while you are off the clock. However, this is common and often in the fine print of a lot of employment contracts between an employer and employee. If you ever want to build a product while you are still employed, you need to understand the dangers, and learn what you can do to both protect your rights to your product and keep yourself out of trouble.

Be Open with Your Employer

Some companies outright do not allow you to work on a business, and you need to find out if this is the case before starting by reading through your employment contract. Other companies are happy for you to have a small side business, as long as you don't compete with your primary employer. You need to find out where you stand. If they are happy for you to have a small business on the side, then you should be open with your employer. Discussing your plans with your employer might not seem like something you want to do, especially if you have been told that they could own your product, but you can save yourself a lot of hassle if you simply discuss your idea or intentions with your employer before you begin. Most employers are going to be happy for you since they want to see you succeed. Chances are, you will know how this conversation is going to go before you even enter your supervisor's office.

The reality of the situation is that there are a lot of businesses that do allow their employees to have a side-hustle. This is something you will be able to find out by reading your employee handbook and contract. Furthermore, even if it states differently in the handbook, there could still be a chance that everything will be perfectly fine with creating your side-hustle. Many businesses struggle to update their employee handbooks annually. Therefore, something like this could bring up the point that it is time to take that fine print out of the handbook.

Before I started my business creating online courses, I used to run another business creating sound design libraries for musicians. At the time, I was working for an internet bank. In their handbook they had a strict rule about not being permitted to be a director of another company while working at the bank. This was part of the overall anti-money laundering regulations. The sound libraries I was making were starting to make a nice little side income, and I wanted to create a limited liability company to protect myself, as I was working with some companies in the US. When I spoke to my human resources manager about this, they said that the rule in the handbook was a blanket catch-all policy, but they were open to discussing individual cases to ensure there was no conflict of interest. I explained that this business was to formalise a sound design hobby of mine, and after a short wait, they wrote me an official letter stating I was approved to create a company based on what I had previously discussed with them.

It was a risk telling them, but it is much better to be honest with your employer than potentially break one of their rules and end up in an awkward situation. Any situation is going to be handled better if you are open and honest. It is also always better to discuss this topic with your employer as soon as you have made the decision to start the project, instead of having them find out about your project through someone else.

You should also consider the risks involved with creating a side-hustle if you work for a public entity such as a government agency. In that situation, you have to deal with the questions of not only an actual conflict of interest, but also potential and perceived conflicts of interest. The latter means that as a government employee, the reputation of, and the public trust in, the government rests on the shoulders of every individual employed by that government. If there's any misconduct or corruption by you in your side-hustle, that also calls into question the integrity of your primary employer. If there is a chance that your business could be seen as conflicting in any way with the business or mission of your employer, even if it doesn't actually conflict, then that is a perceived conflict of interest and has to be formally registered with most government agencies.

If you do register this potential/perceived conflict of interest and permission to run a business is granted, you still need to ensure that all your actions are above board. If it is denied and you choose to run your business anyway, and you are eventually found out, you not only run the risk of dismissal or loss of Intellectual Property (IP) rights to your product, but your employer could also raise a breach under their Code of Conduct, and you could find yourself under investigation by your government's anti-corruption authority. If that breach is upheld, that could mean fines or even criminal charges and will be permanently marked on your record as a public employee, which will likely preclude you from working for any other government agency.

If you don't talk to your employer, you can easily expect them to find out and react hastily out of anger. They may end up feeling like they can't trust you or that you don't respect them. If this happens, you may not only find yourself in legal trouble with your side-hustle, but also without your full time job. No matter what you are trying to do, you always want to protect your full-time job, since this is your main source of financial security until you are able to take on your side-hustle full-time. In my experience and from observing other colleagues, a lot of companies are perfectly fine with you working on a side project, provided you are not developing a product in the same area as your employer, which can cause intellectual property and conflict of interest issues. I think that is fair enough. I did work for one employer many years ago where some of the staff were developing a competing product in their spare time. They were found out and promptly fired from the company.

Seek counsel from a lawyer. One of the best ways to protect yourself is to speak to a lawyer. While many people don't want to pay the fees, taking your time and spending money to talk to a lawyer about creating a side-hustle while currently employed can save you a lot of money in the long run. Not only can they brief you on the legalities within your country or state, but they can also take a look at your employment contract and employee handbook. It may be best to look for a lawyer who specialises in intellectual property or employment law; they might be able to read between the lines and explain any information you didn't previously understand.

Is your current day job worth it? If you have read through the contract clauses and employee handbook, and potentially spoken to a lawyer who told you it is risky for you to create a product while working for your current employer, you might want to consider what you wish to do with your day job. While this will vary from person to person, you might feel that your day job isn't worth keeping if you can't place enough focus on your side-hustle when you are off the clock. Of course, you might also feel that your job is worth keeping because you enjoy it, you have been there for years, and you have worked your way up to a valuable position.

When I started producing my training courses, I was working for a large healthcare company in the UK, and I declared what I was doing to them in the interview, and they were fine with what I was doing. To my surprise, six months later, they were not happy with me working on a side-hustle. I had one manager actually tell me that if I had time to work on these in the evening, then I should be putting more effort into my day job. I was always an employee who performed well and was successful in my employed career, so I was very taken aback by these comments. They didn't tell me that I couldn't work on my online courses, but they made it quite clear they were not happy about it, and over the next six months, I noticed a definite change in their attitude towards me, as they didn't perceive me as a company man. I felt I had a choice to make. On one hand, this was a great company to work for; they were a massive and well-respected brand. On the other hand, I could see the future potential of my new side-hustle, and if I didn't at least give it a go, I felt that I would regret it for the rest of my life. In this case, I decided to find another job and leave. I wasn't earning enough that I could go full time on my courses, so I had to find another job, and I ended up working for a much smaller software company. I declared in the interview that I built these courses, and they were perfectly happy for me to work on them. I stayed with them for nearly two years before I was in a position to support myself full time.

I can't tell you what to do if your current employer does not support your dreams. You have to make that decision yourself, which includes the input from your partner, if you have one. I will say, though, that regret doesn't feel nice—so will you regret not following up on your dreams if you think you have a great product idea?

Create an employment agreement prior to starting your side-hustle. Another way to protect yourself and your side-hustle from your employers taking ownership is to create a business agreement that discusses what can be done and what can't be done while you are in their employment. For example, you can stipulate that everything you create outside of work hours is owned by you and only you. Once your supervisor or the CEO of the company signs this agreement, you are better protected. You may want the added protection of making sure that this agreement is notarised; that an employment lawyer has looked at it and explained it; and that you follow the agreement thoroughly. This means that if it states you are not to use any resources belonging to your employer or request help from your co-workers, then you comply with this part of the agreement.

Be cautious about what you ask your co-workers. Of course, if your agreement clause states you shouldn't discuss your side-hustle with your co-workers, you will need to follow this. However, even if the agreement between you and your current full-time job doesn't discuss this, you still might just want to be careful about what you say to your co-workers and how much information you give them. Even if your current supervisor is fine with you working on the business, you can quickly find yourself focusing more on your own product than your full-time work. This will not only lead you down the path to burnout, but it will also cause you to lose sight of the line you have drawn between your full-time position and your side-hustle.

Consider the higher expectations from your current employer. Imagine that you have talked to your supervisor and you have received the go-ahead to start your side-hustle. You and your employer negotiate a contract that protects your product and any work you do off the clock for your side-hustle. However, you start to notice that your employer is now giving you more responsibilities than before. You also notice that your employer seems to be more critical of the work you complete. While this might seem like they have other motives, the truth is your employer now has higher expectations of you.

You have shown them what you are capable of; therefore, your employer may start to expect more from you. However, some employers might do this because they feel that you need to prove you are still invested in their company, which was my experience in the earlier example. Once you start a side-hustle, no matter what it is, you become a potential threat to your employer. It is an indirect threat because your side-hustle can become successful, which means you will likely no longer work for them. It is also a direct threat if your side-hustle is in competition with their business; and if that is the case, I strongly urge you to leave that company, and seek employment in an industry unrelated to the product you are developing.

Not Separating Your Full-Time Job and Side-Hustle

Another danger of creating a side-hustle in order to build a product is that of not keeping your full-time job and your business separate. There are many reasons why you should do your best to ensure they stay separate. First, it will help you decrease your chances of becoming burnt out. Second, it will help you remain on good terms with your full-time employer. Third, it will help you stay focused between your job and your business.

It doesn't matter if you find that your supervisor is fine with you taking your work laptop home; you should still leave this at your job site. Unless you have work that you need to complete at home, leaving your laptop at your desk helps you create a line between your work life, personal life, and your side-hustle. Furthermore, if you start to bring your laptop home, you might find that using it for your side-hustle is more tempting. Think of it this way: anything you put on your personal computer is specifically for your company. Therefore, if you place information about your product on your employer's computer, you are potentially giving the company a claim to the rights to your product. Ordinarily, this wouldn't matter unless you become hugely successful with your product, but do you want to take that risk?

Keeping your side-hustle and full-time job separate is going to give you better protection for yourself and your product. You will be able to cover your bases more easily if you continue to keep the two separated. Once you start allowing yourself to combine them in any way, you will continue to do this, and this can lead to you not only giving the company the rights to your product but also to you feeling overwhelmed by your work.

Make Sure to Keep Records of Everything. While it might be hard to prove when you worked on your side-hustle and when you didn't, you can still keep your schedule in a daily planner or online. You might be able to find a software program or app which will allow you to keep track of when and for how long you worked on your product. But no matter what happens with your hours, you should always keep track of everything between your day job and side-hustle, just in case something goes wrong within your day job because of your product. This means you will need to make sure you keep all the documents that you and your employer agreed upon; keep records of everything you do while working at your day job, and keep any files saved on your computer, as this will allow you to show when the files were created and modified.

Reaching Burnout Phase

A big risk when working a full-time job and a side-hustle at the same time is burning out. When you reach the burnout phase, what happens is you have become overwhelmed by your work. You become tired, and you have reached a point where you feel like you can't carry on with the work anymore. You may start to lose interest in your product, and/or your job, which you once loved.

Once you reach this phase, it is hard to overcome it. Many people feel that all they need is a vacation in order to get them out of the burnout phase. Unfortunately, this is only a temporary solution. Chances are, you will go back to your same busy and chaotic professional life, and continue constantly working long hours, getting little sleep, and not taking care of yourself. When you go back to this lifestyle, you will find yourself reaching the burnout phase again rather quickly.

One of the biggest steps you can take to protect yourself from burning out is to start slow. Many people come up with an idea for a product, and they want to dive in immediately. They don't fully think about how the extended work hours are going to affect them in the long run. Instead, they think about how much money they will be able to make on the product or how they can continue to work in order to establish their side-hustle as a full-time job. However, this will quickly lead to you feeling burnt out.

Other than taking it slow, you can also create a realistic plan and stick to it. This will take more self-discipline than anything else. However, a plan will help you follow the guidelines you set for yourself, which can include what hours you work on your side-hustle. By effectively planning you might decide to spend nine months creating your product, as opposed to trying to implement it much faster and causing yourself stress.

One of the most common stories you hear from people who have reached the burnout phase is their lack of sleep. Many people come to realise it is easier to work on their side-hustle when their significant other and children have gone to bed. Therefore, they are up until about 2:00 or 3:00 o'clock in the morning, then find their alarm clock going off a couple of hours later. While this amount of sleep can be manageable for one or two nights, you will quickly find yourself struggling within a week. When you are dealing with a significant lack of sleep, you can start to get sick, lose interest in your work and other activities, become easily frustrated and quick to anger. In order to protect yourself from reaching the burnout phase, you shouldn't allow yourself to lose too much sleep.

Becoming Dependent on a Side-Hustle Income

Many people—like myself, initially—keep their day job because it gives them a sense of financial security. You have been able to live off the income from your day job; therefore, anything you find yourself doing on the side is going to be extra income. At first, you might feel that this won't be a huge additional income and figure you can simply put it toward your retirement, pay off some debt, or create savings towards another goal, such as a family vacation. However, you never know what the future will hold, and your business can potentially take off very quickly. In fact, you can come to depend on the income from your side-hustle more than your day job.

Once you find yourself depending on your side-hustle for an income, you risk the chance of losing interest in your day job. This is because you will start to focus more on your side-hustle, which means you might take some vacation days to work on your product or find yourself trying to sneak your side-hustle work into your day job hours, and start using your employer's computer to work on your product.

If you reach this point, where the money you are earning from your own product makes you prioritise that work over that of your day job, then the time has come when you need to make a decision. When I started earning enough that I could leave my job, I hesitated. I thought that I could still maintain the income from my day job as well as the income from my courses. What actually happened was that I was constantly thinking about my own business and my day job had started to suffer. It is at this point you need to consider quitting your day job: both for your own sanity and focus, and for respect of your employer. It is not fair that they are paying you a salary, but your mind is not on the job that they are paying you for. In my case, with my wife's blessing, I resigned from my full-time position and entered the world of self-employment.

Your Product and Tax Evasion

You have probably heard the phrase "getting paid under the table" before. What this means is that you take a side job and get paid in a way (often in cash) that you might not let the tax office know about. Basically, you get paid for work and then don't report that income, therefore avoiding having to pay taxes on it. This can be common practice by some of the more unscrupulous operators in trades such as plumbing or electrical services.

Today, there are at least one in four people in America who have a side job, with most not reporting this money on their taxes. A study completed by finder.com in July 2017 found that about $214.6 billion annually were not reported on taxes. Some of the unreported income came from jobs such as babysitting, freelance work, cleaning, driving services, and manual labour.

The reality is that you need to follow any income guidelines set by the tax office and report your extra income on your taxes. No, it is not fun to do, but you will need to pay taxes on your side-hustle income. Tax evasion is illegal in most countries and can land you in jail. This is one of the biggest ways that can end not only your side-hustle, but also your full-time job and career. On top of this, it is a felony charge, which means you will have trouble finding places to rent, get credit, and a new job once you are released from jail.

The Author's Approach

Throughout this book, I recommend that an excellent way to start a business is to work on it as a part-time venture while still employed. That is what I did. I believe in transparency when running a business while you are still employed. I feel it is right to declare what you are doing and be honest about the process. I used no equipment or software from my employer, and I certainly would never work on my business during the working day while being paid by someone else.

When I started creating and selling sound libraries, I was operating as a sole trader, which meant that any liability from the business landed with me. If anyone wanted to sue me in relation to my work, they would sue me, personally.

My accountant recommended that I create a limited liability company (LTD in the UK). A limited company means that should anyone want to sue, any lawsuits would be brought against the business as a legal entity in its own right, and not me personally. A limited company also means that the business finances are separate from my personal finances. I decided it was a good idea to set up a limited company and began the process.

At the time, I worked full time as a senior software developer for an online bank in the UK. As a banking institution, there are a lot of government regulations and compliance rules to which one needs to adhere. One of those rules is that someone working for the bank, especially someone with influence (which I had in the technology team), could not have a controlling interest in a company that could cause a conflict of interest. I wanted to create a limited company, and because I was and remain the only person in the company, I had a controlling interest.

I went to talk to HR and the company legal team to ask if there was any way I could create the company. Thankfully, they were very accommodating and did not just say no. The very helpful lady in the legal team explained that it was still possible to start a company, especially at the bank. We had a lot of software-developer contractors working in our groups, who all had their own limited liability companies for their consulting work. The legal and HR teams explained that I would have to apply for permission to set up the company and provide a lot of information about what the company was intending to do, how much money I expected to make, and how I planned to conduct business while being an employee of the bank. They were concerned about me starting a company that could turn out to be a conflict of interest. I knew this wouldn't be a problem, but I had to go through the process, regardless.

I had many forms to fill out and then a short wait. Thankfully, I was granted permission to go ahead. While the short delay was annoying, I fully understand why it was important to go through these steps. If I had not been transparent with my employer from the start, I might have created the limited company and then found myself in breach of the government's financial services regulations.

Several years later, I worked as a software development manager for a pharmaceutical company in the UK. By this stage in my side-hustle adventure, I was creating courses for Pluralsight. During my job interview, I declared upfront what I was doing and that I intended to continue making these courses in my spare time. I also guaranteed that I would not talk about my employer or anything I was working on at the company. That is only fair. The company itself was okay with me doing this; there were no issues.

Once I had started at the company and had been there for about six months, I began having some issues with my manager. I was working for a lady who could only be described as an "old-fashioned manager". She did not like me working on these courses, even though it was on my own time and using my own computer and software licenses; and even more crucially, HR and the senior department head agreed with her. Her view was that if I had enough time or energy to work on my courses in the evening, then I was obviously not busy enough during the day. Her answer to this was to have more responsibilities handed to me. I had always been someone that would put in extra hours when needed, especially if there was an emergency or a challenging software release, but I took offence to an attitude like this.

I stayed at this pharmaceutical company for just over two years. When I left, my original intention was to work for myself by spending 50% of my time working on courses and 50% of my time consulting. My earnings from online courses were growing but were not yet at a level that could fully replace my current salary without taking a significant financial hit; however, I was so desperately miserable at this company by this point that I had to leave.

About a week into my four-week notice period, I heard from a friend who was running a start-up, building an online service for the used-car market. I had already spoken to both him and his business partner in a lot of detail and they were both keen for me to come and work for them. They were going the more traditional route with seed funding. Even though they wanted me to work for them, they did not have any budget for me to join them at first. When my friend contacted me after I had resigned from my job, he told me they had just cleared a large round of seed funding, and they wanted me to work for them to help build up their software team to get a prototype of their product released. Seeing as I had already resigned from my job, I spoke to my wife about it, and we decided it might be a good idea for me to work for this other company while I continue to build up funds in my business. What this business was building sounded like a fun project to work on, so I went for it.

For nearly two years, I stayed at this company, helping them get set up with their initial system, before I left to work for myself full time. I had a great time there, and the business owners—one of whom was a good friend of mine—supported my endeavours to build online training. He was a customer of Pluralsight himself and used the platform frequently. I helped them get to where they needed to be, and that extra time building courses enabled me to get to where I needed to be financially.

My main recommendation is to be careful when running a business while you are employed by someone else. Check your employment contract carefully, don't use any company resources, and be transparent with them about what you want to do. Being open and honest has worked for me in the past, and it is essential to know where you stand with your employer. If they have a problem with you running your own business, you need to make an important decision about whether you value your employment more than your potential business venture. I can't answer that question for you; only you can decide what is right for your circumstances.

Summary

This main purpose of this chapter has been to inform you about the dangers of building a product while you are still employed. While you are not alone in this adventure, you also need to make sure you cover all your bases, protect yourself and your side-hustle, and file your taxes legally. You must report all the income that you receive, even if it was a one-time fee and you only made $1,000.

The bottom line is to be safe and smart. Take your time to research, look into your contracts with your employer, and if possible, create a new contract to protect your side-hustle. Being honest with your employer is going to help keep you in good standing, which is always useful when it comes to starting a side project. After all, one of the biggest ways you will get people interested in your business is through word of mouth. Already established entities, such as your current employer, can do a lot of damage to your small business by just talking to a few people. You should look at the bigger picture and all the angles when you are protecting yourself from the side-hustle dangers while still being employed.

Workshop Questions

(1) If you are still employed in a day job, find your employment contract and employee handbook, and try to find any clauses that might limit your ability to work on your side-hustle.

. . .

(2) If you can't find any prohibitive clauses, come up with a plan to discuss your idea with your supervisor. What will you say? How much will you want to reveal?

(3) If there is a prohibitive clause in your contract, research any local employment lawyers who can give you more information and discuss further options. Many lawyers will offer a free one-hour consultation first to assess your case.

9

WHAT TO CHARGE FOR PRODUCTS OR SERVICES?

Good pricing can boost the marketability of your product or service, and while you have the final say in what to charge, you must consider various pricing factors. If you charge too low, clients may consider your products or services to be low quality. On the other hand, if you charge too high, clients may skip your offers and look for alternatives with far more competitive prices. Effective pricing can be hard, but it is vital to get right. In this chapter we are going to look at pricing products and services.

An effective pricing process helps you to recoup your expenses, earn profits, and be able to expand your business. If you want your product to be known for quality, lowering its price to one of the cheaper options on the market will make your branding attempts appear less valuable. If satisfying and retaining your customers are your top priorities, you can give your loyal customers lower prices through discounts and other promotions. When your product is new, your primary concern might be to improve your market share by offering a low-cost yet valuable product. Automatically pricing your product or service low, however, can create a race for the bottom, which doesn't benefit anyone. Do your market research and look at what competitors are offering. Document a detailed features matrix to see what features different competitors offer and then compare their prices. You don't want to price too low, but you may also want to avoid pricing at the higher end of the market; performing this research will help you make an informed decision. It may be better to have ten customers that you charge $1000, instead of a thousand customers that you charge $10.

You also need to be aware of how much it costs to support customers, and factor that into your pricing. Some products, like a software service or application, may need you to provide ongoing support to your customers. Not all products require much support, but you need to think about how much time and cost providing support could take. If you have a thousand customers who have paid $10, you will quickly lose money if you have to provide ongoing support; if you only have ten customers who have spent $1000, you still make the same amount of revenue, but you have fewer customers to support.

An acquaintance of mine, Todd Gardner, runs an online software-as-a-service product called TrackJS, a JavaScript error monitoring tool. He explained to me that they used to have a free developer licence that software developers could use to try out the product, but not use in a live production setting. On the face of it, this seems like a brilliant idea for a developer tool, but what Todd found was that most of the support requests were coming from these users on the free licences, and only a very small percentage of them converted into paying customers. His company only had a few members of staff, and they were drowning in support requests. Ultimately, they decided to remove the free tier of their product. Instantly, their support burden dropped significantly, but their revenue was unaffected, as they still had about the same number of paying customers signing up. This perfectly highlights the point that giving your product away for free to certain users, while it seems like a benefit, can actually cause you more problems than it solves.

Targeting Customers for Products

How much you want to earn should align with how much your target customers are willing to pay. To achieve this, you should first identify your target customers. Determine their age range, location, and employment status. Once identified, think about their potential priorities and their problems that you are trying to solve.

Customer priorities are classified into three key areas: budget, value, and brand. Customers who focus on a lower budget are after reasonably priced offers. Those who prioritise value go for products that provide them convenience by solving a real-world problem. The last customer priority, brand, is about those who want to be associated with a product, brand or company as a way to improve their status or to show loyalty. Apple's brand loyalty is a perfect example of this, as they are seen as a luxury lifestyle brand that people want to be a part of.

You should also try to perform this same research for your competitors. By searching for their products on the internet and online forums, try to determine the key demographic who are using their products. Are they general consumers, software developers, children, senior citizens? Can you define age ranges for your customers from your research?

By researching your product demographics, you are then able to compare against competitors. It could even be that you offer a similar product to another company but target a different demographic, which could open up a currently underserved market to you. A great way of comparing your product to competitors is to seek out user reviews for your competitors' products. Reviews tend to be very honest and direct. From reading both professional and consumer reviews, you can get a great idea of a competitor's strengths and weaknesses. Could a competitor's weakness become your strength? It could open up a valuable niche in which you can start out.

Factoring in Your Business Expenses

Your financial records and expenses will play a significant role in pricing your products, even the expenses that aren't directly required in the production of your product or service. Aside from overall expenses, if it is a physical product, you should also take note of the total cost to produce one item. This means you must take the total production cost and divide it by the number of goods. Of all the factors here, the expenses are one of the easiest to deal with: look at all the regular costs of doing business, from travel, office rent, and bills to software licences or raw materials. You need to make sure your pricing takes all of these into account and adjust your pricing as necessary to cater for them. If your product cost comes out too high, then you may need to recoup those expenses over a more extended period, which affects your break-even point, or try to reduce your total expenses as much as possible.

If you are producing a physical product as opposed to a digital product, then the cost of raw materials will be your biggest concern, and if you are working in small quantities, your costs will be higher. If you can scale over time and generate consistent sales, you can then have better buying power to buy your raw materials in higher quantities, which reduces your per-unit costs. With these cost reductions, and offering your product at the same price, you will increase your profit margins.

Pricing Considerations for Services or Consulting

We have talked about how to price products, whether they are digital or physical. But, compared to products, pricing services such as consulting or training is a bit trickier because it involves factors that tend to be more subjective, such as your relationship with your client. The products you sell, once manufactured, can continue being sold, so this becomes passive income, especially for digital products. However, when it comes to services such as consulting or training, you are charging money for your time, so this is active income.

I feel that in any good business, it is healthy to try and have a mix of active and passive income streams. In my business, I earn passive income for my online courses, as once they have been written and recorded, they continue to sell. I also conduct in-person classroom training from time to time, and this is active income, as I am exchanging my time for money.

Skills are classified into hard and soft skills. Hard skills are those that can be taught and quantified. Examples of hard skills include writing, proof-reading, coding, using specific computer software, operating a machine, and speaking different languages. These can be learned in the classroom and through training.

Soft skills, on the other hand, tend to be more subjective, such as leadership, teamwork, persuasion, motivation, conflict resolution, and time management.

You can demand a higher rate if you have different technical or hard skills, but you have to prove them first by showing certifications or by demonstrating experience. The more advanced your skills, the higher the rate you can charge. As for soft skills, you may have to find ways to show them by discussing specific examples you have experienced which are relevant to the service you are providing. This could be done by writing case studies.

A good way to demonstrate both hard and soft skills initially is to emphasise them on your CV or prospectus when pitching for work. I don't mean saying something like, "At company X, I demonstrated leadership by leading a team of four people." This doesn't tell a prospect anything. You are better writing about the direct benefit your skills gave to your client and the problem they solved. For example, "I led a team of four people to deliver a financial compliance project that reduced legal costs by $350000 per year, resulting in less litigation taken on by the company." Being more specific is much more valuable and more likely to make a prospective client take notice, as not only can they see the benefit, but also visualise how that benefit could apply to them.

Demonstrating experience like this isn't just about the months or years you've spent on a project; it's about the specific projects you've completed, the clients you've worked with, and the services you've supplied and overall benefits that were realised. These can all be quantified. The more you can demonstrate the ability to solve a client's problems and provide a valuable service, the more you can charge. This is why contractors and consultants tend to do so well, as they have the benefit of many years working as a full-time employee, and they can then demonstrate having used their experience to provide value to a client. The more experience you get over the years, the more you can start to charge.

People with technical skills, particularly those that involve software development, tend to enjoy a high demand for their services. Despite the vast number of IT professionals in the market, they can still receive some of the best daily rates, especially if you are working in a big city. The same goes for other professions such engineers and medical professionals. If you have limited hard skills, the demand for your services may not be that high. As a result, you won't have a rate as high as that of an engineer, a doctor or a software developer.

Price Negotiation Tips

Not all clients will accept your initial requested rate right away. Many of them are likely to want to negotiate—or you could be the one asking for a better price. To prepare yourself, let's look at some tips you should apply before and during the negotiation process.

Clients, especially your fellow freelancers and start-up owners, are all after affordable services. Be ready when they start to ask for a rate reduction. When they begin suggesting a price, stick to your preferred rate and remind them about the value you're offering. If they insist, reduce your rate, but it should still be higher than their desired rate as well as the lowest rate you want to accept. Never go in asking for your lowest rate. Once you have determined the lowest rate and ideal rate, decide what an acceptable amount is to add on top of it, such as 10% or 15%. Any potential customer will try to reduce the rate, so that they feel like they got a good deal. If you go in at 15% higher than your ideal rate, there is wiggle room to negotiate. If they play hardball and you need the work, then you have your lowest rate to fall back on, but don't undercut your lowest rate as that sets a precedent for paying you at that lower rate in the future.

When I started working on my business full time, my courses generated a passive income, but I also regularly taught in-person workshops, where I go to either a conference or a private client's site. When I taught workshops at conferences, these were done on a straight profit-share split, based on the number of people that attended. If only two people turned up, I wouldn't do very well, but if 15 or 20 people came along, I would. For private workshops, I used a different tactic. Instead of charging a per-head amount, I would decide what a day of my time was worth and charge that figure, regardless of how many people attended. Let's assume I put that fee for training at $6000 per day. When I start talking to the company about training, I might say my rate is $6500–$7000 per day, knowing full well they will try to haggle on the price. They could then negotiate down to the $6000 a day. I get the rate I wanted, and they feel like they get a good deal.

I will readily admit that at first, going in with a reasonably high day rate felt strange and a bit uncomfortable. When I started off teaching workshops, I went in lower. As my passive income increased from the courses, I didn't actually have to do classroom training. If anything, it became a bit of an inconvenience, as it meant I had to fly to other countries to do the training, even though I do enjoy it. It was at this point that I didn't feel so bad putting up the day rate. I was at the point where I was not overly concerned if they said no, as it meant I could continue working on the courses which earn a good passive income. If the clients said yes to the day rate, it meant I was being fairly compensated for the time away.

Some clients may be too nice for you to reject despite having a lower budget; charities or good social causes fit into this category. If you can fit their projects into your schedule, and you are happy to, then get to know how much they can pay. It's then your turn to negotiate about the project scope. You may not earn much from these engagements, but they can become part of your professional network. If they keep on hiring you and if you continuously give them valuable service, you can renegotiate the rate later, especially when their revenues are increasing thanks to your help.

Working for free sometimes can be a benefit, if used carefully. When I speak at conferences, typically about software development subjects, I very rarely get paid apart from travel and accommodation expenses. Even though this is time away from doing other work, I enjoy doing it, as it helps feed into a community of software developers and the companies they work for. From doing free talks at conferences, I have had several instances after the event where representatives from a company have seen my talk and then booked me to speak at their company for a very good day rate, so sometimes offering your time for free can be a benefit.

However, you do need to balance this carefully. Being able to distinguish between free work for some kind of social good and companies just trying to get some work for free can be difficult to spot sometimes. I am sure everyone is familiar with the stories of the starving musicians asked to perform for free because of the exposure they will get. Exposure won't pay the bills. I speak for free often because I have other income streams that support me. If I didn't have those other incomes bringing money into my business, I would do a lot less speaking for free. Only you can decide where that balance lies for you, but it is something that you need to think about when pricing your products or services.

Consider Staging Payments

If you are offering a consulting service and the project is quite big, it might be a good idea to suggest to your client that payments be made in stages. You can negotiate at which stages you want to get partial payments. For example, your client pays you 10% after you accept the project; they then pay 40% on the middle of the project, and the remaining 50% upon completion. This works quite well if you are not charging a standard hourly or daily rate. This is a useful tool for you to help ensure you secure the project, and it reduces the risk for your client, as they are not laying out the money all at once. If you use this tactic, you must make sure that all the milestone payments are clearly laid out in a contract so there is no ambiguity.

The Author's Approach

When I was creating my sound libraries to sell, I looked at competing products on the market to get an idea of their cost. Sound libraries that were considered genre packs—tech house, minimal technical, funk, etc.—are sold at around the £50 price point for a CD or DVD-ROM. I sold sound libraries in more of a niche area, such as rhythmic sound effects and drones, that sold around the £19 price point. I felt my libraries fell into this category, so I sold them on manufactured DVD-ROMs for £19.99.

Each of these libraries took up a lot of space, three gigabytes of data. Selling libraries of this size online was difficult because of the internet bandwidth costs. I started out selling them as mail-order items from my website. I found a company that let me manufacture small batches of DVDs in a proper DVD case with a printed insert card. The manufacturing cost was £1.50 per disc plus shipping, which was £15 for a box of one hundred discs. A pack of hundred DVD cost in total £165, which gave me a unit price of £1.65. Therefore, if I sold a copy for £19.99,

I was making £18.34 profit per copy. There were postage and packaging charges involved in sending the discs out to customers but they were charged on top of the product price. This was a good profit margin.

The major risk was I had to manufacture 100 discs at a time, and I did not know if I would sell them; but if I sold an entire box of them, I would make £1834 in profit. I sold nearly four boxes of my first sound library called "Electronic Critters", which was a collection of sound effects and rhythmic loops created using a technique called "circuit bending", where old children's toys are rewired to make them sound crazy. I designed and sold five different sound libraries this way. Overall, for a hobby business, this was doing well. After a while, though, managing inventory and sending out libraries in the post was becoming a bit of a pain to keep dealing with. The money made from this venture was not enough to hire someone to help me with it. Also, I didn't want to hire anyone, which sounds scary, and hard work on its own.

After my sound libraries were reviewed in some magazines, I got an email from a company called Sounds to Sample. They had just set up a new online marketplace for selling sound libraries, and they wanted to know if I would sell my libraries through them. Selling sound libraries online was quite rare because of their storage size, but when they contacted me, I was quite excited to try it. Sounds to Sample planned to store the sound library files on their platform, and they charged £19.99 for the library. The commission they set was 50%. That commission was high, but the risks were much lower. I didn't have to worry about manufacturing the discs, packaging them, or posting them to the customer. Once the sound libraries uploaded to their platform, I didn't have to do anything else except marketing. So, even though the commission was relatively high, and my profit margin lower, I could sell in a much higher volume across the globe and not have to worry about inventory management, which was an enormous benefit.

When I started creating training courses for Pluralsight, the pricing factors were not in my control. When I sign a contract to produce a course, we agree on a percentage royalty rate that is used to calculate a payment amount from a larger pot of funds based on minutes viewed. There is no price per course, and apart from the original discussion about the percentage royalty rate, the amount you get paid goes up or down based on how many people watch the courses.

Even though I lack control over the pricing, I benefit enormously from Pluralsight's marketing, which has onboarded millions of individual learners as well as giant corporations who use their platform to train and develop their staff. The sheer size and popularity of their platform more than makes up for the lack of pricing flexibility.

As well as creating online courses, I have written many short books. I chose to self-publish, as this gives you a lot more control over your prices. Most of my publishing has been via Amazon's Kindle Direct Publishing (KDP) platform. Once you are ready to release the book, you pay a manufacturing cost to print each book as it is ordered, and Amazon takes a commission from the sale price. Even when taking these costs into account, your overall profit margin per book is much higher than that from a more traditional publisher. With the lower profit margins available from traditional publishing companies, you need to sell many more books to make up for the difference in profits from self-publishing. I am not disparaging traditional publishing, but if you market your books well, you can achieve good profits through self-publishing and keep your overheads low.

When I was planning this *Path to Freedom* book, I had an entire business in mind, not just the book itself. Initially, I talked to a non-fiction publisher interested in signing the book, but I decided against it. As I plan to build courses based on the same topic, I want complete overall control over the entire process; how the book is released, and when I can issue updates and new content. I know I can sell lots of copies of this book as I have tested the publishing process with my other, shorter books, and know what marketing works and what doesn't.

To set the price, I looked at similar-style books of an equal page count that were on the market, and I set a price that looked attractive alongside them. In my experience, I have found that with books, cheaper doesn't always mean better. People will pay a reasonable price for books if they get value from them. The overall profit margins are higher for the e-book version as there is no inventory to worry about, but I love the idea of having a physical book that someone can buy and hold in their hands.

The print-on-demand market is a fantastic opportunity for authors. The book gets printed only when it's ordered, which means you do not need to worry about storing a large book inventory. This is a huge financial benefit as well, as you don't need to pay for thousands of books to be made upfront. It is also good from an environmental standpoint as you are not using a lot of paper to print a lot of books that you may never sell. The overall cost to print each book may be higher than a mass-manufactured book, but I feel that price difference is worth it in light of the other benefits.

Summary

Pricing products and services can be hard. It is quite common to feel you are charging too much and undersell your abilities. Researching your market is essential as this will show you what the market is willing to pay. If you are building a product, look for similar offerings; are you offering more or less than those products? If so change your prices accordingly. What markets or countries do you want to sell into? Different countries and economies will support different levels of pricing, so it is important to take the physical location of your customers into consideration too.

Workshop Questions

If you are building a digital or physical product:

(1) Identify your closest competitors on the market.

1. What are they charging?
2. How does their offering differ to yours?
3. Identify the key demographics at whom you are aiming your product.
4. Try to identify the same demographics for your competitors' products.
5. For each of your competitors' products, search for both positive and negative reviews. Compile these reviews so you

can determine what their customers like, and more importantly, don't like. Can you build a niche around their customers' complaints?

If you are planning on offering a service, such as consulting or training:

(2) Identify your closest competitors on the market.

1. What are they charging?
2. How does their offering differ to yours?
3. Identify the key demographics at whom you are aiming your service.
4. Try to identify the same demographics for your competitors' services.

10

WORKING WITH A CO-FOUNDER

If you are starting out as a small side-hustle, you may decide early on that you need a co-founder to bring additional skills to your project. Working with a co-founder is a big decision that can have larger consequences further down the line if you choose to take your side-hustle full time. In this chapter we are going to discuss some of the advantages and disadvantages of working with a co-founder.

There are all kinds of important decisions you need to make when running a start-up. Perhaps the most crucial one for you to answer is whether or not you need a co-founder. Evaluating such a question is tough because so much depends on your own personality and your ability to split control of the company.

It is possible to become successful either with or without a co-founder. Google is an excellent example of a company which was jointly founded; but on the other hand, we have successful examples of singly founded companies such as Amazon. Clearly, there's no one right way. In this chapter we will look into co-founders from both perspectives.

First, we'll look at the factors you need to consider when deciding whether you even need a co-founder in the first place. Many businesses simply don't need one, and by making the wrong decision, you will end up paying a lot for your mistake by giving up equity in your business. One part of answering this question is to examine what life would be like if you decide to go solo.

There are pros and cons to this, so you need to take the time to really understand the implications of this decision. We'll also look at the specifics of splitting equity with your co-founder and working together successfully. Conflicts will occur, and how you deal with this will determine the level of success you achieve.

Sometimes, there's nothing to do but break up, and this can be a very messy situation if not handled well. It is important to remain as objective as possible in such cases, and this guide aims to help you do just that.

Evaluating if You Need a Co-Founder

A common approach to answering problems is to consider them scientifically and look at past results to see what has worked. In this regard, having a co-founder is definitely a good option as you have their experience to look back on as well as your own. A large number of companies have benefited from having a co-founder with examples such as OLX, Oracle, and so on.

However, choosing a co-founder is a lot like choosing a partner to spend your personal life with. For every successful partnership, there is a horror story. The reason for this is that a lot about saying yes or no to this decision comes down to your individual personality.

It is helpful to assess what working with a co-founder will be like and to ask yourself whether or not you're ok with this. Every advantage has an associated disadvantage, so let's look at this in more detail.

Trust and Control. Starting a business is hard. You don't need this book to tell you that. Taking a business from its current position to the next level is even harder. It would certainly help to have someone you can trust as much as yourself to share the load with you, wouldn't it?

The key word there is "trust". Picking a name out of a hat isn't the thing to do here.

There have been instances where companies have had four founders and have succeeded and companies with three have failed. No one can predict with any accuracy how you and your co-founder will work together. Ask yourself what you do not want from a co-founder first.

Obviously, you want someone who is committed and dedicated. What about things like retaining control? Do you want someone who can override your decisions? Are you okay with someone demanding more equity in the business if they end up doing more work? Would you mind it if they took longer holidays than usual and worked remotely? Be honest with your preferences and this will help narrow things down.

Specialised Expertise. Does your business have multiple areas that can benefit from specialised expertise? For example, if you're running an e-commerce store, does it make sense to have a co-founder who specialises in accounting? Remember that a co-founder is more than someone who simply puts money into the business.

A co-founder should be someone who shares the same level of passion as you do for the business, and just as you would forego sleep to get things done, so will they. If your business is merely short on funds, bring an investor on board. Set aside the co-founder position for someone who can actually help with execution.

Investment and funding. It is well known that venture capital funds rarely sink their money into companies with a single founder. This is because the risk is just too high. If that person was struck by a bolt of lightning, for example, who runs the company now? This is an instance where co-founders are highly valued.

If you intend to play the valuation game and seek large amounts of funding, it might be worth it to bring a co-founder on board even if the synergy isn't completely there. With the valuation game, you're only looking to garner higher levels of funding and secure an exit before going public. However, if you're truly passionate about your idea, then hiring a co-founder just to appeal to a Venture Capital (VC) fund is a bit like putting the cart before the horse. Your ideas and your ability to execute them should come first in such cases. If someone else can truly help see it to fruition, then go ahead and hire a co-founder.

Problem solving. What sort of a problem solver are you? Do you prefer to work on things alone, without any distractions, or do you work better by having a sounding board to pitch ideas to? You will face a multitude of problems in your business and having a co-founder to pitch your ideas to and share the workload can be a huge relief.

Some people don't need a sounding board as much as a distraction to take their mind off things temporarily. In such cases, having a co-founder is probably overkill. Examine how you like to work and see how you stack up with or without a co-founder.

Stress. Despite the hectic nature of running a business, there is no earthly reason for you to carry around huge levels of stress like a badge of honour. A number of founders make this mistake, and this only leads them to failure in the long run. Different people have different levels of ability to work for long periods of time.

When you work beyond your limits, all you'll end up doing is making poor decisions. In such cases, your ideas become a millstone around your neck, and this is a poor state of affairs to say the least. Having someone who can share the load will be a huge help in such cases.

Control. This is the big one. Are you a control freak? You might be a great delegator at work but how well do you work in environments where decision making is shared, as opposed to being a dictatorship? A lot of entrepreneurs tend to be lone-wolf types, so this is always a hard decision to make. Trying to determine if you are a control freak by yourself can be almost impossible to do on your own; you need to ask someone close to you, like a partner or a best friend—someone who has a track record for brutal honesty and willingness to apply the boot of reason to the seat of ignorance when required—for their honest opinion in this instance.

Examining your need for control over things you can and cannot control is crucial to making this decision easier. Are you comfortable trusting someone else to make good decisions in areas in which you have no expertise? Do you respect your prospective co-founder enough? We often think we know a person but when issues of control come up, we begin to see them in a different light.

When things don't turn out the way you want them to, any lack of respect you have for your co-founder will cause you to blame them for it. How well have you handled such situations in the past? If your business needs a co-founder but your own qualities don't align with this, how willing are you to change?

Evaluate yourself thoroughly using these questions and you'll often find the answers you're looking for.

Accountability. If you're the sole decision maker in the business, everything is going to come back to you, without a doubt. You will be asked to constantly exercise your judgment on matters that are difficult to predict, and your cognitive abilities will be stretched to the extreme. After a while, there is a real risk of burnout and that helps no one.

Having a co-founder share the load minimises the risk of this happening, and if you're someone who likes working in a partnership, you should consider bringing someone on board. If you do bring a co-founder into your company, deciding on a hierarchy is a good idea. If this method of working works for you, then it could give you both flexibility as well as different views of a problem.

Apple, during its early days, is a good example of this approach. However, the flip side of that picture is that Steve Jobs wasn't ready to be the sole head of the company and needed to be removed by the board in order to learn his lessons. There are pros and cons with everything, so take your time evaluating every factor in the decision.

Often, joining a mastermind group of other entrepreneurs will help clarify a lot of the problems and help you unload the stress you face. Going solo doesn't mean you need to be alone. Look to share the load and you'll find that decision making becomes a lot easier. We will be looking at mastermind groups later in the book.

Going Solo! Not Having a Co-founder

The majority of start-ups that progress past being a single-person side-hustle but fail to achieve critical mass, fail due to them hiring the wrong team. Turf wars and egos ruin start-ups far more than market economics. Given that a co-founder is going to be an integral part of the team you hire, it makes sense that a lot of problems centre around having a troublesome co-founder, or not having a supportive one.

Despite the benefits having a co-founder brings, ultimately, having one is neither a maker nor breaker of a business. As we saw previously, there are a lot of things that make a great co-founded company, so it isn't easy to evaluate whether a co-founder will hurt or help.

Having said that, there's no reason you cannot go solo and run your business by yourself. Taking a look at the facts of being a solopreneur will help you make a better decision.

Value vs valuation. Here's the thing: A lot of start-ups turn to co-founders simply because it is easier to find funding from venture capital firms under this setup. This is not to say that you are guaranteed money with a co-founder, but a lot of start-ups with viable ideas hire co-founders to present the illusion of diversification.

This approach, as I mentioned previously, makes a lot of sense for you if your aim is to simply achieve a higher valuation and secure an exit by receiving equity from an acquiring company. This might not be politically correct to say, but the ultimate aim of a lot of start-ups is to achieve exactly this, despite the world-changing disruption theme a lot of companies push.

So, ask yourself what your aim truly is. If you believe in your product and if valuation games do not interest you, there is no need for you to play the games that venture capitalists prefer. You can grow your company organically and take baby steps.

Don't bring a co-founder on board just because you think you have to find funding. If your business is self-sustainable and doesn't have diverse work areas, going at it solo is a perfectly valid approach.

Flexibility. Being a sole founder allows you great flexibility. A lot of decisions can be made more quickly, and you need not spend time in meetings with your co-founder or waiting for their sign-off on things.

Decisions taken to overcome problems require brainstorming and viewing the issues from different perspectives. This is often easier with a co-founder since two minds are better than one. The trade-off is that the decision-making process is slower. If your joint decisions are regularly better and more efficient, this compensates for the delay in decisions.

Attacking a problem from different perspectives often leads to novel solutions but sometimes, a problem doesn't require multiple perspectives. That just complicates things. A lot of start-up founders find themselves in a dilemma where the decision is clear, but they still find the need to delay it to avoid upsetting the co-founder.

The dynamics between you and your partner are what matter the most, so if you're considering flexibility as a pro of going solo, do not ignore the other side of the coin.

How to Be Successful with a Co-founder

Choosing to go down the co-founder path can be a lucrative decision for a lot of reasons, especially if you have a genuine need for one. Working with a co-founder is a lot like any other human relationship. It takes work to maintain and doesn't take care of itself. At one point or another, a fight or disagreement is inevitable, no matter how much you respect and admire each other.

Before getting into the ins and outs of working with a co-founder, I'd suggest that it is a very good idea to first work with your prospective co-founder on a smaller project *before* pitching them your idea and splitting equity. When the stakes are low, you can evaluate one another to see if there's a match. The best co-founders have usually worked together at another company prior to setting one up for themselves.

Once that is done, make sure that you follow the tips below to ensure that you maintain a good working relationship between you and your co-founder/s.

Complement one another. The best co-founders have skills that are complementary. Entrepreneurs are extremely independent by nature and if you and your partner have skills that are concentrated in the same area, you will be interfering with each other's work. Bringing someone on board who has skills in another area will help you move your business forward. A typical mix is one founder who is technically focused and develops the product, while the other partner handles the outward functions such as sales or funding.

The homophone of complementing also applies here. Take the time to appreciate your co-founder's work. Be sincere about it and don't compliment them just for the sake of it. Once your company grows bigger, you will have less time to work with one another, so make the time to catch up with each other in a casual environment and just talk.

Communicate. Do not assume that your business partner knows what you're talking about, or that what you meant to say was obvious. They are not a mind reader, and you should always communicate any grievances immediately. Set aside time each week for both of you to catch up alone and discuss the state of things.

Ask them explicitly if there was something you did that they are not happy with, or if there is an issue in the business they would like addressed. Honesty and promptness in communication are very important, since these little things have a way of coming up at the worst possible time. A relationship doesn't end due to a huge mistake, but rather by a thousand tiny cuts.

You will notice I'm using language here that can be used interchangeably for a marriage. A co-founder relationship is a lot like a marriage due to the stakes involved. A business is a lot like a child and requires a lot of nurturing and care. Neglecting your relationship for the sake of the business does not ever make sense.

. . .

Equals. A co-founder needs to be on the same footing as you. This doesn't mean equity needs to be split 50/50, but there shouldn't be a huge mismatch. In such cases, the dominant partner is the CEO and their decisions will never be questioned. Such setups are not real co-founder relationships, even if the minority partners adopt the co-founder tag. Facebook is a good example of this.

Don't make the mistake of bringing in a second partner in the later stages of your company's growth unless absolutely necessary. When this happens, divergent priorities emerge, and this is a recipe for disaster. Right at the start, ensure a fair share of the equity that everyone is happy with. This communicates respect to one another and places both of you on a fair footing.

Objectivity. When choosing your co-founder, be as objective as possible. It is a good idea to develop a scorecard and grade yourself and the other person on it with respect to the qualities you're looking for. It might be tempting to go into business with a friend, but this will most likely result in a friendship lost.

Similarly, resist the natural instinct to start a business with a family member. There are a whole host of emotional issues when it comes to family, and we're not the most rational when it comes to them. Place objectivity above all else by simply avoiding emotional traps.

When selecting a co-founder, look at how they handle problems and whether they can deal with them in an emotionally mature way. Are they capable of being honest about their feelings? Or are they insecure and lash out at inopportune moments? Your business will prosper the most when it is objectively run so always make that your ultimate goal.

Splitting Equity with a Co-founder

You might think that once you've decided to bring a co-founder on board, all that needs to be done is to shake hands and get to work. However, there's still the prickly issue of equity to be dealt with. The how, what, and why of equity splitting will have long-term ramifications to your business, and you should take the time to weigh all your options upfront.

A lot of entrepreneurs simply decide on a 50/50 split at the start and never really have the conversation about equity. This is understandable. It is a tough conversation to have and if not discussed in a structured manner, it can seem as if one person is attacking the other when negotiating for a larger equity share.

Handled incorrectly, this discussion can result in one partner feeling undervalued, and they might consider quitting the business before it has even begun. Such concerns are valid but are not a good enough reason to simply agree to an even split. You must take the time to consider a whole host of factors.

Contribution. This is an obvious one. If one partner is going to be working full time on the business but the other is part time, the person working full time deserves a greater split. Even if both founders are working on things full time, what happens if one founder decides to do things in a way that is counter to the objectives of the business? The case of Mark Zuckerberg and Eduardo Saverin is a good example of this.

Saverin kept a large stake in Facebook, which grew on the back of his having invested capital when the business was small. Despite not working on the business full time and pursuing ideas that weren't in line with what Facebook wanted, he held onto his large stake. Zuckerberg's attempts to reclaim that equity landed him in court and led to a messy split.

Capital is often a reason for one founder receiving an outsized stake, but this is the wrong way to do it. Instead, issue preferred stock to the person contributing the most capital, and issue equity on an effort basis, with the ones putting in the most work receiving the highest split.

A good idea is to use the Founder's Pie calculator (https://cofounders.gust.com), which weighs various factors that go into the decision and spits out a number that indicates a fair equity split.

. . .

Expertise vs idea. Expertise comes in two forms. First, a person could have expertise in the field that the new business aims to operate in. Second, a person might have experience taking a company from fledgling status to a successful exit. Such people should receive fair equity compensation for the value that they bring to the table. Such people often end up butting heads with those who had the idea in the first place.

Ideas don't count for much, to be honest. Unless the idea involves a patent, the person bringing the idea should not automatically receive a large share. Execution is what matters the most, and it is the person with the most experience that is going to bring the idea to fruition. Claiming a large equity stake for simply having an idea is a sign of immaturity, and you should watch out before partnering with someone like this.

Commitment. A common problem most start-ups face is that one of the founders decides enough is enough and packs it up. Running a start-up is hard work and involves sacrifices. It is impossible to know in advance how things will go and what issues you will encounter.

Therefore, it is a good idea to have a malleable partnership agreement at the start. This agreement can contain clauses that allow the partners to adjust the equity stakes after certain time periods or business maturity levels. The benefit of this is that everyone will know and have experience with how the business really works. The resulting split will be based on objective principles.

However, having this conversation at the beginning is a lot like discussing a prenuptial agreement before getting married. If this becomes too uncomfortable, use the power of vested stock and options to enforce commitment in a small way.

Having stock vest at different time intervals will ensure that your co-founder doesn't leave the company after a short period of time with a significant amount of equity. Usual structures involve 25% of the overall share vesting after a year, another 25% after two years and so on. This way, your co-founder needs to remain involved for at least four years in order to realise their full equity stake.

. . .

Dilution. Consider the effects of dilution as your company grows. You will need to leave equity for future investors and employees. In such situations, the minority partner will see their stake significantly reduced, so it is important to have conversations about this. Perhaps they will want their stake to be a certain guaranteed level or some psychological monetary threshold. Air these issues out at the beginning and do not let them fester.

Dealing with Conflict and a Bad Co-founder Relationship

The biggest reason why most start-ups fail is due to the breakdown of the co-founder relationship. Often, success hides existing fault lines and co-founders who don't take the time to address and communicate their concerns with one another risk seeing their business fail. An adverse side effect of such in-fighting is that employee morale often hits rock bottom, and this puts the company in a death spiral from which it can never recover.

One of the best ways to deal with conflict is to actively accept it. Running a business is stressful and there will be many times when you will be called upon to do things at a time when you're not at your best. In such moments, it is inevitable that tiny differences between you and your co-founder will be magnified and will give rise to conflict.

Expecting this to occur and having processes in place to handle this before it eventuates is the best and most realistic method of dealing with this. When starting out, you and your co-founders should take the time to sit and talk about everyone's behaviour. There are certain idiosyncrasies that everyone has which irritate others, and during stressful times it pays to be aware that minimising these behaviours can reduce conflict.

Some level of conflict is a healthy sign, since it shows that everyone involved cares about the business. This is not to say that a complete lack of conflict is a bad thing; most of the time, though, it is more realistic to prepare for conflict than to assume that the two of you will sail along smoothly.

Addressing conflict during the initial stages is important, so watch out for the signs mentioned below and take steps to nip them in the bud.

Avoidance. Do you skip down another path or change direction when you see your co-founder walking towards you? Do you find some of their behaviours irritating but brush them under the rug, thinking that it isn't important? Do you find yourself complaining to your friends or spouse that your co-founder isn't pulling their weight? These are some early warning signs that your relationship could soon be on the rocks. As with everything, communication is the key and you should always keep those lines open.

Remember that honesty between the two of you is paramount. However, make sure you have the emotional intelligence to recognise when *radical honesty* is a bad idea. Often, problems arise when personal issues exist. If someone is going through a tough time in their personal lives, it is unreasonable to expect them to be fully committed to their work. Make it clear that you will always lend a sympathetic ear to one another and ensure that guidelines exist for dealing with such situations.

Argument. Arguments by themselves aren't a bad thing; however, arguments on certain topics are. If you and your co-founder routinely disagree on idea ownership, or if one of you feels patronised by the other, and if there's a lack of accountability within the team, this is a huge warning sign that you need to bring in professional help.

The reason this is a bigger issue than mere avoidance is that these kinds of arguments signify that the trust between you and your co-founder is deteriorating, and that something needs to be done quickly. If left unaddressed, this will likely end up ruining the company the two of you have worked so hard to build.

Respect. No matter what the surface-level issue is, if one of you feels that the other doesn't respect the process or the business, chances are that this relationship is not salvageable. You need to either bring in professional help immediately or cut the cord. Lack of respect often manifests as one partner feeling that they are clearly doing more work than the other, one co-founder sabotaging the efforts of the other or undermining them in public, and so on.

When this happens, it is time to deal with the fallout of having entered a relationship that didn't work out.

Breaking up with a Co-founder

There's no easy way to end a relationship. This applies equally to when the two of you share a business together. If both of you were pulling your weight but just can't seem to get along, well, it's going to hurt, but it needs to be done—both for the sake of the business as well as for your own sakes.

Having an agreement similar to a prenuptial agreement before you go into business together is essential. Make this agreement as comprehensive as possible and detail the various clauses that will or will not be triggered when one of the co-founders leaves the company.

Vesting is a good technique to ensure fairness. Having a stock-vesting structure as described earlier is a good way to ensure that the co-founder who remains gets a fair share of the proceeds. If possible, do not burn your bridges, since this is often detrimental in the long term. It might be tempting at this moment to air your grievances and you may feel as if you're the wronged party, but with time, things will change.

Priorities. Remember that your business is your first priority. Do not, under any circumstances, air your dirty laundry to either your employees (if you have any) or your suppliers—and least of all, to your clients. Resolve the matter between the two of you. Handling things amicably is a sign of maturity, and it will improve your prospects in the long term.

Typically, when one partner leaves, there will be options to buy out their stake, so make sure the business can support this purchase. Often, cash is scarce in start-ups and the last thing you should do is to use investor money to buy out your old partner. Generally speaking, a lump sum payment is better than instalments.

This is because if the breakup needs to happen, it's better to do it as soon as possible before it turns into something else. As long as the business can handle the payments, do it. Meanwhile, remember that you still have a responsibility toward your employees and your clients. Make sure that no matter what happens, they are not affected by these changes and that you continue to be there for them.

Doing it the hard way. If you don't have any prenuptial-style agreement and if you cannot keep it amicable, there's not much hope of this breakup being painless. You may have to go to court and sometimes, your board and investors might even force you into mandated lawsuits. This is going to cost you legal fees and lots of emotional pain. Seek the best quality legal help during such times. Do not pick the lawyer with whom you're on the friendliest terms. Seek help from professionals who have dealt with these situations before.

Once you're done with the courts, you will still need to make sure that everything is documented and that your bridges aren't too badly burned. Don't worry, though. A bad breakup is hardly a reason for failure. Facebook had quite likely the ugliest possible breakup, and yet still thrives. It is hardly alone in this matter.

The best way to deal with a breakup is to simply avoid one. Here are some tips for you to ensure that you don't have to deal with such a situation; and if you do have to deal with one, how you can do so as amicably as possible.

- Seek complementary skills and don't encroach on one another's territory.
- Choose someone you've worked with in the past. Don't choose someone just because they are friends or family.
- Have an agreement in place that details contingencies. Even better, make provisions to reassess equity splits and control of the company after a certain period of time, once both of you have a fair idea of the work involved.
- Address all disagreements immediately via weekly or daily sessions.
- Spend time with each other alone periodically to discuss things. Keep communication lines open.

- Monitor for signs of a deteriorating relationship.
- If the breakup has to happen, do it as quickly as possible and in the least disruptive manner possible.

Ultimately, everything comes down to good preparation and open communication. Like with any other relationship, you need to work hard at it and should not ever assume that things will be easy.

The Author's Approach

When setting up and running my business, I decided against having a co-founder. The main output of my business is content; video content and written content. As my business is based on my personal brand, a co-founder made little sense.

My podcast co-host, Kevin Taylor, who runs the company *Steel Beam Calculator* and *Timber Beam Calculator*, is the opposite. Kevin runs his business with a co-founder, and they both have complementary skills. Their "beam calculator" suite of products is designed to help structural engineers and people drafting construction plans. Their software lets you enter measurements from a technical drawing plan and tells you what beams you need to install to ensure the structure is safe. In their business, Kevin is the subject-matter expert and qualified structural engineer; co-founder Nick is the software developer who organises all the code, software development, and deployment of the platform.

In their case, being co-founders works out well. They both have complementary skills between them to allow them to run a successful business. Kevin provides the business and domain knowledge, and Nick delivers the software development and technical know-how to build the product and deploy it.

Summary

Choosing to work with a co-founder can be an immensely rewarding experience. Often, working with a partner whom you respect and who has abilities which you don't possess can boost your business results to the next level. There's also the benefit of it being easier to find funding with a co-founder than as a solopreneur.

That being said, ease of funding should never factor into your choice of whether to bring a co-founder on board or not. Above all else, the needs of your business come first and if your business truly has varied areas of operation, you should seriously consider bringing someone on board. Going solo is not the end of the world, although it is harder. The choice of partnering with someone or going solo really comes down to your personality.

Evaluate yourself using a scorecard and rank yourself on how you score in metrics such as needing control, communication, emotional stability and so on. Do the same for your prospective co-founder and evaluate whether the two of you will be a good fit.

It will be tempting to work with someone in the same field as yours since we usually form better bonds with people with whom we share similarities. However, this is not a good idea, since your skills should complement those of your co-founder/s. This way, both of you will retain independence, and you won't step on each other's toes, which is a common reason for co-founder breakups.

Success in any relationship requires communication and work. It is easy to get lost within our own worlds, and this can cause us to assume that the other person is a mind reader and should know our thoughts automatically. A lack of open communication causes issues to be swept under the carpet, and these will rear their heads at the worst possible moment when you should be working together.

Having a detailed partnership agreement will save both of you a lot of headaches in the future. Think of this as a prenuptial agreement between the two of you. Yes, it is difficult and prickly to talk about, but you will emerge from it stronger. The best way to discuss such agreements is to assume that trouble will strike at some point because it usually does.

How will you handle conflicts? Will you seek professional help? How do you propose to conduct yourselves with one another, and what are the warning signs you should look out for? Discuss all of this in detail. It might seem like overkill at first but given what's at stake, it's worth it. Implement a vesting scheme so that stock doesn't get automatically allocated at the start.

Use start-up equity calculators to determine who should get how much. Do not, under any circumstances, simply decide to split the equity into halves, since this will only lead to stagnation. If you arrive at an equal distribution at the end of your discussion, then that's fine. Just don't agree to it because you are trying to avoid looking at it in detail.

Keep communication open between yourselves and nip all conflicts in the bud. Air out even those issues which seem trivial. Do not assume that these small things will go away. They will crop up at the worst times and damage your relationship. But, if things do get out of hand, do not hesitate to cut the cord and get out of the relationship.

If you have prepared well in advance, via a legal agreement, things should go as smoothly as they can. If this agreement is not present, then you can expect turbulence. Always keep your business above everything else and make sure it suffers the least disruption possible.

Working with a co-founder to build a business can be one of the most rewarding things that you can do. Make sure you go about it the right way, though, so that your business can run like a dream and not like a nightmare.

Workshop Questions

(1) Write down all the skills that you feel you bring to your business.

(2) Write down skills that you feel you lack, such as marketing, software development, accounting etc.

(3) Based on the answers to questions 1 and 2: if you were to take on a co-founder, what would your ideal co-founder look like to complement your skills?

(4) Would you be happy to split creative control on your product or service? Or are you looking for someone to handle the finance and marketing side of the business?

. . .

(5) If you are thinking that a co-founder is right for you, how much equity would you be prepared to offer?

    1. If you have invested a certain amount into the business that represents your total stake in the company, how much would you want a co-founder to pay into the business for their stake?

11

PRODUCT-LAUNCHING STRATEGIES

Starting a new side-hustle can be quite intimidating, especially if you need to hold onto a full-time job or when you are low on finances. The fear of rejection associated with starting a new venture can be nerve-wracking. Once you clear these basic hurdles and become a seasoned veteran, other challenges will come up. You might not have sufficient funds to expand your business, or you might run out of ideas that make you stand apart from your competitors. In this section, you will learn about certain strategies you can use to launch a successful side-hustle without incurring any debt or looking for external funding.

As a business owner, you should be proud of the service or the product you offer. However, you must not let this hamper your selling ability. Understand that your target audience has specific needs and problems. By offering a fixed solution, you are effectively preventing yourself from incorporating any helpful feedback into your sales pitch. This will reduce the effectiveness of your sales pitch in the future. Keep in mind that most of your customers will be uncertain about their needs. Salespeople usually think that if they can gain enough trust from their customers, they can make a sale. However, your aim must be to *close* a sale, not just make it.

Launching Strategies

It is not a good idea to target a broad market, especially while getting started. Although it may sound counterintuitive, you can increase the effectiveness of your sales pitch when you are aiming at a niche you thoroughly understand. When you target a specific market segment or a niche that shares similar problems, you can address their problems more effectively. Apart from this, it also makes the sales process rather easy. When your sales increase, along with various resources at your disposal, it becomes easier to uncover any new insights from your targets. A combination of these factors will help increase the effectiveness of your sales pitches.

It might sound like a great idea to aim for the stars. However, when you opt for a specialised niche, it is easier to get positive results. Select a market segment that appeals to you.

Get in touch with the decision makers. A good value proposition is only a part of the equation. You not only must know how to make a good sales pitch; you also must ensure that you are presenting it to the right person. You need to spend some time to research your potential clients, determine who has the authority to make purchasing decisions, and reach out to them. Once you have identified the key decision makers, concentrate on developing a good relationship with them. The best way to do this is by providing as much value as you can upfront without focusing on an immediate return. By building good relationships with the decision makers, you can almost guarantee return sales for your business.

A good pitch. If you think a sales pitch is all about making a twenty-slide presentation and spouting off facts or figures, then it's time to reconsider. Statistics and numbers are important, certainly, but when it comes to developing a sales pitch, you will only have about a minute to make your point as persuasively as you can to your prospective client, so it has to be convincing, appealing, and above all, concise. In that 60 seconds, you have to grab the prospect's attention and then hold it, so try to provide some basic information that covers answers to all general queries a prospective customer might have. Spend some time doing the necessary research, crafting the ideal pitch, and then practicing it. This is essential—you might have a great sales pitch, but if you lack conviction or confidence while delivering it, all your expertise will be of no use. You only have one opportunity to pitch to a prospective client for the first time, so make the most of it.

An effective sales pitch is one that will convince any prospects that buying your product or service will solve a problem that they have. If you are focusing on a specific niche, then you are targeting a specific demographic of people. If you can't demonstrate what problem of theirs you are solving, you will find closing a sale very difficult. One of the most effective ways of demonstrating problem solving is to weave in a story. Ever since the advent of human language, storytelling has been a highly effective way of entertaining and persuading. A powerful technique is if you can relate the story to yourself as the owner of that product and service. Not only does this weave a story into your sales efforts, but you can make the whole process much more relatable by including these personal references.

Make those calls now. A common challenge faced by entrepreneurs is that they are scared of making sales calls. If you want to make your side-hustle a profitable venture, then you must overcome your fear, pick up the phone, and start calling prospective customers. Making the first sales call might be scary. However, it is time to bite the bullet and make the first call. Eventually, it does get easier. As your business grows, you can hire a dedicated sales team to do all this for you. Until then, you must do it!

Selling yourself. The products or services you offer do matter; however, your business is more than just this. You might have the best product in the niche, but that won't serve any purpose if your prospects cannot relate to your business or to you. If you want to be successful, you must work on selling your ideas convincingly. Selling is a subtle art that depends on trust, which is something you must build with your prospects. To do this, you need to be upfront about your business. Share your story, create a human side to your company, and don't worry about admitting any setbacks you face. You must be able to sell your idea and ideals to convince the prospects about your business.

Minimum Viable Products and The Lean Startup

The Lean Startup is a method created by Eric Ries. It is designed to provide an approach to create and manage a start-up to get your products into the prospect's hands as quickly as possible. You can engineer the success of your business by following this process.

Most start-ups begin with the idea for a product that they think that others will want. Once they have this idea, they spend a lot of time—months, or even years—to perfect that product. They do all this without showing the product or its initial design to their prospective buyers. When they fail to win their audience, it is usually because they never asked whether their product would appeal to their prospective customers or not. When their brilliant product is met with customers' indifference, it leads to the failure of their business.

The Lean Startup method helps create order instead of chaos by providing the business owners with the necessary tools to continuously test their product vision. When a start-up does all this, they will have an established market for their product by the time it is ready for distribution.

A start-up is a place that proposes to offer a new product or service. However, there is a lot of uncertainty surrounding any idea a business proposes. By using *The Lean Startup's* process, it not only allows you to test your business vision, you can also reduce your costs along the way.

The premise of this model is quite simple. It encourages entrepreneurs to work smarter, instead of harder. However, if you are aiming for success, then the question you must ask yourself isn't whether a certain product can be produced or not. Instead, start by asking yourself whether such a product even needs to be built. To launch a successful product, you must understand that the product you want to develop not only has to sound good on paper, it has to be profitable, too. If the idea turns out to be successful, then you can start working on streamlining the production process, concentrating on the marketing campaign, and then on developing the product. When you follow these steps, you will essentially have a market for your product by the time it is ready for distribution.

An important concept proposed by *The Lean Startup* method is the "build-measure-learn" feedback process it creates. The first step is to determine the problem or the needs that your product will address. The next step is to develop an MVP (minimum viable product) to start the learning process. You will learn more about MVP in the next section. After this, the start-up can start working on fine-tuning the production process. It involves the measurement, analysis, and understanding of certain actionable metrics, which help steer your product toward success. If you go through this process, it will help you understand whether launching the product is a good idea or not. If the results aren't favourable, then you can make the necessary changes without incurring any huge loss or damage.

Let us look at an example to help you fully understand the concept proposed by *The Lean Startup* method. We'll assume that you are a meal delivery service that provides healthy meals, that usually targets single twenty-somethings in cities. You discover that targeting thirty-something new mothers in the suburbs is a good idea. Your business will then need to change its delivery schedule along with the menu offered to fit the new customer profile. You might also want to add meal options for their spouses or partners, and maybe children. If you follow *The Lean Startup* model, it will prompt you first to identify a problem that your business can solve. Then, it encourages you to think about developing a minimum viable product that you can introduce to receive feedback from your potential customers. Doing this is more cost-effective and helpful than developing the final product and then obtaining the feedback. It helps reduce the risk of uncertainty while allowing you to test the effectiveness and profitability of your business idea.

Minimum Viable Product

Starting a business can be tricky. You must come up with a brilliant product idea, develop and produce the product, and then invest in marketing and advertising to ensure that the product reaches your target customers. These are the steps followed by any business.

A Minimum Viable Product (MVP) is essentially a product with only a couple of basic features that helps capture the attention of an early adopter. This makes product development easier as you can test ideas early, which leads to rejecting bad ideas and building on successful ones. You might have heard of successful companies like Zappos, Uber, and Dropbox. All these companies started out as MVPs and gained the power and influence they wield today. An MVP is a great way to do the following:

- Release your product into the market within the shortest timeframe.
- Reduce any implementation costs.
- Test the demand for your product before full-fledged development and release of said product.
- Avoid any chances of capital loss or chances of failure.
- Gain the necessary insight to decide what works and what doesn't.
- Work directly with your target customers and analyse their preferences and needs.
- Increase your customer base.

In 2011, Eric Ries released a book, *The Lean Startup*, which went on to be a bestseller. In this book, he described his experience working with start-ups. It not only influenced the start-up industry but also introduced a vital concept, the MVP. An MVP is a product that only has certain basic features, which are released to test the success of the business idea. It is used to gauge the reaction of the target customers. The idea is simple—obtain customer feedback *before* working on developing a full-fledged product and launching it in the market. An MVP can help a business reduce the chances of incurring a capital loss and avoid failures.

The concept of developing a minimum viable product seems rather straightforward; however, a lot of people tend to misunderstand it. Instead of developing an initial *version* of their final product with basic functionality, they tend to make an initial product, which is either complicated or doesn't include the final product's key features. Please remember that the MVP must effectively convey the essence of the product and provide a brief overview of the product in its most basic form. It is almost like a teaser for a movie. Due to the variety of products as well as services available today, MVPs can be quite different. Let us look at the different types of MVPs.

Piecemeal MVP. A piecemeal MVP is a brilliant way to introduce a new product to the target customers by keeping the investment at the bare minimum while developing the product. This model of MVP uses only existing tools or resources for creating a product or service. It is usually an amalgamation of components from various sources to form the basic version of the final product. For instance, if you are interested in developing a rental marketplace for designer bags, then it is better to test this idea on an existing marketplace, instead of directing your resources toward an idea which might or might not work. You can use an online platform like Mirakl or Arcadier to do the same by creating marketplaces with a minimal of financial or time investment.

Groupon, the popular American marketplace that connects potential customers with local retailers, grocers, and other businesses, used a piecemeal MVP to test their idea. Groupon has certainly become quite popular these days, but this wasn't always the case. Groupon offers deals that are available only for a specific day and can be activated by purchasing the deal from said platform. Initially, the creators of Groupon used WordPress to update their customers about any deals, because it was a free service and it gave them a chance to test their idea. Once they realised their idea was viable, they went ahead and took steps to implement their business plan.

Concierge MVP. The concierge MVP model allows you to test the viability of the solution you offer and to see whether there exists any demand for your product. You must first find out if there are any takers for the service or product you wish to offer. Once you have an audience, you must test your idea on them and obtain their feedback.

One of the best examples of using a concierge MVP model for launching a product is 'Food on the Table'. This is a mobile app which collects information about the user's food preferences and suggests recipes along with a list of groceries required to cook such dishes. Apart from this, the app also provides a list of nearby grocery stores which provide a good discount on the products the user will need. This brilliant service was developed by Manuel Rosso. Initially, this service had neither a website nor an app. It was a personal concierge service provided by Rosso. To check the validity of his business idea, he did a trial run. He decided to gather certain participants, interviewed them and made a list of what they liked along with their grocery budgets. He used all this data to compile simple shopping lists along with recipes he thought they would like. He also gave them coupons from the local grocery stores for the list of products the participants would require. Once this idea clicked, he worked on automating his business idea.

This type of MVP helps you understand what your customers really want and is a good way to validate your product idea without burning a hole in your pocket. Since you have a chance to work with your target customers directly, it becomes easier to understand whether the idea will work or not.

Wizard of Oz MVP. A concierge MVP is based on the premise of delivering an experience to real customers without making any qualms about showing that the product isn't fully developed. A Wizard of Oz MVP concentrates on creating an impression that the product is complete even while still in the development stage. It is also known as Manual-first MVP. Zappos is an ideal example of a Wizard of Oz MVP. The creator of Zappos, Nick Swinmum, started this brilliant website with a simple idea. He went around clicking pictures of different shoes he found at stores. Then he simply uploaded them onto the internet to see if he would get any takers. He was merely testing an idea which proved to be a goldmine! His idea paid off and his efforts were worth it.

This form of MVP is a good way for a business to test whether or not the services it wants to offer will have any takers. The product might seem like it is fully developed, but behind the scenes, it is still under construction. This MVP allows you to directly work with your potential clients and analyse their behaviour and needs or preferences.

An MVP is essential if you want your start-up to be successful. It helps launch a product, keeps investment costs low, mitigates the risk of losses, and even helps acquire the validation for the business idea.

Dealing with Failure

Anyone who launches a new product wishes to see that their product is successful in the market and has plenty of demand. Whether the product was launched for a start-up or to increase the revenue of an existing business, no one likes to see their new product fail or get rejected by the market. However, it doesn't always go as planned. You might have noticed that some ideas tend to do extremely well while others fail terribly. Why does this happen? In this section, you will learn about the common reasons why product launches fail. When the product launch is successful, and it goes smoothly, it is all good. However, if the product launch fails, it can send your business packing in no time. The tips given in this section will help ensure that the product launch isn't a flop, but will also help ensure that if it does, you will have a contingency plan for any recovery.

Failing to understand customers' needs and demands. Demand for what your business offers is based on the customers' needs and your product's ability to satisfy at least one of those needs. If the product doesn't do so, then it will fail.

In the 1970s, AT&T had come up with a brand-new PicturePhone. They launched this product after spending several months on research and test runs. The product was launched into the market in the belief that it would be successful. However, due to the lack of customer interest, this product was scrapped by the company three years after its launch. What were the reasons for this failed product launch? The management didn't pay any heed to the negative feedback which they obtained during the trial phase. They proceeded to launch the product instead of working on fixing the negative feedback. Not only this, the product also had an overwhelming number of features which didn't appeal to its target audience and prevented them from having a wonderful viewing experience.

A good example of how a company changed its product after testing its MVP is Coca-Cola. In 2004, it introduced C2, which was quite similar to the regular Coke. The only difference was that it came with only half the calories and carbohydrates as regular Coke. During the MVP stage, the company realised that the product wasn't targeted at the right audience. They used this insight and came up with Coke Zero, which proved to be quite successful.

If you want your business to be a success, then you cannot ignore the needs and wants of your customers. Do plenty of research, conduct surveys, seek expert opinion if necessary, and obtain feedback before you think about launching the product.

Wrong pricing. Deciding the product's pricing is a crucial step in launching your product. There exists a direct relationship between the demand, need, and the value associated with the product by the customers. It is a relationship that you cannot afford to ignore. Selecting the wrong pricing can be a deal-breaker. If the product you are offering has certain existing alternatives in the market, then it is even more important to get the pricing right. If you set the wrong price, and customers consider it too high, the chance of them abandoning your product in favour of your competitors' products increases drastically. If the product in question doesn't belong to the luxury market segment, this is doubly true. For instance, in the early 1990s, the Apple Newton PDA came with a hefty price tag of $700. This proved to be the primary reason why this product was scrapped by the company. Few customers could afford the product and weren't keen on spending so much when cheaper and equally efficient products were available.

The price of the product must be decided according to the customer demand for the product and the value placed on it by customers, along with the supply of the product. For instance, if your target audience is in the market looking for luxury bags or any customised product, a low price will not do your business any favours. People splurge on luxury bags and designer products because they offer exclusivity, which is the value which is being delivered to the customer. So, if a Hermes Birkin bag is priced at only $500, it simply loses the exclusivity it offers.

Don't fix a non-existent problem. If you have to turn on your computer, what will you do? You will click on the power button. Now, would you need another product to help you with this? Of course not—no one needs assistance in this process. While developing a product, you must ensure that it addresses an existing need or a problem. Don't try to fix a non-existent problem if you want your product to be successful. The demand for a product is based on the *existing* needs of customers, or any real problems they wish to solve. For instance, if XYZ is in the market looking for a product that will help heat up their food instantly, there exists a need to heat up the food and keep it warm. So, XYZ starts looking at different microwaves available in the market to meet his needs.

Regardless of the reasons why you are developing a product, if it is designed to solve a problem that doesn't exist, be prepared for it to fail. You don't have to worry about working on marketing strategies, because the success rate of such products is negligible. For instance, Maxwell House came up with Ready-to-Drink Brewed Coffee in 1990. This product was created with the aim of providing customers with a new and convenient way to enjoy coffee instantly without having to make it at home. It could be purchased from a supermarket and used; however, the user needed to pour it from its packaging and then microwave it before it could be enjoyed. Why would the target audience want this product, when it wasn't *instant* coffee as it was marketed? This was the reason why the product had to be scrapped by the company.

. . .

The wrong audience. There's some truth to the saying "You can't please all of the people, all of the time". Certain products will only appeal to certain segments of the market, and there's no one product that appeals to everyone. No matter how long you spend developing the perfect product, if you aren't marketing it to the right audience, it will fail. For instance, it isn't a good idea to market comprehensive security software to a grocery store, or to market organic fertiliser to famous fashion houses. Do you remember Apple's iPod? This device developed by Apple was certainly a ground-breaking innovation. Have you heard of the Microsoft Zune? Chances are that you probably haven't. In 2006, when iPod's popularity was at its peak, Microsoft came up with the Zune. It was intended to be a competitor to the iPod; however, Zune failed because Microsoft was trying to capture a market audience who was already taken with Apple.

The reaction of your target audience to the products you develop can at times be tricky to ascertain. Therefore, it is essential that you do a little market research before deciding to launch a product. When you obtain customers' feedback, try to make the necessary changes if required. If you receive only negative feedback, it is time to scrap the project and start afresh. It is better to cut your losses initially than to go ahead with a poor idea and suffer an even bigger loss later.

Poor preparation. If you want your product to stand a fighting chance in a competitive market, then you must prepare accordingly. A successful product launch that captures the attention of your target audience will take a lot of groundwork, not to mention significant time and attention. You cannot skimp on it if you want your product to succeed. So, what are a couple of things you cannot afford to overlook? You must continue to test the product, conduct proper market surveys, analyse the data and use it to devise your game plan. You have to stay involved, hold a lot of meetings, and build your customer base. Be prepared to put in the necessary time, effort, and money to give your product launch its best chance of success.

. . .

Must be adequate. If the product has any technological flaws or is inadequate in any way, then it will not stand a chance in this high-tech world in which we live. Who would want to pay for or have time to deal with a product that is technologically flawed? The answer is, "No one!" Technological flaws don't have to be related to the product, they can be related to the production or marketing process too. For instance, if you offer a brilliant product, but your business website accepts only one form of payment, it can be a potential turn-off for your customers.

Recover from a Failed Product Launch

Now that you are aware of the different reasons why a product launch can fail, you must learn to deal with the failure, too. A superficial autopsy will not help you understand the real reason why the product launch wasn't successful. Perhaps some important features were left out and some unnecessary details were added. However, to unearth the reasons for product failure, you must dig deep. In this section, you will learn about a couple of simple tips you can use to overcome a failed product launch.

Analysing the data. You must collect data which will help you understand the reasons why the product launch wasn't successful. However, your job doesn't end once you collect the data. You must carefully review the data and information you gather. Why is this important? Well, any snags in the customer journey can also be the reason for the failure of a product launch. For instance, while analysing the data, you might notice that a lot of customers don't complete the sale. On further examination, you might realise that the checkout process is too cumbersome, or that it doesn't offer sufficient payment options.

Regardless of how trivial a detail might seem, it can be quite important. You can use different tools like Google Analytics to study all the data you gather. A couple of metrics that you must analyse are the bounce rate, entry pages, and exit pages while using Google Analytics. The bounce rate shows the percentage of users who land on a specific page and then exit the website without visiting other pages. It helps identify the pages that are the weak links. The entry pages are the entry points for visitors. It helps you to understand which of the pages need to be optimised, whereas the exit pages show the point where customers become disinterested. By reviewing all this data, you can understand the steps you must take to ensure that your customers stay engaged and close a sale.

Talking to the audience. Talking to your target audience is a great way to not just acquire their feedback, but to understand the reasons why the product wasn't a success. A simple survey is the quickest method of obtaining customer feedback. You can use a service like SurveyMonkey to create a questionnaire for conducting your survey. You can also ask for feedback on any social media platforms used by your target audience. You can include questions like the following in the survey:

- Which features did you like in the product?
- Are there any changes you would like to make to it?
- Does it fulfil your requirements or address your needs?
- Is there a feature you didn't like about the product?

You are free to include any question that you want, provided it helps you understand the reasons why the product flopped.

Harness the Power of the Sales Funnel

If you are just starting out as an entrepreneur or are getting ready for a product launch and you aren't quite sure how you are going to get people to part with their money, then you are in the same position as the majority of small business owners.

It takes time to understand how business and specific industries work. Unfortunately, while you are learning, you could be losing sales. There is one tool, though, that has become a must-have in any entrepreneur or side-hustler's marketing toolbox, and that is the sales funnel.

You've likely heard the term mentioned before, and perhaps you aren't quite sure how it works, or more importantly, how you can create a sales funnel for your own business.

What is a Sales Funnel?

A funnel is used to ensure that whatever is put in the top moves smoothly through into a container and we don't lose any of the precious contents. So, how does that apply to sales?

Picture your buying customer base as your container. If you aren't using a funnel to direct prospects into your business, then you're just grasping at thin air and hoping for the best. That doesn't sound like the most efficient way to be operating, does it?

Directing Prospects. If you are about to undertake a product launch, then you likely already know that there is a market for your product or service. The key now is to ensure that you have a strategy to direct those prospects through the various stages of the buying process until they are ready to purchase. Sales funnels are a marketing concept or process that you build to direct those prospects.

Buying Stages. Anyone with even limited knowledge of marketing understands that most prospects are not ready to buy on day one. You can recognise that from your own purchasing endeavours too. Buyers go through four stages, and it's your job to make sure they get through all four and make it all the way into your business. The four stages of buying are:

Awareness of need: This when your prospect realises that they have an unfulfilled need. They don't need to come to this realisation on their own; the whole point is that your marketing efforts should help them to get there.

Interest in solutions to that need: After your prospect becomes aware that they have an unfulfilled need, you need to present your product as the solution to that need and create interest.

Decision to choose the right solution to their need: At this point, the prospect knows they have a need, and they are aware that your product or service may satisfy that need. Now, they are weighing up their options. If you have played your cards right, your product should be at the top of their list.

Action is taken to fulfil the need: After having weighed up their options and, hopefully, being strongly pulled toward your brand, the prospect now makes the decision to take action and purchase.

How Do I Apply This to My Service or Product Launch?

Your first step, which would likely already have been part of your product development process, is to be really clear about who your ideal customer is. By developing a customer persona, you will know where to aim your funnel and exactly what type of process will be most effective to move your prospect through the buying stages.

Your sales funnel needs to be split into four different strategies that target each of the four buying stages. To develop this funnel, you will need to identify what type of outreach works best at each stage.

Outreach Types. Before the advent of digital marketing and online business, marketing outreach looked very different from how it looks today. If you were marketing your business physically, you would use strategies like cold calling, promotion stands in supermarkets or at expos, and even product samples.

When your business is solely online, those strategies still apply; they just look a little different. Marketing strategies for online sales funnels use content marketing to attract and retain prospects.

What Type of Content Should I Use for My Sales Funnel? There are several content types that can be used in the different buying stages; these include blog articles, lead magnets, videos, and webinars. The key is to develop these content forms so you are addressing the stage at which your prospect is, and so that each content form (and thus stage) leads the prospect to the next one.

Blog articles, for instance, are excellent for the awareness and interest stages of the buying cycle. The key to good blog articles is not to use them to push your product. Although that may sound counterintuitive, what you are doing with your blog is providing value to future prospects with interesting content. When done well, blog articles help to start building a relationship of trust with prospects, and also hint at the unfulfilled needs they may have that you can fulfil.

Lead magnets can be considered the free samples of the digital marketing world. It's just like the person in Walmart giving you a taste of the latest cheese sausage brand, except, in this case, the prospect is exchanging their email address for the free content. Lead magnets help to create interest after awareness is gained, and they should be valuable pieces of content that will leave the prospect wanting more.

Videos are a great way to get your message across to prospects who may not be big fans of reading—and let's face it, many people aren't in today's fast-paced world. This versatile medium can also be used in all four stages of the buying cycle—awareness, interest, decision, and action. According to data gleaned by Google, 70% of internet users are watching at least one video in their purchase cycle.

Webinars are most commonly used in the decision and action phases of the sales funnel. Like lead magnets, you want to be creating valuable content here that gets your prospects interested in your product and answers all their questions.

How Do I Activate My Sales Funnel?

Once you have decided which forms of content you are going to use in your funnel, you will need to decide how you are going to put that strategy into action. Think about your sales funnel strategy as the body of a car; now you need to pick a motor to power it. Three of the most popular ways to get sales funnel content in front of your customers include email marketing, social media, and websites or landing pages.

Ideally, you will want to use a combination of these three methods to cover all your bases, but social media does tend to have the highest engagement rate of all three.

Keep in mind that although you are designing your funnel to target prospects in all four buying stages, not all of your prospects will be in the same stage at the same time. Your strategy, therefore, needs to include a continuous flow of content from all four levels.

Of course, software does exist to automate the sales funnel process, but it doesn't create the content or close the sale for you. For that, you still need a human being, i.e. you!

An Example of an Assembled Sales Funnel

Let's assume, for our example, that you have just started your own dog training business and you are about to launch your *Citizen Kanine* product, which will help customers to train their dogs at home.

In order to create awareness, you have decided to use your blog. You'll be writing articles, carefully worded for SEO (search engine optimisation, which will help get you prospects. We will explore SEO later in the book), on several topics related to unwanted behaviour in dogs. Within those articles, you will hint at the importance of training to correct these behaviours.

At this level of the funnel, your prospects are becoming aware that the behaviours you are referring to are things they are struggling with in their own canine friends. You have made them aware of their pain and hinted at a solution.

These articles can link to a lead magnet that will provide solutions to simple behaviour problems. Prospects that have identified their needs in the first stage will gladly provide their email addresses in order to receive a partial solution to their problems.

Now that you have your prospect's email address, you can target them through email marketing and either invite them to follow you on social media or provide them with the videos you have created for use at this level.

Your prospects are now aware they have a problem, they have identified your service as a possible solution, and now you just need to close the deal by providing a call-to-action. Discount vouchers with limited time offers work well here.

In a webinar or similar platform, you will be able to provide social proof—testimonials from happy clients—and answer any remaining questions your prospects may have. This services the action phase of the buying cycle.

Sales Funnel Stats

Over 95% of visitors to your website will not complete a purchase on their first visit. This is one of the reasons it is so vital to have a sales funnel in place; because you are still maximising your chances of keeping those visitors in your funnel if you have a plan to get their contact information.

On average, it takes five contacts with a prospect to make a sale, but 44% of entrepreneurs say they stop after the first attempt. In terms of a sales funnel, you are setting up those contact points upfront.

About 30% to 50% of buyers say they will end up buying from the first vendor that responds to their request. The fact is, though, that while you can't be available 24/7, your sales funnel can. When a prospect is typing a pain they have into a search engine, your sales funnel jumps to life by providing the content they are looking for.

Furthermore, if you have set up the flow of your content items correctly by using calls-to-action and links, your prospect could guide themselves all the way through the funnel. Even though you are not physically responding, your brand is still responding to the need and you fulfil the requirement of being the first to respond.

If your users find you organically through a search engine, it automatically adds a level of authority to your business. In order to do this, you need to harness SEO capabilities in all your content formats. Even the simplest SEO tactics in your content can measurably boost the efficacy of your sales funnel.

The Author's Approach

Back around 2011, I worked for a financial service and consumer loan company. I was the lead developer on the team that maintained the payment collection and debt management platform. I remember one meeting where we had the head of the collections department call a product review meeting with the IT heads. She wanted to discuss building a system to help encourage people, who were behind on payments, to make a small payment using positive reinforcement. Her idea was that instead of using the threat of a phone call from a collection's agent, we would instead try to encourage them to pay small amounts. We wanted to avoid imposing negative or stressful feelings onto the person in debt.

The premise was that some people fall into debt for reasons outside their control, and when they are stressed and anxious about debt, they can try to evade calls from the collections team. When you are in debt, the last thing you want to do is talk to someone from the company you owe money to, even if you have good intentions to pay.

The issue was the policy that once a debtor reached a certain level of lateness on their payments, their account would get sold off to a debt collection agency. This incurred a sizeable financial hit for the lender and was also an unpleasant situation for the debtor. Our head of collections genuinely wanted to help people who had fallen into debt, as well as recover money for the company.

The head of collections wanted to run a series of experiments by building a lightweight version of a payment portal. By running these experiments, we could analyse the results to see if the company wanted to invest in a more in-depth version of the platform, with deep integration into the rest of the loan and collections systems.

Our approach to this project fell nicely into the principles of *The Lean Startup*-style "Minimum Viable Product". They tasked me with putting together a small team, and we had a small budget to cover this piece of work. We treated this team as a small internal start-up to enable us to move faster. We had me, two software developers, a designer, and a member of the collections team who was also a compliance officer. Having someone from compliance involved was vital, as we still had to make sure we followed financial services regulations.

The MVP we built featured an online portal that a debtor could access. The company would send out an email or SMS message to the customer with a link to the portal. We took the customer through a series of security screens to authenticate them. We then presented them with a screen showing their total outstanding balance and a slider. The slider started at a minimum payment of £5, and incrementally increased to the maximum owed value. As they moved the slider, we would show a series of positive reinforcement messages about the benefits of paying down their balance, including how much interest they would save and what the benefits would be to them. We also mentioned that if they made a payment, even if it was only the lowest payment, the company's debt collection team would not contact them to chase payment for another 30 days. Once the customer had picked an amount to pay, they could then make that payment using a debit card. They weren't allowed to use a credit card, as that is paying a debt with a debt.

It took us three weeks to develop, test and deploy this portal onto a production server. Once our compliance team was satisfied with the solution and its security, the collections team prepared different debtors' target cohorts to contact. This included over 30 days late, 60 days late, 90 days late, and finally 180 days late. At the 180 days late stage, they were about to be sold off to a debt collection company.

Part of the experiment was to observe people's behaviour when presented with the portal. If you are given the option to make a payment and not have to talk to anyone, would they go ahead with that payment? There are still many stigmas associated with debt, and when someone is in that situation, the last thing they want to do is have a conversation about it. We were giving them a way to make a payment and avoid having that awkward conversation.

When we started contacting different cohorts of customers, we were not sure what the uptake would be. We targeted people who had been difficult to reach and have conversations with, so they would ignore the messages, emails and letters from us. To our surprise, the adoption rate was very high. A large proportion of customers paid the minimum payment of £5 or an amount near that.

With debtors that were late with payments, or even near the point of being sold off to a debt collector, we noticed quite a few of them made large payments, or sometimes cleared their debt entirely. We were not expecting that at all. Without physically talking to the customer, we could only guess that being offered a way out of the problem without the awkward conversation, prompted them to clear the debt and remove the problem. These were exceptional cases and not the norm, but they surprised us to see it happen.

Even though this project was not my business, we treated it like a start-up within the company. While we were solving a problem for the company, it was also great practice and education for everyone involved in testing an idea with a smaller solution can be a significant advantage. We learned from this small prototype, and all the data we collected could inform an extensive work program into alternative payment mechanisms.

When looking back at some products that I have sold through my business, I have used a number of different tactics for launching products. When I started making sound libraries, I used to release small libraries for free from my website. From there, I could look at the download statistics to see what was more popular. Using these numbers, I could decide which commercial libraries to release.

Training courses were harder to use any data for initially. In deciding what classes to teach, I went with the utterly unscientific gut feeling of teaching what I know. When I started working with Pluralsight, I said that I would only do courses that interested me. Creating these courses is a lot of work, so I would only work on something that I was interested in myself to keep myself motivated.

As courses were released and people started watching them, I could look at feedback from those viewers and the retention data to see if I could identify any problems. The most direct feedback would be from people's comments on the courses. Their feedback would always help me try to improve on my next and future training material.

When creating and publishing books, I took more of a "minimum viable product" approach. My goal all along was to write this very book you are now reading. It is a reasonably hefty book and took a considerable amount of my time to write it. Along with this book is a YouTube channel, where I create lots of advice videos. At some point in time after this book is released, there will also be an online workshop version of the material that people can take, which is designed to be very practical. All of this is a significant investment of my own time and money to start this business. It all starts with publishing a book, for which I formed my own publishing brand instead of using a traditional publisher.

I wanted to go down this route because I want to own all the rights to the material and be able to easily update and release new versions without being stuck in the very slow machine that is traditional publishing. Releasing and promoting a book is hard, so I didn't want my first attempt at publishing to be with this book. When I first started working full time, I knew I wanted to write a book like this, so I began writing a series of shorter guides of around 80 to 100 pages.

The idea was to practice the publishing process with these small books, meaning that if I were going to make any mistakes, it would be with those books and not this one. Conceptually, the publishing process is not that complicated, but as with most things, the devil is in the details. Writing the books is the first stage, but then you have formatting, cover design, writing book descriptions, keyword selection and search engine optimisation, and lots of other minor tasks that you need to get to grips with.

By far, the most challenging part of releasing a book is promotion and marketing. At one point, I talked with a publisher for this book, because marketing support would have been the one area that would have made me consider going through a traditional publisher. What I found out shocked me, though. The amount of marketing support an author gets these days from a publisher is minimal. At first, I thought it might have been just that publisher, but no, this is not the case. I am fortunate that I know many people who have written books, and after talking with a lot of them, there is a common theme. Unless you are a high-profile name and already well-known, you will hardly get any marketing support—you are expected to do a lot of it yourself. I don't mind paying for marketing and promotion, but only if I see its benefits on the back end. The margins through traditional publishing for a book like this were not very good.

The Path to Freedom project will adopt a sales funnel similar to what we discussed earlier in this chapter. At the top of the funnel, I have content at no cost to an end reader or viewer, which is designed to deliver a lot of value. This includes a YouTube channel with weekly videos and a weekly email newsletter that people can sign up for. In this level of the funnel, I will let people know about this book, but even if they have no intention of buying it, they should still get a lot of value from the video and email content.

The next level down on the funnel is this book. If people like enough of what I talk about on YouTube, then they can purchase this book, which offers a lot of valuable information. From there, I will have the online workshop on the next level of the funnel, a high-cost product offering. The number of people converting to this product would probably be much lower than those buying the book, but that product costs more and has a higher profit margin.

From there, on the next level, you could have coaching and consulting. The idea is to bring someone into the funnel, offer them a lot of value, and gradually try to promote them to the lower layers. Not everyone will, and that is fine. Those people are still great to have around watching content, and over time they may convert to buying the book or the course.

Summary

When it comes to planning a launch for your product, targeting to broad a market can make it very hard to compete; especially if you are a very small company compared to your competitors. Your best initial strategy is to focus on a niche for your market and implement that well. When it comes to launching a product, you can test your ideas early using The Lean Startup techniques. By producing a series of minimal viable products, you can test your product's initial market worthiness before investing too much time on the complete solution.

A sales funnel is a vital sales and marketing tool for all businesses and product launches. While large businesses may have complex and intricate funnel structures for various areas of their business, entrepreneurs and side giggers can get equal value out of their own self-developed funnels.

For online businesses, content is king in the buying process, and it is important to select the correct type of content for your audience and their buying stage. The time it takes to develop a sales funnel is paid back in enormous dividends as it helps your prospects to find your product or service and ultimately results in sales.

Workshop Questions

(1) If you have a product or service idea already, think about ways you can test that idea without spending too much time on a full implementation.

1. Are there products on the market that you can use to test your product idea, such as existing online marketplaces, or lead page generation tools?

(2) Try to write some sales text that describes what your product or service does, and what problem it will fix for the customer.

1. Think about how you can weave in a personal story into the sales copy to make it relatable to the customer.

12

THE WORKING ENVIRONMENT

I don't know what's better about not having a boss. The fact that I can start work when I want, or that I can dress however I please with no formal expectations. But with all the good comes the bad as well, such as finding a good place to work. Because you no longer have an office or a designated cubicle in a grey, drab building, you'll need a new, productive place to work. There are plenty of options, all with their upsides and downsides, pros and cons, joy and sorrows—whatever you want to call it. There is one major factor that you need to take into consideration when you are deciding what's best for you. Are you a social butterfly or a hermit?

My mother always told me that I was her hermit child. I used to stay in my room and read, write or play games without so much as making a peep. If it weren't for food and bathroom breaks, I would have stayed in my room all day, every day. But there's a sort of comfort in knowing that you're not alone. The best thing was always knowing that if I left my room, there was someone there willing to give me a smile or make a snarky comment about being a hermit. As great as living on your own can be sometimes—being able to do what you want, when you want, and walk around in your pyjamas—after a while you may start to notice how quiet it is.

When you work at an office with co-workers, it's easy to forget that your home is empty. But once you begin freelancing or taking your start-up from side-hustle to a full-time hustle; staying at home the entire day, you'll notice it right away. If you don't have family living with you, the silence can become deafening. It's hard sometimes, even for someone who has been considered a hermit their entire lives. Just knowing that there is someone else in the house makes a huge difference.

The other issue is that it can be hard to find the discipline needed to work for yourself. With a boss, it's easy to get things done because you have set deadlines and you have to keep to them. When you are a freelancer and get more space to breathe, it's easy to procrastinate and leave work for the next day, and the next, and the next. It's important to take these things into consideration when you are deciding where you want to work from.

It might take some trial and error and could even cost more than you anticipated but finding the perfect place to work is important to get your work done and be as productive as possible—while keeping the better part of your sanity, of course.

Advantages of Working from Home

Working from home is fun, it really is! But before doing this, there are some pros and cons you need to weigh.

No commute. The first thing that comes to mind when you are working from home is that you save yourself the effort of commuting. Whether you drive or use public transportation, working from home eliminates those annoying trips and traffic jams.

Saving time and money. When was the last time you checked the price of fuel? Not to mention the services that your car requires when you're frequently driving long distances. It also saves on start-up costs if you don't need to rent or buy a separate office space when you are starting your own business.

It's comfortable. Who else can say that they can go to work in their pyjamas? Although it's not necessarily the preferable working attire—if someone comes over unannounced you don't want to be caught in your Batman pyjama bottoms—it is quite comfortable. You are very much allowed to do whatever you want. You can get refreshments or have comfort breaks whenever you need them, and you don't have to wait until a scheduled lunch break to whip out that delicious lunch.

Food. I've personally found that working at an office is an excellent excuse to buy food from vendors; but after the first month, it felt as if I had gained 14 pounds. An advantage of working from home is that you can make your lunch much healthier. It can also be a lot cheaper, and you have the flexibility in your schedule to be able to spend a couple of hours one day a week chopping and prepping vegetables to store in containers in the fridge, so that you can throw together a fresh lunch salad in a few seconds. There are a lot of health benefits to preparing the right food at home. But be careful; it's equally easy to fall into the habit of making poor lunch choices. Once you start, it's going to be far too easy to continue eating unhealthy foods.

Regular exercise breaks. When you are working from home, you have the perfect opportunity to think about your fitness levels. From the comfort of your own home, you can take regular exercise breaks without it impacting your productivity, which is hard to do when you are working from a traditional office with colleagues. The great thing is that you do not have to do much to improve your general fitness levels from home. You could take a short walk around the block during break time. You might take some time over lunch to do some yoga from your lounge. You could even keep a small set of dumbbells or weights next to your desk and do a few repetitions throughout the day. You can do this without it impacting your workday tasks too much, and by doing a little every day, you will keep your body healthier, provided you don't reach for the doughnuts straight after your workout.

Regular exercise like this is much harder to do from an office surrounded by your colleagues. You may get a few strange looks if you suddenly start doing yoga, or curling weights in the middle of the office. Going for a walk is still very much possible, but when your colleagues are going to shoot some pool in the lunchroom, or your work friends are having a chat, it can be hard to break away to get that walk when you would rather have some fun.

When working from home, there is less of an issue with your colleagues enticing you into doing something other than a little fitness. It would help you to have the willpower to go out and do something active, instead of reaching for the TV remote control or the game console controller.

Flexibility. Have you ever had a dentist appointment and had to step into your boss's office with your tail between your legs to ask if it was okay to go? Some employees are too afraid even to ask. When you're working from home, you don't have that problem, and it makes running errands so much easier. When the weather is terrible, or you're feeling unwell, you can sleep in, stay inside and work at your leisure if you aren't on a deadline. Don't get into the habit of sleeping in, though—that can soon turn into an excuse not to do work, which isn't an excellent foundation for starting a business.

Reduced stress. I have a friend whose work environment was incredibly stressful, and she suffered badly from it. She jumped whenever someone spoke too loudly or showed up unannounced at her desk. Having so many people constantly around her made her very anxious and stressed, and no amount of medication could calm her down without turning her into a zombie. When she finally decided she'd had enough, she quit and started working from home—and she became an entirely different person. It's fair to say that your working environment has a significant impact on your stress level, and it's something that can be improved when you are working from home. Everyone is different, though, and working from home comes with its own set of stresses, which we will explore a little later in this chapter.

Family time. When someone has a full-time job, it can be easy to fall out of touch with their family or loved ones. It's hard to maintain a good relationship when you hardly see one another. Sometimes, even when you do get to spend time together, it can feel rushed as you can only see that person at night or weekends—and that's if you aren't working overtime. As a parent, this is particularly hard when you have to drop your child off at day care so someone else can raise them during the day. It causes you to miss out on the critical milestones in your child's life. When you are working from home, you have the opportunity to have your child with you at all times, or even send them to day care for half a day; if you worked full time, you would have to make special arrangements for your child to be looked after until you got the chance to pick them up. A lot of new mothers like working from home for this reason, and my wife was the same when we had our two children. You don't have to miss out on time spent with family as you have a flexible schedule, and you can figure out what works best for you and the people around you. Having your kids at home can also be a distraction as much as it can be a benefit, though, so be careful not to throw your schedule out the window entirely just because it suits other people. A child can be distracting when you are trying to work from home, so unless they are sleeping, chances are you will have to entertain them.

Disadvantages of Working from Home

For all the advantages of working from home that we have just discussed, there are also some distinct disadvantages that you need to take into account as well. Of course, one person's disadvantage might be another person's advantage, but it is worthwhile taking all of these factors into consideration.

. . .

Isolation. Of course, you can call, text and email as many people as you'd like, but it's not the same as having face-to-face human contact. Loneliness is one of the biggest cons of working from home, and sometimes there's not much you can do to prevent it. When your friends are at work and conversing around the water-cooler, you're alone at home. It's not as easy as just popping out for a quick lunch break together when all of your friends work full time. Some people don't seem to mind the isolation at all—for example, I have no problem being alone for days at a time. If you are like me, you shouldn't have much of a problem, but if you rely on companionship for your mental well-being, you will need to think things over very carefully.

Difficulty communicating with the outside world. Occasionally, I have noticed that people who work from home can start to lose the ability to communicate properly with the outside world. I saw this with remote workers that I managed when I was in a full-time job, and I have also found that to be the case with myself. People can become nervous and fidgety, simply because they are no longer accustomed to having others surround them, or being able to talk to someone in person. It's often much more comfortable to communicate via social media or phone calls, and if you don't leave the house to interact with people very much, you can get out of practice in talking with people face to face.

Distractions. Distractions are the worst of the lot: those notifications about your favourite YouTuber's new video don't help when you're in the middle of writing reports or articles. "Just this one video" can so easily turn into "One more won't hurt", and the next thing you know, the day has turned into night and you still haven't done what you were supposed to accomplish. Distractions are horrible, and you need a lot of self-discipline to avoid them as much as possible.

Lack of productivity. When you are in a workplace, it's easier to get things done overall as you have more pressure from your colleagues and managers. You have to get certain things done at certain times of the day, or by more structured deadlines, or even in relation to the work being completed by others. When you work from home, it's easy to leave a project until the last possible moment.

Undervalued. "I work from home" is a phrase that can make others think you do nothing. Some people don't understand that "working from home" actually means that you are doing just that—working. You might have a different type of office, but you have the exact same workload—if not more—than that person. Sadly, it's something that likely will never change. Working from home when you work for a company where office working is the norm may always carry this stigma. Luckily, when you make the switch from working a job for another company to running your own company, that stigma goes away, as working from home when you are an entrepreneur is more typical.

What is interesting, though, is that when the COVID-19 pandemic started taking its grip on the world towards the start of 2020, a lot of people who ordinarily worked in an office were forced to start working from home at short notice. As a large part of the working population started getting to grips with homeworking, the attitude that people don't work as hard seems to have changed. Whether that remains to be the case when the world has returned to a regular routine will need to be observed but having a lot of people forced into homeworking may help the original remote workers feel more valued.

Switching off can be a problem. It's a proven fact that working and resting in the same place can be problematic. Switching "work mode" off along with your computer is not as easy as it sounds. Being in your work environment will cause your brain to carry on working, even if you aren't. It can cause many, many sleepless nights. I had this problem after nine months of working from home full time when I started my business. When you are supposed to have finished working, and you have downtime, it can be very tempting to finish off a piece of work—you feel obliged to do it as your home is your workplace.

Advantages of Working from Co-working Spaces

A common alternative to working from home is renting a co-working space. Co-working spaces have both good and bad qualities, just as working from home does. It all comes down to your mental state concerning isolation, and whether you are okay on your own for long periods. It's worth giving it a try as spaces or desks are most commonly rented out on a weekly or monthly basis. If you feel it's not for you, you can pack up your things and leave. It's as easy as that; you have no lease binding you to the desk for years. The following are some advantages and disadvantages connected to co-working spaces.

Routines. It's easier to fall into a routine when you work at an office with other people. Naturally, you want to keep up your image with others, and slacking off is not an option if you are determined to keep up the image of a dedicated freelancer or entrepreneur. When you have a scheduled time that you can get into the co-working space, and a specific time you need to be out of the building, you'll be forced to fall into a routine and get the work done while you are on site. You are also paying for the desk, so if you are not utilising it, it's going to be wasted money.

Sense of community. Working in an office with other freelancers can be fun. Everyone is trying to make it on their own, doing what they love and what they can to make their businesses succeed. They know the struggle of getting work, dealing with clients or deals that never work out. They understand the joy of landing a client, and they know how to console you when you don't. It will give you a sense of community, and that's very important. There will be people in the same office space with whom you will get along and form friendships.

Productivity increases. One of the biggest problems of working at home is that productivity is never constant. When you are at an office with other co-workers, you will more likely be inspired to work, as everyone around you is busy getting on with their own businesses. Other people's productivity tends to rub off on you, which is why working in a co-working space can be advantageous to you. Nothing will be left for the last minute, and you'll have a head start on your next project. If you are a writer, though, you need inspiration. It's not as easy as simply turning on your computer and writing. Sometimes being alone can spark creativity; sometimes being around other creative individuals might do the trick.

Distractions. There aren't as many distractions at a co-working space as there could be at home. The other freelancers at the office might talk a lot, but it's not as easy to switch Netflix on and binge-watch a series. Other co-workers might encourage you to put your phone away and focus on the task at hand. Also, there's no time or place for a nap. It forces you to stay at the office and get your work done.

Disadvantages of Working from Co-working Spaces

As we can see, working from a co-working has many advantages that will help you be more productive. There are also some downsides to co-working spaces that you need to consider.

It costs more than working from home. The biggest con of working at a co-working space is the cost. There can be a broad price range in office space rentals depending on where you are renting, but the fact remains: it costs money that might not have been necessary to spend. If it improves your mental health to be in an environment with other like-minded people, there is no doubt you will benefit from spending the extra money. Still, if you are indifferent to having company and you find you are not getting the work done because of the other disadvantages discussed in this chapter, maybe it's time to reconsider the space that you will be using.

. . .

Working hours are restricted. When you have a tight deadline and need to put in a few extra hours, it can be quite tricky when there is a time limit on access to the office. When you are working and have a space that you enjoy working in, it's hard to then get your laptop out at home and get back to work; especially if you seek a separation between your work and home life. Everyone has a space that they enjoy working from the most. Whether it's an office or the kitchen counter, when you are in that space, you get the job done faster and more efficiently. In this case, your working space is the co-working office; so, when you are at home, you may find it hard to simply grab your laptop and get to work. You are not in your working space—you are in your relaxing area, and you need to adapt before you can deliver the quality of work you are accustomed to.

Co-workers. As beneficial as working in a co-working space is, it can be distracting if you are working with like-minded individuals who enjoy talking about the same things you do. It's no secret that co-workers like to hang around at each other's desks and chat, and without supervision from a manager, that can become a distraction. Some boundaries need to be set between working and socialising, and that can be hard sometimes when there are so many creative folks around. When I hired a desk at a co-working space, I also enjoyed chatting with my co-workers; I learnt a lot from these conversations. We also had an unwritten rule at the co-working space: if you had your headphones on, then this meant you were concentrating, and no one would disturb you unless it were absolutely necessary.

Dealing with Isolation as a Lone Worker

Working from home may sound great, but it does come at a cost. The mental health of someone working from home can be a tricky thing to handle and regulate. Every person reacts differently to isolation, and the best thing you can do is avoid it if you feel like it's suffocating you. If being isolated at home is affecting you, then taking the advice earlier in this chapter and renting a desk at a co-working space could be very good for you, even if it is an additional cost. Being alone at home the entire day can get lonely even for the person who claims to be a hermit or introvert. Your home will start to feel like a prison after a while, and it will make it hard to relax. You will want to replace the silence with anything that sounds even remotely like human contact—the radio, YouTube, or Netflix. The need to have voices surrounding you can become overwhelming.

During the 2020-2021 COVID-19 pandemic, a lot of people were suddenly forced into working from home at short notice. People who were used to interacting with colleagues or customers in person were suddenly forced to reduce all human contact and conduct business via video conferencing software. For many, this sudden reduction in social contact caused a feeling of isolation, and for people living by themselves, a lot of loneliness; this was something I found particularly hard as a small business owner.

My wife and I, like many families around the world, suddenly had to balance the running of my business and her job from home while trying to homeschool two children. It was very challenging. As a business owner, I was also worried about the economic effects of the pandemic on my business, on top of the stress of homeschooling. Even though I run my own business as a single-person company, I have never enjoyed working from home. I always preferred using hot desks at co-working spaces and, eventually, renting my own private office, as I still like the routine of going out to work in the morning. For me, loneliness wasn't the issue; it was more the fact that I need a quiet environment to work. A quiet environment was one thing I was not going to get during the lockdown, as the house was chaotic with two children who were both a bit resistant to being homeschooled.

While I wasn't lonely from the "physical people in the house" point of view, I did feel isolated. There was a continual assumption that because I work for myself, that I could drop everything and focus more on homeschooling the children. Flexibility is part of the benefits of being self-employed, but I still had online course deliverables that I had signed contracts for, and they still had to be delivered on time. The assumption that I could drop everything because my wife had a traditional nine-to-five job did cause some stress. I had to put quite a few projects on hold for about four months, including the writing of this book.

One thing I found hard during the pandemic was not having like-minded people to talk to. My wife coped better with this because she still had colleagues she could talk to—office banter didn't go away for her, it just went online. Having other adults to talk to during work hours helped her keep a sense of normality. I didn't have that, and I must admit I did begin to find that difficult, so I started relying more on some online communities to get some adult professional conversation.

I wrote the original draft of this chapter before the COVID-19 pandemic, and most of the advice I talk about focused around "normal" times. The pandemic was certainly not "normal"; it was very disruptive, and it put a lot of restrictions on daily life, but I didn't want to change all of the advice because of a single, unconformable event. I want this book to have a long lifespan that goes way beyond a time where our lives were disrupted from the pandemic, so I have kept the advice the same because life will return to normal, and it most likely already has by the time you are reading this chapter.

Working from home takes getting used to, but there are things you can do to make it easier to cope. Here are a few tips for coping with loneliness and isolation when you are working from home.

Make changes. Rearranging your office or working in the garden instead of at your desk can make a massive difference to your mental state. It's easy to feel trapped when everything around you stays the same, so try moving your desk from facing the wall to facing the window, so you have something different to look at. If you are feeling the need to change your house around, do it. Try mixing up your routine a bit, too; instead of going to the gym after work, go before. Go out and meet a friend for coffee or lunch from time to time. It's essential to keep things exciting and different. It's too easy to get comfortable in what you are accustomed to and fall into a rut. That can lead to you spiralling into a hole that's hard to crawl out of, which can affect your mental health.

Know that you are not alone. There are many freelancers and entrepreneurs that feel the same way you do when starting out running a business. There is a lot of fear of the unknown when the comfort of a regular salary has gone. Some might even struggle more than you. You can help ease this fear by joining an online community for individuals working from home, or you can join physical meetup groups where you can network with like-minded entrepreneurs. You'd be surprised how many people feel the same way and how much you can relate. Quite often, running a business means you're staying in your house and not communicating with people enough, and that can lead to you thinking that you're alone. But other freelancers and small business owners are in the same position; make an effort to meet them! Otherwise, you will stay lonely, which can cause anxiety and lead to depression.

Emails, IM's, phone calls and video calls. When you can't have physical contact with people like you did in a full-time job, social media is a great way to keep in touch with people. Don't be afraid to chat with your friends or call your parents or family to catch up and share some news. It's nothing like the real thing, but it's a good alternative. It is also worth seeking out local small business communities, or groups who operate in the same area as your expertise and joining those. Before I started working for myself, I joined several local communities using the Slack communication tool, and I make sure I regularly contribute. I have made many friends in these groups; some of whom I have never met in person, and others I have met in real life. Online communities are a great way to minimise the effects of loneliness, as you have people to talk to and help answer questions if you are struggling with anything.

Take a walk. Getting out of the house for a walk is a great idea when the walls start closing in. Putting your work aside for a bit and going for a walk will cost you less time than struggling with it because you are uncomfortable. In the past, I have suffered from cabin fever while working from home, and I have found this to be the best solution that always helps me. It allows you to get a change of scenery, some fresh air, and a little exercise. Walking is also a proven way to boost your mental health, by getting out into nature and getting the blood and endorphins flowing. If I find I am stuck on a work-related problem, going out for a walk is perfect for helping me with problem solving. When I walk, I listen to music or a podcast, and the problem I was struggling with gets filed to the back of my mind. By the time I have finished my walk, I have either thought of a solution, or the answer comes to me quite quickly after going back to work. By distracting your mind and not actively thinking about the problem, it gives your brain a chance to process why you are stuck and come up with a solution.

Go to a coffee shop. Going to a coffee shop to write is one of my favourite things to do. I don't need to socialise or sit with anyone. I am perfectly content alone in a corner with a cappuccino. It's the ambience that gets my creative juices flowing, and just being around other people makes going home to an empty house feel better. It might give you a dose of socialisation, or it might remind you why you don't need people around. Either way, it's an excellent place to go to work. If I am working on something challenging, I have found the ambience of the coffee shop helps me to concentrate. That may not be the same for everyone, but it is worth trying. From years of working in a coffee shop, I have also started getting friendly with a lot of the regulars who also like to work there, and I will frequently make small talk. If you are struggling with loneliness while working from home, these small social interactions can help to break up the day.

Keep things tidy. There is a lot of truth in the saying, "Tidy desk, tidy mind." When your home is a mess, it's easy to get discouraged and depressed. It's essential to keep things tidy at all times when you're working from home. Wash the dishes, vacuum, keep your trash cans empty and organise your files. You'll be surprised to notice the difference in your morale when you are in a tidy environment. Some people differ in how they like to keep their desks. I love my desk to be neat all the time and as minimal as I can make it. My wife, on the other hand, has a desk that I can only describe as pure chaos, but that's how she likes it, and it works for her. No matter how you want to organise your desk, keeping the rest of your working environment and house tidy while you are working there sets you up perfectly to do a good day's work, as you are not fretting about completing the household chores. You will also find it easier to relax at the end of your workday if you are coming back to a tidy home, rather than a list of things that need to be done.

Consider a pet. Everyone has heard that a dog is a person's best friend, so when you don't have friends and co-workers around you, why not replace them with a new friend? I know it's a big responsibility to take on, especially when you are just starting a business or giving freelancing a go for the first time—not to mention the financial strain.

However, pets are fantastic for inspiration, and pick you up whenever you are feeling particularly down or lonely. Nothing makes a person feel better than a cold nose pressing against their leg or a warm little body curling up on their lap. Having something to love like a person is nearly as good as loving a person when you're alone.

The Author's Approach

I don't want to talk about working from home during the COVID-19 pandemic again as I have already covered that. In that situation, most of the population didn't have a choice, and had to work from home where possible.

When I started working for myself, I worked from home. It was fun and still felt like a bit of a novelty. I remember back to the first day I was in this position. It was a Monday, and I had finished my notice period and left my previous employer the Friday before. I sat there in front of a tidy desk, full of excitement but also a little nervous about my new situation.

I set my office up in our dining room at home, as to be honest, we never used it for that purpose. We have a home office at home, but my wife uses that, as she has been a home worker for over 15 years. As far as home offices go, I really like my dining room setup. I have the patio doors leading to the garden on one side, and double doors leading into the lounge area on the other side. I get lots of natural light in this situation, so I really like it.

After nine months, I started working in the lounge more often and putting the TV on while I worked. I would spend half the day at my actual desk and the rest sitting on the sofa with the TV on in the background. I wasn't slacking off; I was working on writing course scripts and preparing slide decks, but sitting on the sofa, no matter how comfortable it is, is not great for my back.

Even though the TV was on as a little background sound distraction, I started watching the comedy show, Big Bang Theory. After what felt like a short while, I had completed seven seasons of the show. I realised I needed a change of scenery. I was productive, but this was turning into a bad habit.

Another problem that was brewing was that I was resenting both living and working at home. I found it difficult to separate between home life and work life and they often became blurred. Once I had picked the kids up from school, I would make their dinner and help with homework, but I would also be thinking about work and feeling guilty if I hadn't completed something I was working on.

Many people can be quite disciplined with the work-life balance aspect of working from home. My wife is a good example of this, as she has been balancing work and home life for a long time, but I struggle with it. I was feeling cooped up and suffering from a bit of cabin fever. I started being hard on myself. On one hand, I am in this dream scenario of working for myself and having more freedom, but on the other, I was not liking the homeworking aspect of it as much as I thought I would. Something had to change.

I did some internet searches to see if there were any co-working spaces near where I lived, and I found somewhere that was a short ten-minute train journey from my home. They had an option where you could rent a fixed desk so that you can leave your monitor and keyboard setup on the desk. I went to visit them, and they let me work there for free for a day to get a feel for their facilities. Going out to this co-working space was just what I needed, so I signed up for a fixed desk.

Even though I enjoy working for myself, what I was missing was the physical act of getting up in the morning and going out to work. By renting a desk at the co-working space, I was going out to work; getting a full day completed and then leaving to go home. For me, this was a much better position to be in. In the room in which I was working, there were eight people in total. Each person was in a similar situation to me; they were working on their own businesses. By being in a room together we had the normal office conversations that you would get in a regular company, but with none of the office politics normally associated with working at a company.

After a short while, they offered me a private office, which was not too much more expensive than what I was paying for the fixed co-working desk, so I jumped at the chance. Having a private room that I could set up as I wanted to run my business was fantastic. I had a place to go, set up the way I wanted, that was private and perfect for concentration. I fixed the problem of needing the routine of going out to work, which helped with the mental separation of work and home life.

I am quite an introverted person, so being in a room by myself to concentrate was perfect for me. I know that people who are more extroverted would hate the idea of being by themselves all day, but for me, this situation worked out great. I regularly met with people from the co-working space for coffee, and each month there was a co-workers' lunch at a pub, so there was a professional social life too.

My routine now has me working in the office three or four days a week, and the other days I do still work from home. By mixing it up like this, I find I can keep myself motivated by the changes in the work environment. If I were to spend every day in my office, I would suffer the same problem with cabin fever that I faced originally at home. By splitting my time between working from the office and from home, the change of scenery keeps my working week feeling fresh, where I continually look forward to both working from home and going into the office.

Summary

Whatever location you choose to work from, remember to stay in touch with the people who have supported you while you were deciding to start your own business. It's easy to become distracted by new things and new people in your life, but don't leave the loyal ones behind. Go out with them if they invite you for coffee, and don't be shy to ask them. I speak from experience when I tell you that one tends to lose sight of the important things when you are starting a new venture.

When you are always on your own, you don't think about going out or keeping in touch. You can lose yourself in your own little world, and that's not healthy in the long run—not for you, or the people who have always supported you. Whether you decide on a co-working office or working from home, remember that you need to do what works best for you and keeps your routines consistent and effective.

Every advantage and disadvantage that we discussed in this chapter depends on the person. Just because it is a disadvantage to me, doesn't mean it will be for you, too. Do your research thoroughly and do what will make your venture a success. Choosing a location won't make you succeed by itself, but it will help you along the way to success.

Workshop Questions

If you are considering working from home in the future, or if you have already started working from home, consider these following questions.

(1) Are you an extrovert who feeds off the energy of others, or an introvert who likes to spend time by yourself?

1. If you work from home, how would being alone for long periods of time affect you?
2. Who could you talk to during the day if you need to have a chat with someone?
3. Where could you go for a change of scenery? A coffee shop, co-working space, walking routes, etc.

2.Think about the best place in your home that you could use as an office. Where possible, you want to work in an area that you don't relax in, like the bedroom or lounge, as this can make it hard to separate between work and downtime.

13

BEING A DIGITAL NOMAD AND LOCATION-INDEPENDENT WORKER

Do you have the itch to travel but worry about your responsibilities, such as how you will be able to pay your bills? Not sure where to visit or where to stay? Add to that your bank account telling you to stay home because you can't afford a trip across town, let alone across the ocean? Thanks to the many advances in technology, people can now work from anywhere at any time of day. Millions of people are taking advantage of this benefit, creating a new wave in the workforce known as the "digital nomad lifestyle."

A digital nomad is a person who travels from country to country and may not have a permanent home. The phrase became popular after Tsugio Makimoto and David Manners' 1997 book, *Digital Nomad*. Digital nomads generate their income through remote freelance work while using technology such as a smartphone, laptop and cloud-based applications. Most digital nomads will travel to foreign countries and work in coffee shops, hotel rooms, or any place they feel comfortable. While most people picture digital nomads as bloggers or freelance writers, any type of remote work is available to them. Many companies hire employees to work remotely; you can have an average nine-to-five job, or you can decide to become your own boss through your freelance career. You don't have to be a freelancer, either. If you are building a business that doesn't need to have a fixed location, like a software-as-a-service business, then there are no limits on whereabouts in the world you work.

While the possibilities are endless, there are still general guidelines that digital nomads need to follow. First and foremost, you need to ensure that you have a reliable internet connection. You won't be able to get much work done if you aren't able to connect to Wi-Fi. Second, you need to be organised when it comes to different time zones, which will affect you more if you move around often. Some nomads will stay in one location for a few months, while others move on after a few days. Whatever you choose, think ahead so you can guarantee that you will make your deadlines. Third, you have to focus on time management. You need to consider that the amount of time spent travelling will affect your workflow. For example, say you are freelancing for a company, and your next project is due in three days. During this time, you are flying from South America to Africa, which is about an 11-hour flight. Once you land, you still need to find the location where you are staying and settle in. This can easily add another couple of hours onto your journey, if not more. You need to schedule your work time and your travel time to make sure you will meet your deadline.

If you have an itch for travel and think the digital nomad life might be for you, then there are a few steps to get started. First, you want to be certain that it is the right decision. If you aren't entirely sure this is what you want to do, you should do a trial period. Take a couple of months and travel. Please don't sell your house, but you can rent it out to give you a little extra money. If you haven't started your business yet, you could begin to work remotely and find a freelance project to work on, but there is more financial risk taking this approach if you don't have a business that is already generating income.

After your trial period has ended, and you are certain you want to travel, the next step is to make it a reality. You might want to sell or rent out your home. While renting might feel like the best option as it will give you a monthly income, you also need to keep in mind that you are still the owner of your property—this means you will need to make repairs, keep everything up to date, and work with the tenants. This can be difficult while you are in different countries. You may want to think about hiring a manager to take care of your property while you are away; however, this does mean another expense.

Before embarking on a full-time digital nomad way of life, you should make sure you have a good stream of income coming in each month; have savings as a backup for when times are lean; and have adequate traveller's insurance. You'll also want to sell or store the possessions you can't bring with you, such as furniture, and secure your valuables. As a digital nomad, you will carry only the essentials and possibly a couple of possessions that are unique to you.

Above all, as a digital nomad, you'll need to be safe. It would be best if you researched the highest crime areas at your destination. Once you know this, you will be able to look for accommodation in a safe location. Many people worry about travelling alone because they view it as dangerous. Solo travelling is not dangerous if you take the proper precautions, and millions of people do it every day. The key is to be smart about where you go and what you do. Always ensure that someone, whether it is a family member or friend, knows where you are. Anything can happen, whether you are in the security of your home or living life as a digital nomad. Be safe, but don't let the fear of something happening to you keep you from living your best life.

Popular Digital Nomad Destinations

You probably have a lot of places you want to visit. You may have added these locations because you've heard other people talk about them. They might be places you've always wanted to see, or the country your ancestors emigrated from. When you choose your destination, you want to ensure you keep various factors in mind, such as Wi-Fi access and safety. You need to research your location so you can make sure it fits in with your profession. For example, if you have a YouTube channel or you are a travel blogger, you won't want to visit a dull place. You will want to make sure there is a lot of excitement and beautiful scenery for your video, pictures, and content. No matter what career you choose, there are three essential features you will always need.

. . .

Your location needs to inspire you. You can have a travel hotspot list of places to visit, but if your locations are random and have no inspiration or meaning for you, they won't be the best choices for your profession. Not only do you need the inspiration to get your creative juices flowing, but also to interrupt the feeling of loneliness. Many digital nomads travel alone, which can lead you to feel lonely in your new journey if you're not careful. If you spend your time meeting people and taking in some of the most magnificent scenery in the world, you're going to have a better time.

You have to have an internet connection. There are some locations throughout the world where getting online is challenging. Some places have a slower internet speed, which means getting your content or project uploaded is going to be difficult. If your work depends on your ability to hit deadlines, this could cause you to lose business from clients.

There might be locations where the internet connectivity is sporadic, so you'll want to check with the hotel or wherever you're staying about intermittent internet service. I have fallen into this trap before when I did some travelling around eastern Europe; finding a stable internet connection in some places was quite tricky. Part of the work I did while travelling was editing videos for a new course. I needed to upload the videos to a server, but the upload speeds were very slow, making it hard to submit content and make online backups. Luckily in this situation, I had plenty of time on my deadline, and I had USB drive with me to make backups; but if I had been close to the wire on the deadline, it could have been quite inconvenient.

It's always best to go cheap. While some digital nomads don't need to worry about their finances too closely, many do. If you are starting a business and decide to do a lot of the work on the road, being cost-conscious is always a good idea, as you never know when that revenue will start flowing in. Therefore, you need to ensure that your destination is going to be cost-effective. No matter where you decide to travel to, you should ask yourself some basic questions: "Is there a safe, yet cheap place I can stay?", "Are there any discounts available for long-term residency?", etc.

The world is a vast place with lots of fantastic locations to visit while working on your business. Here are some great places for digital nomads that I have been to that may give you some inspiration.

Bangkok, Thailand. Not only is Thailand a beautiful country, but Bangkok has several working places available to digital nomads. It is also one of the busiest cities in the world, home to over eight million. With so many people, you will be sure to meet a fellow digital nomad or two on your journey and form great relationships with other like-minded founders.

Bangkok isn't Thailand's only popular destination for nomads. About 430 miles (700 km) from Bangkok, you will come to Chiang Mai, a city that holds ancient temples. Chiang Mai is a great city to visit if you are interested in finding some extra work and want to stay somewhere affordable.

Barcelona, Spain. There is always something to do in Barcelona. Furthermore, the city is highly accommodating to the nomadic lifestyle. You will have no trouble finding a café with excellent Wi-Fi. These areas are often filled with other digital nomads, so you will be able to take breaks and talk about different locations you've visited. After work, you will be able to join in on Barcelona's nightlife. The only drawback to Barcelona is that it's one of the more expensive places to visit, live and work.

Budapest, Hungary. If you've ever wanted to take a trip on a ferry, take a look at Budapest. This city is known for its history and culture. You can get two cities down in one trip as the Danube is across the river. When compared to other European cities, Budapest is one of the cheapest. You will be able to find excellent Wi-Fi all over the city and see some fantastic architecture.

. . .

Playa del Carmen, Mexico. Playa del Carmen is one of the best destinations because of its affordability. While the digital nomad population is a bit smaller than the previous destinations I've discussed, the city provides you with magnificent scenery. Everything a digital nomad needs is available in Playa del Carmen. The only downside for me was the climate; I found the heat and humidity stifling. This is definitely something to bear in mind if you prefer or are used to milder weather, but it is still a lovely place to visit.

Advantages of Being a Digital Nomad

After considering so many amazing destinations, it's obvious that one major advantage of the digital nomad lifestyle is the places you will be able to visit while you are working. But this isn't the only advantage.

Work environment is less stressful. Do you find that you often feel stressed when you walk into your office or work area? You look at the piles of work and your busy schedule and immediately feel anxious. You look out the window and wish you could leave and enjoy the wonderful sun and scenery. As a digital nomad, you can! You will be able to find the most enjoyable place to work every day. Not only will this help you feel less stressed, but you will become more productive.

You create your own professional path. As a freelancer, you have the freedom to choose what you want to do, where you want to go, and the hours you want to work. You get to establish your rules; this means you can decide to work in the morning, take a couple of hours to sightsee during lunch, work a few more hours, and then take in the nightlife. If you're tired of the nightlife, you can choose to work later and check out the city during the day. The biggest challenges many digital nomads face are self-discipline and time management. However, if you are determined to live as a digital nomad, you can accomplish anything.

. . .

You will become more flexible. We often become accustomed to our daily schedules. We fall into a routine and don't often get away from it, and this can leave us feeling trapped. While some people enjoy this type of lifestyle, if you are itching to see the world, you are going to enjoy the digital nomad lifestyle much better.

When you travel, you will push yourself from your comfort zone. You will learn about new cultures, history, and adapt to new environments. Through your experience, you will become a more flexible individual. Pushing yourself out of your comfort zone like this also helps prepare you for facing challenges and obstacles in your new business career. When running a business, there is no such thing as a regular routine, so learning to adapt to routines that are alien to you is excellent preparation.

Meet people and make friends. As a digital nomad, you will meet people from all over the world and create lifelong friendships. You will meet people from the country you're visiting, and other digital nomads from various parts of the world. This will expose you to more cultures than you can imagine. I really cannot overstate how important it is to have friends and acquaintances from different countries and cultures when forming a business. Diversity in your friendships and acquaintance groups will naturally make you better at working with people from all different backgrounds, which is an essential skill and benefit when starting up a business. Most of my closest friends are people I have met through my travel around the world, and they are people I hope to be friends with for many years to come.

It can be a financial advantage. You can use working remotely across the world as a way to increase your financial wealth and make your money go further. You do this by staying at less expensive cities than you are used to, that still offer you the essential services you need. As an example, if you are used to living somewhere like London, then one month's worth of expenses that you pay there could last three or four months in a country like Thailand or Vietnam. If you have no family ties to hold you to a more expensive city, then choosing another, more affordable destination could be a great way to let your money go further while you are starting a business. Nomadic working is especially beneficial if your business is not location-dependent, like an online software service.

Learn more about yourself. As you work and travel, you will begin to learn more about yourself, just like when you moved out of home for the first time, perhaps to go to college or university. You will grow with your experiences, and this personal growth will hopefully reflect on how you run your business and collaborate with other people.

Living with less. We live in a materialistic world where we want the best, whether it's a vehicle or a new appliance. When you are a digital nomad and travelling around, you won't worry as much about material possessions. While you may have a few sentimental items, such as pictures of your family and friends, you will typically only travel with what you need. This doesn't mean you sell all your possessions, but you might ask a trusted family member or friend to take care of your belongings or put them into storage if you rent out your home. As you grow with your digital nomad lifestyle, you will learn that material possessions aren't as important as you might have originally thought. You will begin to value your experiences more than objects or money.

Live a healthier lifestyle. Without the stress of being in an office, or working from home, you will naturally start to feel better physically and mentally. Because you can create your schedule, you can take it easy if you are not feeling motivated, or if you feel like taking a day to relax and see the city you're working from. With so many food options, you can choose the healthiest meals available. Additionally, you will get more exercise from all the walking you'll do when out sightseeing. And having a change of scenery is a great way to mentally and physically recharge yourself. If you find you've grown tired of one location, you can move on to somewhere else.

Disadvantages of Being a Digital Nomad

Whenever there are advantages, there are disadvantages. Any digital nomad will tell you it's not all fun sightseeing and having great experiences. It is important to note that this section isn't intended to discourage you from the digital nomad lifestyle. It's here to give you a complete vision of the lifestyle and make you aware of the disadvantages, so you can make an educated decision whether or not you can learn to live with them.

Lack of daily mentorship. We often need to find someone who inspires us to be a better person, to work harder, or who helps us through our business challenges. It is quite common to have a business mentor, which is something we will be discussing later in this book. When you are a digital nomad, your daily mentor is likely thousands of miles away, making face-to-face meetings with them impossible. You can use all the modern technology that enables you to be a digital nomad—email, chat clients or video calls—but there is nothing quite like physically sitting next to the person. There is also the issue of time zones to consider, which can make keeping in touch more difficult to manage. This lack of daily mentorship can be a disadvantage as it can make you feel lonely from time to time.

You must have self-discipline. Self-discipline and knowing when to say "no" to yourself and others are essential as a digital nomad. You need to be able to put off having fun in a new country until it's time for you to go sightseeing or go out to enjoy the nightlife. You also need to tell people that you aren't able to take on specific projects if they will interfere with your travelling or create too much work for you.

When you are starting out—as a freelancer in particular—it is tough to turn down work. I experienced this when I started as a full-time creator of online courses. It's a great feeling when work starts piling up, as you feel validated in your decision to go into business in the first place, but there is only so much you can manage at a time and produce high-quality results. The situation can feel amplified when you are travelling, too, as you can't get as much work done while moving from place to place. If you are going to be spending the next 14 hours on the road, but you have a client expecting work to be finished, or they require something redone, it can add to your stress levels, and travelling can be stressful enough as it is.

Freelance pay isn't always great. If your business is freelancing, you can struggle to make a living as a digital nomad, which means you will need to get very good at saving money and living lean. If your freelancing work is coming from a more prosperous economy while you are living in a less expensive country, you can do well. On the flip side, if you are taking freelance work locally, the rate you get might be more suitable to the local economy, which means you could be earning a lot less than you would expect. This is one reason why it's always in your best interest to have backup savings that you can access from anywhere in the world. Another downside is that if you use websites like Fiver, Upwork or Remote, work can be sporadic—and work from those websites tends to have more competition and therefore lower rates. This doesn't mean you won't be able to find consistent work as a freelancer. Sometimes you have to work on building up your resume to retain a consistent workflow.

You can become burnt out. When the freelance pay isn't great, and you still have to pay your travelling expenses, cell phone bill, and all other bills, you can find yourself picking up too much work. If that happens, you might become stressed as you try to finish everything by your deadlines. You can quickly find yourself working during your downtime. While many people can pull off long work hours every day, it will eventually burn you out. If you don't take the time to take care of yourself properly, you can find yourself wishing you were back home.

Homesickness happens. You may have had a home for decades, whether this was with your parents, on your own, or both. You always had a place to call home, and now you are travelling. Your view of home needs to change, and this is a process. It won't just happen overnight. Also, you might find you are missing your family, friends, and old home, and this can make anyone question their choice of becoming a digital nomad. While many people feel homesick from time to time, it generally goes away after a while. If you find that it doesn't, then it's time to re-evaluate if the digital nomad lifestyle is the one for you.

Work or vacation? Many people believe if they travel while they work, they are always on vacation. This should never be the reason you want to become a digital nomad. It would be best if you treated it as a profession. Unless you have endless savings, you are going to need to work. While you can always take time off to go sightseeing, you shouldn't think of it as a vacation.

A vacation is the time you spend at leisure, when you don't have to worry about the work you leave behind. When you are a digital nomad, you are usually carrying your laptop with you, which means you are always attached to your work. You might find yourself sitting on the beach, trying to enjoy a part of your day, when you take out your laptop and start working, at least until your battery runs out or you need Wi-Fi. Just as work can always be on your mind at home, it will generally be on your mind as a digital nomad. In fact, many digital nomads work seven days a week.

Typically, you will spend your working hours in a coffee shop, restaurant, or the room where you are lodging. While the scenery might be nice, it's not the beach that everyone imagines. The beach can be a difficult place for a digital nomad to work anyway, because the sun makes it hard to see your screen, and you can become too distracted.

A digital nomad lifestyle requires you to make a lot of changes in your thinking. You used to think of work as being at your office. Now, you have to think about work being everywhere. Yet, you don't want to work absolutely anywhere because you still need your hours of relaxation. Therefore, if you love the beach, for example, it's best to not work there because then you can leave this area as your relaxation place.

You need to ensure that you keep "work" and "vacation" quite separate in your mind. You are not on a lifelong vacation as a digital nomad. You are on a remote job, where you still need to work long hours and make deadlines to receive a pay cheque. Your bills don't disappear with this lifestyle; most of them simply change. Instead of making a house payment, you are paying for hotel rooms. Instead of making a car payment, you are buying aeroplane tickets.

Taking a vacation as a digital nomad. Working as a digital nomad doesn't mean you can't take a vacation. However, you might find it helpful to schedule a vacation, just as you would at an office job. For example, if you know you are going to be in China for three months, look at which week would be good to take off work, and set this as your vacation. Make sure you don't schedule any projects to be due that week, and get ahead of your workload before your time off is due to start; this will make it less likely that you will start working during your vacation.

You should also set up an "out of the office" email alert during this week, which will notify your clients that you will get to them the following week upon your return to work. Turn off your notifications for your email, any work apps, or any programs on your laptop. Let your clients know ahead of time when you will be taking a vacation, and stay away from your work. Leave your computer in your room and schedule your days with adventure.

Another tip to follow when taking a vacation is to invite one of your friends or family members to your location if you can. Spending time with someone who doesn't work remotely will help you keep your mind off work and on vacation.

Being a Digital Nomad When you are Older

There is a myth about digital nomads: that you have to be young to live this type of lifestyle. In truth, you can become a digital nomad at any age. More retired people are starting to sell their homes, purchase an RV or a caravan, and travel across the country, or move to apartments in the sun. While they don't often go from country to country, it's still possible. Most digital nomads are older than you might think.

The only thought that often holds people back when it comes to the digital nomad lifestyle is believing it's not a possibility. Of course, there are additional factors that older digital nomads will need to take into consideration before they start their journey.

No matter what age you are as a digital nomad, you should always have health and travel insurance. You should never take any chances with your health when you are travelling, no matter what age you are. Your life and business could be going perfectly; but if you suddenly fall ill, and if you don't have medical insurance, you could have a huge bill to try and pay. Before you travel, make sure you have comprehensive travel and medical insurance, and make certain you are covered for the countries you wish to visit; the risks of going without the correct insurance is just too high.

Noise is a consideration. When you get older, you naturally start to enjoy peace and quiet; I know I do. Because of this, some popular digital nomad destination places might not be appealing to an older crowd. While you can still go, you might enjoy staying outside of a city more or finding a quiet location in a town. You will also want to think about the type of accommodation you're choosing if you want a quiet neighbourhood. For example, if you are looking into a hostel, you will probably want to make sure you can get a private room.

Think ahead with your prescriptions and routine medical check-ups. If you have health issues, you should do your best to keep to countries where healthcare is better for your circumstances. When it comes to your regular annual routine check-ups, you will want to plan ahead. A lot of countries don't have the medical advances and equipment you will need for your regular check-ups or any health issues. If you are on any medication, such as insulin for diabetes, ensure you have a large enough supply for your journey and any necessary paperwork for taking the medication on a plane, and a resupply plan for when you are away.

Unfortunately, it can be hard to get your prescription medicines when you are a digital nomad; this is something that you will need to think about before leaving for your destination. If you are travelling to a different country, talk to your doctor and pharmacist so you can get everything you need before the trip. They can also advise you as to what to do if you run low on medication.

Travelling with kids.

It's a myth that you cannot be a digital nomad with children. There is nothing to prevent you from taking your children with you; however, you will need to be aware of several factors.

World schoolers are a community of people who travel for one reason: they have children. They want their children to experience the world in a hands-on way, especially when it comes to education. They don't believe in placing their children in a building to learn for six to eight hours a day at a desk.

Most world schoolers will have one general location where they spend a good amount of their time, but they also travel. This doesn't necessarily mean they travel just when school is on vacation. They can decide to travel any time they want, and it won't affect their children's education.

Unschooling. Just as some parents travel to give their children the best education, some parents don't focus on formal education. When you live in a country where sending your children to school is mandatory, it is hard to imagine this. However, when parents focus on unschooling, they believe that their children's experiences will teach them everything they need to know.

Unschooling doesn't mean their children aren't educated. Instead, they learn at their own pace and when events naturally occur. They are also taught the basics of reading, writing, and mathematics naturally. For example, if you are in front of a sign with your five-year-old, you will stop and teach your child how to read the sign. If you are in a grocery store, you will take the opportunity to teach your child math skills.

Of course, you always have the option to place your child into a local school, as most countries are accommodating in this regard. You might also pick a specific destination because of the school system. You should include this as part of your research.

If schooling like this is something you wish to consider, you must check the law in your country to make sure you follow any rules. In the UK, for example, it is mandatory to send children to school, and if you withdraw them, you are liable for prosecution and hefty fines. Home-schooling is allowed, but there is a process you have to follow, so make sure you check your local laws before proceeding.

You will still need to think of work. Travelling with your children doesn't mean you won't work as a digital nomad. It could mean that you are more cautious about how much you make with each job, or how much you have in savings just in case you are low with your income for one month. Like a single-location, independent worker, you will want to schedule work time and leave the rest of your time for family and yourself. It will be helpful to ensure your children understand when their parents are working, just as they would if you were to leave home and go to an office.

Don't overpack. It's easy to pack for yourself when it comes to the necessities. It can also be easier for you to let go of material possessions, because you are an adult and understand the sacrifices that come with being a digital nomad. You know you can't travel with everything. Young children are not going to think the same way. If you decide to start living the digital nomad lifestyle after having children, it is going to be a more substantial process when it comes to selling your material possessions.

At the same time, you can't allow yourself to overpack. Of course, your children are going to need a couple of toys with them, and your teenagers might want their electronic devices. You will be able to find plenty of ways to entertain your children as a digital nomad family. Keep your packing to only what you absolutely need.

Medical facilities. Another important factor for a digital nomad family is to know where the emergency rooms and clinics are. When you are in a new area, find out this information right away—or preferably, research it before you even arrive. This is always a good idea for any traveller but is more important when you are travelling with your family, as there tend to be more emergency room trips with children.

Being a Part-Time Digital Nomad

Many people feel that if they commit to becoming a digital nomad, they have to commit full time. This is false, as many digital nomads do it part time. Many digital nomads will go from full time to part time simply because they feel that travelling part time works better for them. There is nothing wrong with this. If you are finding that you can't live out of a backpack anymore, look for a home base. This can be in any country around the world, or back in the place where you grew up.

You might also become a part-time nomad because you have fallen in love and want to start a family. You and your spouse might have decided not to travel with your children, or not to travel with them until they are much older. Therefore, your story might become similar to mine.

When you become a digital nomad, there are a lot of factors you will need to think of that we've already discussed. For example, researching your destination and finding a safe place to stay. It doesn't matter if you are staying a few days or a few weeks. Safety is always the number one priority. You will also want to continue working and making sure you can afford to take the time away from home; not just you, but your family as well.

Don't think that the online communities are only for full-time digital nomads. They are for everyone, whether part time or full time. It will help you just as it would anyone else to join an online community. Being a digital nomad is a specific lifestyle that not everyone understands, and an online community can help you connect with people who can offer you advice.

Many part-time digital nomads feel this is the better end of the bargain because there is a lesser chance of burnout. Furthermore, they often feel their time away from home is more valuable because they aren't travelling full time.

If you are looking at the part-time digital nomad lifestyle, you will want to have a clear delineation between work and vacation. This can be a bit harder for a part-timer because you still have a home and possibly an office location, unless you work from home. Therefore, it is easier for you to fall into the trap of thinking that a trip is a vacation and you are not there to work. This can decrease your motivation when it comes to the work that needs to get done, which can be damaging to your career.

The Author's Approach

I never desired to commit to a full-time digital nomad way of life, as I like where I live and want to stay, but I do travel a lot around the world and visit lots of new locations when I am attending conferences. When I started creating online courses, I also started public speaking as a way to promote my courses and keep my name out there. I began speaking in the UK, but after a while I was being selected to speak at conferences overseas. As a speaker you are rarely paid to speak, but a fantastic benefit is that your airfares and accommodation are covered for the event.

Once the conference has finished, I like to stay in a place for a week or two. I want to get to know the local start-up scene there and hang out with other like-minded business owners, which is great for networking. Taking this approach has worked out well as I get to work away occasionally, which I really enjoy, but I am still based at the family home in the UK. I can't travel too much since having a family, but when I do travel, I try to make the most of it and see the sites, work from cafes and co-working spaces, and meet as many people as I can.

When I first started speaking at international conferences, it was a novelty and I tried to do as many trips as I could. At one point I was away for nearly five weeks speaking and doing workshops. While my wife accepted it at the time, I wouldn't want to do that again. After a while, the novelty wears off and you start to not enjoy being in airports as much, so I dropped the number of conferences I speak at to no more than five or six in a year.

During the COVID-19 pandemic, the number of overseas trips naturally dropped to zero, and most of the conferences at which I would have spoken moved online. I still spoke at many of these online events during the pandemic, but they are nowhere near as fun as you don't get the same level of interaction from the audience as you do in a real conference centre, up on stage.

For me and my family, uprooting the kids and world-schooling while we travel has never been an option. While it works for some people, the travel involved in just taking the kids on holiday for two weeks is stressful enough, let alone travelling frequently. I can see the appeal for others, but it was never for us.

Summary

By now, you should have a better understanding of what the digital nomad lifestyle is. You know what it means to be a digital nomad. You understand that it isn't a vacation, but a profession. Just like any job, it comes with advantages and disadvantages. For example, you can see the world; however, you are also mainly on your laptop, working to generate an income. This can easily lead to burnout, which can make you decide that living the life of a digital nomad on a part-time basis instead might be in your best interest. This is a common theme when it comes to digital nomads, and if you find yourself going from full time to part time, there is nothing to worry about. Instead, focus on living your best life, no matter where you are located at the moment.

You also understand that anyone can become a digital nomad, no matter what age they are. If you are in your forties and have always dreamt about travelling, but have a home, spouse and children, talk to your spouse. Together, you should be able to come up with a solution to your travelling itch. You might even find that they also have a yearning for travel!

Children are not meant to hold you back from living a digital nomad lifestyle. You can have children and become a full-time nomad; however, there are certain factors that you will need to think about. For example, what type of schooling do you want to look into for your children? Are you going to focus on world schooling and unschooling? You might also want to look into all the public or private school options in the country you are planning to visit, especially if you are going to be there for some time.

No matter what your digital nomad lifestyle is like or who it includes, you should always focus on these factors *before* you start travelling:

Safety. Safety is always number one. No matter where you are staying, you want to make sure it is in a safe area. When you are researching your trip, take time to look at the crime rates in the different areas you are looking to stay at.

Insurance. While this is something that a lot of younger digital nomads don't think about, it is essential for everyone. You can feel like the healthiest person in the world, and something can happen to you. Always take time to look into health insurance as this will be extremely helpful if you get sick or injured. Life insurance is also essential, especially if you have a family.

Mental health. People often forget about the importance of their mental health, and this is something that you need to pay attention to, as it can become affected through your digital nomadic lifestyle, especially if you are travelling full time. When you are feeling homesick, you can find yourself becoming depressed if you don't take care of your homesickness by talking to your family or friends. Getting burnt out is another problem for your mental health. You need to take care of yourself and that means making sure that you schedule relaxation time, even if you are feeling a little stressed about making bills.

Workshop Questions

If you like the idea of one day working from anywhere in the world, use these following questions to help you decide if it is right for you.

(1) Write a list of reasons why you would like to travel the world and work.

(2) Write out any reason that would prevent you from being a digital nomad.

　1. For each of the reasons listed, how could you mitigate those reasons?

14

GETTING SUPPORT FROM A MASTERMIND GROUP OR A MENTOR

Running a small business is a tough task. You will need to wear multiple hats, whether you have expertise in specific areas or not. Often it can feel as if you're alone and that there's too much to cope with. In some ways, this is true. After all, it's your business, and you are the only one who can change its course. Business success ultimately comes down to the actions you choose to take or not take.

However, thinking that you are entirely alone is false. You are not the first person to run a small business, and certainly won't be the last. There have been many people who have undergone what you're going through right now. So why reinvent the wheel, when you can simply improve upon the existing one? In other words, learn from the experiences of those who came before you.

Reading books and biographies of famous businesspeople is one method of achieving this. However, the written word is limited, in that there is no chance for receiving feedback to your questions. Another limitation is that business conditions change.

Therefore, it is essential for you to connect with like-minded entrepreneurs and to access their collective brain. This is what has come to be known as a mastermind group. Napoleon Hill made this term famous in his books "*The Law of Success*" and "*Think and Grow Rich*". Hill identified the collective power of the mastermind as being one of the reasons for the success of some of the richest men who have ever lived.

Another way of accessing the power of the mastermind is to engage a mentor to guide you through the pitfalls of business. A mentor is someone who has already experienced what you're going through and has achieved the results you wish to manifest in your business. Mentorship has an advantage over a mastermind group, in that you will be directly in touch with someone who can tell you exactly how things should be done.

In this chapter, I will be talking about the various aspects of a mastermind group and how you can use it to boost your business results. I will also be talking about mentorship and how to evaluate whether you need it.

What is a Mastermind Group?

There are many forms of networks calling themselves mastermind groups out there. Let's take a more in-depth look at what a mastermind group is. Traditionally, a mastermind is a group of people who share a collective purpose, and promise to hold each other accountable in their journey towards that purpose.

The meetings that are held are a combination of accountability, goal setting, problem solving and brainstorming. They are run by people called facilitators, who direct the general flow of conversation and set the agenda for that meeting by gathering everyone's input.

The point of the meetings is usually to help the individual members set goals, for their business or personal lives, and to then hold them accountable for the achievement of those goals. Mind you, while the group will help the individual solve obstacles and provide advice on how to deal with them, it is up to the individual to work and achieve their goals themselves.

Therefore, joining a mastermind group should not be seen as a shortcut. Your work does not get done for you. Instead, it makes your path a lot easier, and often, shorter. The reason mastermind groups work is that the coming together of many minds produces exponential rewards, not linear ones.

Process. The first step taken in a mastermind group is to set goals. There can be goals set at the group level as well as at the individual level. Given that the group is usually assembled by people who share a common purpose, the group's goals usually match or complement the individual's goals. The next step is to plan how you will achieve that goal.

Here, the other members will help one another lay down markers of progress and devise plans to this end. Furthermore, the group will also hold the individual accountable with regards to their actions and their progress towards the goal. All success is enthusiastically celebrated, while problems are brainstormed over to solve them. The only thing that is usually not tolerated is laziness on the part of its members.

A mastermind group requires a lot of commitment, since it isn't just about you but the entire group. While you will receive input on how to run your business better, you will need to be invested enough to return the favour. This is where the facilitator plays a huge role in maintaining the balance and the spirit of the group.

Qualities. There are a few simple qualities that a good facilitator will reinforce throughout the sessions. The first of these is accountability. Accountability is a powerful motivator to get things done. Often, we put aside tasks that are important because carrying out the task is too painful. Your mastermind group will hold you responsible and help you through the toughest and most unpleasant tasks you need to do.

Having access to the collective mind also has another benefit. Your group may well uncover opportunities to which you are blind. Other entrepreneurs will often have skills and modes of thinking that you don't have, and the mastermind group can be a great way of connecting with and tapping into those resources. This also extends to problem solving. A common mistake people make when encountering an obstacle is to try and solve the problem right in front of them.

This sounds counterintuitive, but the best way to get rid of an obstacle is to clarify instead what the actual problem is in the first place. This begins with asking the right questions. Often, we get too caught up in the details and miss the bigger picture. Having a group of like-minded people who are invested in your success enables you to properly clarify and define your problems. When this is done, often the solution is found to lie in plain sight.

We are deeply influenced by the environment we're in. This might be a holdover from our earliest survival mechanisms, where the inability to adapt to a different environment might have resulted in death. These days, death doesn't entirely threaten us the way it used to, but the reflex survives. Prolonged exposure to a set of habits and certain types of people causes us to adopt their mannerisms and thought processes.

The mastermind group allows you to trade up to an environment which is better than the one you're currently in. The saying that you are ultimately most like the five people you spend most of your time with is very true. It is far easier to find creative solutions to your problems in an environment which is dedicated to improvement and success.

The problems that your mastermind group members will encounter will often be quite similar to your own. This is because the group will be formed to address a common theme between the members. For example, a mastermind group focused on helping e-commerce entrepreneurs is likely to highlight challenges that ring true for all the members involved in the group.

By clarifying problems for others and finding solutions from an observant role, dealing with your own problems becomes a lot easier. When simply observing a problem, our minds are not as emotionally involved in it and therefore, we can apply a greater cognitive function to find a solution.

So now that you know the basics of what a mastermind group is, let's look at how you can go about starting one.

How to Start and Run a Mastermind Group

Starting a mastermind group is easy enough. Ensuring that it meets its goals is a whole other thing. A lot of mastermind groups can disintegrate a short while after they are formed due to mistakes made in the initial formation. Avoiding these mistakes will increase the chances of your group being useful for everyone involved.

Before starting a mastermind group, it helps to outline what the group is not; this will not only help you clarify your own goals but will also give you an easy screening process for prospective members.

Firstly, the mastermind group does not exist to provide cross-promotion opportunities or sales leads of any kind. While these things may happen by themselves between members, they are not the overriding purpose of the group. Your group isn't there as a workshop for learning new subjects either. You may invite speakers on specific topics occasionally, but members are primarily there to help each other.

Finally, the meetings are not an opportunity for the facilitator to teach or instruct the members. This is not a group coaching session; the point of a mastermind group is to enable the members to help each other and themselves. The facilitator helps monitor the flow of conversation and prevents the dialogue from becoming dominated by a few individuals. Now that you know what to avoid, let's look at what you need to do to start a successful group.

Define the purpose. What do you want your group to be about? Start off by thinking of the niche within which your group will exist. Is it a group that is dedicated to entrepreneurs? Digital nomad entrepreneurs? Entrepreneurs in a particular location?

You can create a group about virtually any topic out there—define the group, though. The more specific your group's definition is, the better. Creating a group for entrepreneurs in the affiliate marketing space who are currently located in Chicago is better than simply starting one for entrepreneurs. Of course, if you end up going too narrow in your focus, you also risk filtering out people who could help you.

To avoid this, define your own objectives and problems. What is it that you are looking to improve upon in your business? Is your business esoteric enough that only those people who have experienced it can provide qualified advice? Or is it broad enough to share attributes with other companies?

For example, if you're a foreign exchange trader, there isn't much help a small online service can provide you. They might help on a general basis, but really, there isn't much of an intersection. However, if you're an e-commerce entrepreneur selling physical goods, there is an intersection even though your respective sales avenues are different.

Write down a mission statement for your group. The statement should define everything you wish to achieve and should be specific enough for prospective members to glance at and see whether they would be a good fit for the group.

Define the rules. You want your group to be as engaged and helpful for its members as possible. Problems will inevitably arise, such as disagreements and differences of opinion. A lot of mastermind groups make the mistake of not having set processes to deal with these problems. As a result, they end up causing more significant disruption than they would have if they had laid out the processes to deal with disagreements in the first place.

Group members will be using the meetings to improve their business results and will seek input and creative challenges which help them. Having someone disrupt this by being unprepared or late puts off other members from turning to the group for answers and as a result, engagement levels drop.

The rules of engagement also help you define the balance of interaction between members. Will you have a "hot seat", which is a single member taking the majority of the time to describe their challenges? Or would you rather spread it out in every meeting? How often will you meet? If the members wish to change the frequency, how do they go about it?

Payment to join, to create a mastermind group fund, is a great way to get people to commit to the meetings. The payments collected could then be used to pay for a venue, or a drink and food fund if you meet in a bar or restaurant. Of course, the value proposition of the group needs to be significant enough for people to do this. You will likely find resistance to this idea, but the good thing is that the requirement to pay tends to filter out a lot of the problematic members before they can even join.

Make sure to write all of this down in detail so that each member knows the rules. Brainstorm problematic issues and come up with contingencies to deal with them. Being prepared is the best course of action.

Choose your members. The first two steps will do the majority of the heavy lifting for you when it comes to identifying people who will be a good fit for your group. Start small and expand from there. If you're not experienced enough at masterminding, then consider adding someone else as a facilitator. Remember that the facilitator's goals need to align with the group's goals, too.

When choosing members, always look for people who are willing to take and give feedback. You want them to recognise what "constructive feedback" means. One good way of figuring this out is to see if they can take what they give. Positive, forward-thinking entrepreneurs usually can.

There is a tendency for some people to provide feedback that is sometimes too hard-hitting for some, so try to include members who have basic emotional intelligence, unless one of the group's tenets is extreme rationality. Whatever you do, make sure that the group meetings provide a challenge for everyone involved.

Meet and tweak. Once your membership is finalised, it is time to meet! You should have decided by now whether or not you would like to meet online or in person. In this day and age, online meetings are par for the course, with a yearly or quarterly meeting in person. In-person meetings provide a great bonding opportunity for members, and if your group is engaged enough, you will find yourself looking forward to this.

Take notes during meetings and require each member to be honest about their struggles and with their feedback. The group only works if every member commits 100%, so remind everyone of this fact. Be honest about the level of help everyone is receiving and check to see, with the group's permission, if there is anything that could be changed.

Once in a while, you can invite a special guest to inject some fresh ideas into the group. Above all else, enforce the rules and spirit of the group. Be open to experimentation and change things up if they get too dry or unhelpful.

Advantages and Disadvantages of a Mastermind Group

Not everything is perfect with mastermind groups. While there are many advantages to joining or running one, there are some disadvantages you should be aware of. A lot of these disadvantages happen due to a lack of definition during the planning stage.

It is hard to think of a single disadvantage of joining a mastermind group that is a good fit. Yes, it requires a lot of commitment, and it might even require money to join, but don't let this deter you. If you feel that the group is a good fit, you should join it wholeheartedly.

If the group is not a good fit for you, you might begin to notice some of the negatives listed in the following sections.

Experience mismatch. Getting the membership of a group right is an art. The key is to have members within a few steps of one another. Having someone who is too far behind or someone who is too far ahead disrupts the dynamic of the group. A person who is too far ahead of the rest will feel cheated since no one in the group can help them. Even worse, those too far behind will find it challenging to get the help they need.

When joining a group, first and foremost, evaluate the person who is organising the meeting. The organiser is usually the facilitator, and their experience level will tell you a lot about the group's aims and the way the group will be run. Ultimately, no matter what the mission statement says, the organiser's nature tends to come through in the way things run. So always look at it as though you are evaluating the person and not the group itself.

Mission mismatch. There are a few high-profile mastermind groups out there which suffer from what I like to think of as a mission mismatch. Often, you will see mastermind memberships being offered to qualified students of a particular business coach. These sessions cost a ton of money—usually, five to six figures per head—and people buy them enthusiastically, thanks to the coach's credibility.

Once you join, you find that this isn't a mastermind event as much as it is a group coaching session, with the guru only interested in telling everyone what they need to do. Additionally, the ego of the group leader or coach often gets in the way of true mastermind learning potential. A lot of the famous mastermind networks operate this way. Ultimately, masterminds are good business, and there is no shortage of charlatans out there who seek to take advantage of people this way.

This is why it is crucial to start with small groups and network your way up. Usually, the bigger groups already have hundreds of participants, and it is unlikely that you will receive any face time with the organiser or feel any real positive impact. An alternative to these guru-type groups is a professionally managed group, but even here, it is difficult to get the right fit for your needs.

Ultimately, start small and grow slowly. As your network builds, you'll find yourself in better situations to run a productive mastermind.

Lack of organisation. Running a mastermind is hard work. A lot of groups do not take this seriously enough, though, and this leads to a lot of irritation due to disorganisation. Many groups suffer from this unless there is a strong leader present who keeps everyone in line and on the same page. On the other hand, you also have groups that are just too large to make sense and are merely marketing events posing as mastermind sessions.

The person who screams the loudest indeed tends to get the most attention. Usually, these screamers run the least effective groups. This is not to say that they're all bad, but if someone is running a business organising masterminds, their primary incentive is to have as many people on board as possible. This is in direct opposition to your goals, which will be better served to have as few people on board as possible, usually no more than five or six. So, ask yourself: what are their real incentives?

If the organiser is someone who used to run a ten million-dollar company (revenues), has run multiple businesses in the past and now does this full time, what is their true incentive?

I don't mean to be overly negative here. There are many advantages to joining a mastermind. Just make sure you avoid these negatives. As for the positives, well, let's take a look at them now.

Overcome impostor syndrome. You used to be a janitor and are now a CEO. Are you sure you're worth the title? These sorts of negative thoughts plague entrepreneurs everywhere. Impostor syndrome affects everyone from established company founders to freelancers starting out for the first time. A lot of us identify with particular labels when it comes to our careers, and even when you manage to find success, it can be tough to let go of that feeling of unworthiness.

A mastermind group serves as a timely reminder that you are worth it and that you do add value. The notion that we evaluate ourselves by looking at every single action but evaluate others by looking only at their highlight reels is true. You might be overawed when you join a mastermind by people you respect; when you consider that they look at you as an equal, impostor syndrome vanishes pretty quickly.

Efficient networking. Networking is what helps businesses thrive. It helps broaden your customer base and puts you in touch with prospective clients. A lot of networking sessions are dead ends, though. A typical networking session is full of sales managers more interested in pitching their product to you, instead of listening to what you need the most.

Mastermind groups help you network better by eradicating the sales component. You know that people are committed to helping you improve and aren't there to take advantage of you. This enables you to connect with other people's networks on a more legitimate basis, and this can lead to better opportunities.

Other advantages. Aside from the positive effects mentioned above, masterminds will help you stay accountable to yourself and prevent you from becoming lazy about your goals. Often, we tend to not follow through after brainstorming sessions for a variety of reasons. Most often, life gets in the way, and a lot of ideas seem ridiculous when viewed in the light of cold hard reality.

We are susceptible to having our opinions changed depending on our moods, and this is what causes us to view some of our best ideas as being pieces of trash. A mastermind will save you from this. It will also keep you from your own biases which cause you to view a terrible idea as being a great one.

By being part of a mastermind group, you gain access to knowledge that grows at an exponential rate. The combined understanding produces a total that is far beyond the sum of its parts. This is a characteristic of exponential systems everywhere, and a mastermind group is no exception.

In-Person or Virtual Mastermind Groups?

There are two forms of the mastermind group: in-person and virtual groups. Virtual groups are extremely popular, but there is no denying the power of physical interaction. However, in-person interaction groups tend to cost more in terms of both time and money, so there are pros and cons to each option.

Flexibility of a Virtual Group. In terms of flexibility, it is hard to argue against a group that meets regularly using the internet. This makes it easier to adhere to your calendar and increases accountability since the attendees might be in different time zones and have to consciously make time to attend.

While physical groups also enforce accountability, it does limit flexibility quite a lot, and it might be hard for some people to attend due to other commitments. If you are a digital nomad, you will also struggle to commit to a physical group if you travel around a lot. One of the benefits of a mastermind group is that you build up a relationship with the group over time, which is hard to do with a physical group if you move around different countries a lot. As a result, the burden might prove to be too much, and the group might not last long.

Open Borders of a Virtual Group. The internet has opened the world up in more ways than one. Nothing is stopping you from accessing the markets and minds of a place that is on the other side of the globe. The more diverse perspectives you are exposed to, the better suited you are to deal with change and adapt to the way the world works.

In-person groups have an obvious difficulty in this regard. It is difficult for someone living in Australia to fly over to New York once a month on a particular date. It just isn't feasible—unless the participants happen to be incredibly wealthy in the first place and own their own jets.

No Substitute for a Physical Connection. Nothing beats talking to a person face to face to understand their motivations and their problems honestly. Not only will you be able to provide better feedback, but you will also receive better recommendations and solutions to your problems.

If you run an online mastermind, make it a point to organise an in-person meetup at least twice a year if you can. This gives everyone something to look forward to and rejuvenates the energy within the group.

Getting a Business Mentor

Sometimes, your problems get too big for your mastermind group to address and what you really need is the expertise of someone who has "been there and done that." This is the role of a business mentor, and you should consider finding yourself someone to mentor you, especially if you are in the initial stages of your project.

Your mentor should be someone who has already had experience in what you're going through, and experience achieving the goals you wish to hit. The trickiest bit about mentorship is that it is a personal relationship, and it can be tough to find someone. Often, entrepreneurs reach out to someone successful in their field and request a mentorship.

This sort of request displays a very low emotional quotient, and it shouldn't come as a surprise that such requests are usually rejected or just ignored. A mentor-mentee relationship is something that develops organically, with the mentee recognising the value of the mentor's advice, and the mentor seeing the potential in the mentee and wishing to impart some of the wisdom they have accumulated over the years.

Networking, and thereby increasing your professional reach, is the best way of getting someone to mentor you. Now, not everyone has access to an extensive network of highly successful people, so this can be tricky to do. This is where informational talks and books come into the picture, along with articles online.

Gather as much wisdom as you can from these free resources and build your knowledge as much as possible. While it is unrealistic to think that you will find solutions to specific problems, you will learn a great deal of information with regards to your field. As your expertise increases, eventually, someone will appear who can help you overcome specific obstacles.

Another good source of mentorships is mentoring programs like *Y Combinator* or *500 Startups*. These groups are typically limited to companies in specific sectors or particular stages of their life cycles. It isn't easy to enter these programs, so this makes it crucial that you learn as much as possible from the internet, books and workshops to soak up as much wisdom as you can from popular resources.

One phenomenon that has emerged in the online world is the role of the paid mentor. Whatever they may call themselves, these 'mentors' are really just paid advisors or coaches, so treat them as such. A true mentor is never paid since it is a rewarding relationship. Do seek to compensate your mentor for their time but be aware that paying someone every month is not necessarily true mentorship.

Good mentors are hard to come by, so don't jump the gun and appoint someone as your mentor without taking the time to get to know them personally. Finding the right mentor will do wonders for your business so it is worth your time pursuing one. Just trust that someone will appear in your life at the right time and follow your instincts.

If the current obstacles are too large, consider hiring an advisor to help you past these problems.

The Author's Approach

Along my journey, I have received help and advice from people all over the world. When I started creating courses for Pluralsight, I met lots of clever and interesting people who eventually became good friends. The more experienced course authors were generous in giving me and other new authors advice on how to create and promote our courses.

When I rented a desk at the co-working offices, I met lots of like-minded people and we discussed running our businesses. Sharing knowledge with like-minded people is fundamental to your own business and to collaboration. Throughout my career I have been mentored by some amazing people, and I have tried to return the favour by being a mentor to others.

Learning from other people is fundamental to success, no matter what it is you aspire to do with your business. We progress in business and in life by learning from others' experiences, and this is something for which I have been grateful, and with which I have tried to help other people. With that said, I haven't been a part of a formal mastermind group like those discussed in this chapter. While I do have a close group of friends that I talk to, we don't keep each other to account.

My co-host on the *Side-Hustle Success* podcast, Kevin, takes part in a formal mastermind group. Within their group, they share their business goals, and the rest of the group hold each other to account on those goals.

No matter whether you decide to attend a mastermind group or not, I recommend networking with other like-minded entrepreneurs. It doesn't have to be a formal mentoring arrangement; just having someone who can help guide you and offer the wealth of their experience will be of great benefit to you.

Summary

Mastermind groups are the best way out there to turbocharge your business results. As Napoleon Hill said in his books, the power of the mastermind is exponential, in that it gives you access to a sum of intelligence that is far greater than the sum of the individual intelligence of those around you.

Masterminds also help you place yourself in a supportive and positive environment for your business. The environment around us deeply influences us, often reflecting back what the people around us believe, and we also tend to mimic their behaviour. The best way of improving your results in any area of your life is to change your environment.

The first step to creating a mastermind group that sustains itself for a long time is to decide what you wish to achieve with this group. The more you can define this purpose, the better. For example, if you're looking for better results in your business, seek to niche your mastermind group by defining the sector your business is in, by the objective or by the location, and so on.

This is a great way to get people to self-select themselves for your group. Ideal group sizes are around three to eight people, so don't worry about gathering huge numbers. Consider implementing a payment requirement to gather higher levels of commitment from your members. Ultimately, the members in the group must be honest, so you should communicate the group's aims and codes of conduct clearly.

Deal with problems before they occur by defining processes to address the most common issues, such as members who are not attending nor preparing for the session. Define processes which help you maintain harmony within the group and expel troublesome members as quickly as possible. Usually, defining the group's goals and processes does this automatically, but problems do occur despite this.

Beware of large organisations which conduct organised mastermind groups. Always examine the incentives of such organisations, since larger groups often turn into group coaching camps. Your mastermind group does not exist to teach you new skills, nor does it exist to learn from some guru. Ideally, the group size will be small, and every member will be within a few steps of each other.

Masterminds are a great way to battle impostor syndrome which affects entrepreneurs at all levels. By associating with people you respect and having them view you as a peer, you reaffirm the honesty of your vision. In addition, this respect will prevent you from slacking on your goals and will hold you accountable. The relationships you build will be of a higher quality and any business opportunities you receive will automatically be better.

Consider implementing or joining a virtual mastermind group.

Despite the perceived limitations, the truth is that there are advantages and disadvantages to this model. Physical meetings might place too big a load on people's schedules, and it does reduce your geographic reach quite a lot. The internet, by contrast, opens the whole world up to you.

Sometimes, the problems you encounter will be too big for your mastermind group. In such cases, consider obtaining a mentor or hiring an advisor. A mentor-mentee relationship is an organic one, and it isn't easy to find a good mentor. Networking is the best way to do this. The vast amount of free information available on the net is also a useful resource for this.

A true mentor will help you past obstacles well beyond your business. They will change your life and the earlier you find one, the better. An advisor is someone you pay to increase the quality of your business, and you should not treat such people as you would a mentor.

All in all, mentorship and mastermind groups enable you to access higher levels of information and intelligence. Remember that growth is exponential and not linear. These methods will help you realise this in your business faster and will propel your results to the next level, no matter where you are currently.

Workshop Questions

(1) Create a list of people that you know locally that are like-minded, that you could form a mastermind group with.

(2) Search for existing mastermind groups in your area using a tool like meetup.com.

(3) Think about what you would want to get out of a mastermind group. Is there anything you specifically need help with?

15

STAYING MENTALLY AND PHYSICALLY FIT

Just because you're a busy business owner and entrepreneur doesn't mean that you are exempt from taking care of your health. Life isn't going to take it easy on you just because you happen to be very ambitious, especially when it comes to your career. In this chapter, we are going to cover some of how you should be looking after yourself. Granted, this might be both the most important and most challenging aspect of staying healthy. But it's not entirely impossible. Heck, even former President Obama talked about how he always found at least 30 minutes to an hour every day to dedicate to his fitness, and this was the most powerful man in the free world we're talking about. If he could do it, then so can you.

You don't always have to have such lofty goals when it comes to your fitness. Sure, you can have bigger goals like training for a triathlon or whatnot; however, you also have to be realistic with yourself. If you're busy being an entrepreneur, you might not have the extra two or three hours every day to be training. At the very least, all you need is 30 minutes to an hour. You don't even have to go to a gym.

Don't Overcomplicate Your Daily Fitness

There are various home or office workouts that you can do on your own with minimal equipment. A nice little one-hour yoga session in the morning could even be enough.

Keeping your gym bag handy. Every night, before you go to bed, make sure that you have your gym bag handy. This way, when you wake up in the morning, all you have to do is pick up your gym bag and go. If you're planning to go for a run outside, then ready your running shoes, shorts, and shirt. If you're going to a yoga class, then have your yoga mat ready when you wake up. This way, you are priming your mind to work out as soon as you wake up.

Walk as much as possible. Whenever possible, try to walk; this is especially important when you become a small business owner. Walking can be a very effective way of burning off extra calories and staying fit. Also, try taking the stairs more often. I live in Derbyshire in the UK, which is a national park, so I enjoy going out walking as much as I can. In the town where I live, I have planned out various walking routes that will take me anywhere from 30 minutes to two hours to complete. I try to walk most days, even if it is only for 30 minutes.

You can incorporate walking with learning by listening to podcasts or audiobooks. Not only are you exercising your body, but your mind, too. I do a lot of software development as well as online course creation and find that walking is also a great way to solve problems that I am struggling with at my desk. If I get stuck on a problem, I leave my desk, go out for a short walk and listen to some music. When you are out on a walk and giving your mind a rest instead of struggling with the problem, more often than not, the solution to the problem will come to you more swiftly.

Set up a standing desk. The chair is probably the poster child for modern obesity and poor health. The human body is designed to run, jump, climb, throw, lift, catch, and do all sorts of other amazing things. And yet, most of us have condemned our bodies to sit in chairs all day. Granted, you want to get work done at the office, and for that, you need a desk. Try having a standing desk instead so that you are forcing yourself to stay on your feet.

I was initially sceptical about standing desks until I tried a desk that a friend owned. Having the flexibility to be able to stand while working helps you with your posture, and it also helps to keep you more alert and awake, especially in the afternoon when energy levels can start waning.

With a standing desk, it is a good idea to strike a balance between sitting and standing. Too much of either can cause discomfort, but a sensible blend of the two will give you the best results. When I go into my office in the morning, I start the day with some administrative tasks like mail, finances etc. I always do these standing up. For work where I need to concentrate, I sit down for a lot of it, but I will always try to stand for at least 15 minutes in every hour. When I am recording voiceovers for a training course, I always record these standing up, so I can get more air into my lungs while talking.

Out of all the measures I have tried for keeping my weight in balance, using a standing desk has had the most impact. You can incorporate it into your daily work routine so that it doesn't require much effort—and low-effort exercise is always preferable, as then you are more likely to keep it up.

Plan your meals. Meal preparation is critical when you want to get your diet on track. You can consult a nutritionist and get their advice, but you can also do your own research to see what kind of nutrition plan would work best for you. Some people go full plant-based vegan nutrition; or there's intermittent fasting plans, keto or paleo regimes, and many others. All of these diets have varying levels of effectiveness for different people—it's all a matter of what suits you best.

Part of planning your meals is also ensuring that you don't engage in any unnecessary snacking throughout the day. If you're spending the majority of your time at a desk, you are going to want to limit your calorie intake as much as possible. So, the little bites of crackers, chips, or candy bars that you may have between meals should be a big no-no at this point.

However, this isn't a book about dieting advice! Suffice to say that when you are working, and potentially under pressure to complete work, it can be very tempting to snack, but if you prepare all your meals and keep snacks away from your work area, you will be less tempted to reach for the biscuits.

Get a good night's sleep. Never underestimate the power of a good night's sleep. You would be surprised at how much healthier and more energetic you become just by practising proper sleeping habits. Try to have a consistent sleep and wake-up time that you follow strictly every day. Resist the urge to hit the snooze button and make an effort to get out of bed early in the morning. The sooner you wake up, the more time you have to do more work throughout the day. However, being able to wake up early also depends on you going to sleep early at night.

Having a good, regulated sleep pattern can be easier said than done, especially for parents of babies and small children who are brilliant at sabotaging the best-laid sleep routine plans. If you are in a position to get a good night of sleep without being interrupted by darling little sleep terrorists, then there are a few things you can do to help get a better quality of sleep, so you feel refreshed for a productive day.

The first is to reduce your screen time for at least an hour before going to bed—and this includes phones and tablets as well as laptops and desktop computers. I know in this modern, connected world that isn't always possible, or even desirable, but it does help.

Bright light—particularly blue light, but all colours will have an effect—suppresses your brain's production of melatonin, the hormone that tells your body to get tired and sleep. Without that melatonin production, your body's internal clock is thrown off its normal schedule, and you will find that you aren't able to fall asleep at your normal bedtime. Lowering the brightness of your devices and screens can help counteract this effect. Using dim red lights in your house in the late evening will also help, both to wind down for the night, and to reduce eyestrain after looking at bright screens all day. However, it will not stop your mind racing if you are trying to do something mentally taxing, and this can make it very hard for your brain to switch off before going to sleep.

An excellent technique for helping with sleep is to read for at least 30 minutes before bed. This could be a fiction novel, or you could also feel productive by reading a non-fiction book, but the routine of reading is a great way to prepare yourself for a good night's sleep. It's a good idea to make sure that you're reading a traditional paper book or on an e-ink device like a Kindle Paperwhite, rather than a brightly backlit tablet or phone, otherwise you're back to square one with the screen light issue.

Avoiding caffeine anywhere near sleep time is a good idea, as it is a stimulant that will likely keep you awake. The same can be said for alcohol, as while this may help you initially fall asleep, you will have a more restless night if you have consumed a lot of it that evening. I am not trying to be a big party pooper, but not drinking the night before you need a productive day is a good idea.

Looking After Your Mental Wellbeing

Being an entrepreneur can be an incredibly fulfilling journey that's going to have a lot of high points and low points. Part of what usually makes up an entrepreneur's low points is the toll that particular challenges can take on a person's mental health. Sometimes, the problems that are involved with being an entrepreneur can burn a person out to the point where they want to give up. You can try to avoid this burnout by making sure that you are always taking care of your mental health.

We've already talked about how important it is for you to be taking care of your body. Now, it's time for you to learn how to take care of your mind. After all, your mind is your greatest weapon in amassing success and achievements in your life.

Confront your feelings and emotions. Don't discard the fact that you are a human being and that you are an emotional creature. You are bound to deal with all sorts of emotions when you're an entrepreneur. You will be happy, sad, excited, disappointed, optimistic, and even downright angry every so often. It's important that you validate all of these feelings and that you don't keep them pent up inside.

As an entrepreneur, it can be very easy to bottle up our emotions and try to hide them from other people, as you don't want to give the perception that you can't cope as a business owner. This couldn't be further from the truth—you can cope, but like everyone else, sometimes you need a little help. It is essential to talk to people; your partner, loved ones, friends, or a trained counsellor. The saying, "A problem shared is a problem halved," rings true here. Just by sharing any problems you are having, you remove the burden of carrying it all by yourself from your mind, and hopefully, someone else can help to fix the issue you are facing.

A healthy work-life balance. A good work and life balance is critical. It can't be all be work and no play, or the other way around. Establishing a proper balance between your work life and your personal life will help you avoid burnout and depression. If you are working from home, finding that balance point between work and life can be hard. I learnt this when I first quit my job and worked on my own business from home. Even though I had a room set up for working in, I always felt compelled to get one more task completed. Even after the kids went to bed, I would frequently continue working. I am not saying putting in extra time is completely bad; it is normal for people to put some extra effort in when it is required. If you do this all the time, though, you will soon be out of balance, and your mental health will start to suffer.

If you are working from home, it helps to have a separate room you can work from that is different from your living space. Not everyone has the space to do this, but if you can, it is recommended to give yourself a dedicated work area. When you finish work, instead of putting your computer or laptop to sleep, try powering it off; this will make it harder to go back on the machine to complete a task when you should be relaxing. If you don't have a separate workspace in your house, then make sure you put your laptop away at the end of the day, so it isn't just lying around. Placing the machine out of view makes it less tempting to go back onto it.

For me, I found the most significant help was by using a co-working space for work, so that I was out of the house. When I was at the co-working space, and eventually my own office, I was working; when I was at home, I was not working. The physical act of going out to work and then coming home again introduced enough of a routine into the day to be able to successfully separate work from home life. You may not be ready to go to co-working spaces or your own office at the very beginning of your business's life, but it would be beneficial to have it as part of your broader vision to aim toward.

Not everyone struggles with a work-life balance, but I have found that people working on their own business tend to struggle with this the most, as there is more pressure to succeed and start making the business profitable.

A healthy attitude towards failure. While you would generally want to avoid failure at all costs, it's something that you can't always run away from. Failing isn't the worst thing in the world. What's far worse is allowing your failure to own and control you. Have a healthier disposition towards failure, and you will find that it can be turned to your advantage.

A good mindset to get into is that failure is an opportunity to learn. Failures come in all shapes and sizes, from small mistakes through to catastrophic failures that can cause your business to collapse. While you don't want a catastrophic failure, you still have an opportunity to learn from it once you have licked your wounds.

No matter how big or small a failure or problem is, try not to react straight away. It is always best to try and take some time to think about what has happened before you put in any response. This also goes for analysing any problems to learn from them. If you try to take the lesson in the heat of the moment, you will lack the ability to explain what went wrong critically.

You can think of this like the scientific process where a scientist has a hypothesis that they test by running experiments. Sometimes their hypothesis might be proven true, sometimes false. Does that mean it is a failure? No, it means they have disproven an idea—which is still a successful outcome. Let's look at this from a scientific method point of view where you make an observation, ask a question and form a hypothesis, make and test a prediction, then use the results to form a new hypothesis.

Make an Observation: You will have an idea for something you believe will be good, such as a product or service. In other words, you observe a need or a gap in the market. This could be a gap identified from your experience, or what you observe in the market at large.

Ask a Question: You will perform some research to determine the viability of the idea. Does my product/service truly fill this gap?

Form a Hypothesis: Based on your research, you decide the idea is solid and you want to pursue it further.

Make a Prediction: You devise your plan to test the market and establish your success criteria. You may use some of the *The Lean Startup's* techniques that we covered in an earlier chapter.

Test the Prediction: You invest time and money into the execution of the idea and launch it.

Use Results to Form New Hypothesis: You measure the idea's performance against your success criteria. If the execution and implementation fall short of your expectations, you can let the dust settle and then look at what went wrong. From there you can either try again, factoring in what you have learnt from this experiment, or you might decide that the idea wasn't valid after all, based on what you now know. Both could be valid outcomes.

Rinse and Repeat: Trying other things to make your product/service a success.

In some fields, there's an almost optional extra step: *Communicate your results.* This would be where you would discuss your results and findings with a mastermind group or with a mentor.

From testing your predictions and hypothesis several times you may decide that the product idea is worth pursuing, or you may decide that it is not worth pursuing. The critical point is, don't treat all failures as something terrible that you should try and run away from. Use any failure as an opportunity to learn and improve yourself and your business.

Dealing with Stress

Stress is something that can be incredibly damaging to your health. Please make no mistake about it—as an entrepreneur, you are going to be exposed to a lot of stress when you run a business. It's essential that you know and understand just what you can do to manage the stress in your life. It's not all that uncommon for entrepreneurs to be working as much as 50 or even 60 hours a week. This kind of workload can put an individual under a lot of stress, and failure to manage that stress would make that kind of working pace very unsustainable. Ultimately, some level of stress is inevitable, and this is why it's so essential that you learn to manage it effectively. There's no way that you would be able to get rid of stress in your life—and, in fact, the right amount of stress is good for you, as it tunes up the brain and improves your performance and overall health. But if you learn to manage any excess stress properly, then it shouldn't present a problem for you. Here are a few things that you should do as an entrepreneur to manage the stress in your life.

Say no when necessary. It's essential that you learn how to say no when necessary. Sometimes, you need to know your limits as an entrepreneur. You're not Superman. Heck, even Superman had to let Batman do some of the work sometimes. You don't always have to do everything that you are told or asked to do. When you feel like a project or a task is far too onerous or complicated, then you need to be able to turn it down. You don't want to bring that unnecessary stress, pressure, and anxiety into your life.

At the start of your business's life, it is normal to feel you should say yes to every piece of work that comes your way, especially if you are a freelancer. As you build up a client base and stabilise your business over time, it is then that you need to make a concerted effort to assess the benefit of each piece of work to all of your other work. If a piece of work comes in that you know will take up a considerable amount of time compared to the reward from it, or the customer has been very difficult to work with in the past, it is okay to say no. You owe it to yourself to make these decisions.

. . .

Learn to delegate. Whenever possible, learn to delegate. One of the biggest problems that entrepreneurs have when running a business is falling victim to the founder's syndrome, where you feel as though you have to do everything for it to be done correctly. Remember, as you try to grow your business, you may have to recruit the help and services of other people, either as full-time employees or freelancers. You need to learn to let some work go and trust other people to do it for you. You don't need to do everything on your own. Learn to hire good people you can trust to help take some of the work off your plate.

Disconnect and unplug. Now and then, take some time for yourself. This means that you need to unplug and disconnect yourself from the outside world for a bit. The advent of the smartphone makes you so accessible to so many people. However, this can also be a considerable stressor. Try to go incognito every once in a while, to recharge and rejuvenate your soul. We talked about walking earlier on in this chapter, and that is a fantastic way to get some time to yourself, especially if you leave your phone at home for a few hours so no one can phone you, and you are not tempted to check notifications, email and social media.

A healthy exercise routine. As we have already discussed in this chapter, exercise has benefits that transcend the mere physical benefits. Sure, you get a better physique and healthier body, and you reduce the risk of disease when you exercise. But you also get the chance to relieve the stress that is in your life. Remember that exercise triggers the release of endorphins, the happy hormone, in your body. One of the kindest things you can do for your body is to set aside time for exercise, even if it is only 20-30 minutes a day; you will feel physically better, but also happier.

The Author's Approach

Before I left my full-time job to work for myself, I didn't take physical or mental fitness that seriously. I am lucky that I have never suffered with depression, and apart from being overweight, I felt fine, even though I spent most of my time sitting. I have always enjoyed walking, and each year I set a New Year's resolution that I would try to walk more while at work on my lunch breaks. Of course, that doesn't last long, and because of being busy and under pressure, I just reverted to old habits of eating my lunch at my desk and not walking.

When I started working for myself, I decided I wanted to make sure I got more exercise each day. Each day I would go out for a walk in the morning or the afternoon. Some days this might just be half an hour, or on other days I might go for a longer hour or even a two-hour walk. Extended walks every now and again were possible as I didn't have a boss hovering behind me, making sure I was working all the time. If I was busy getting ready to complete a deadline, then walks would be shorter, but if I didn't have any immediate pressures and I was progressing well with work, then I would go for longer.

The town where I live in Derbyshire in the UK is near a national park, so we have a lot of hilly countryside that has become a natural exercise machine within a five-minute walk from the house. After a year of taking these regular walks, I felt very good; more energised and generally more alert. I have never been someone who enjoys going to the gym, the idea just doesn't appeal to me, so I was happy I found an exercise routine that works for me. If you are someone who does enjoy going to the gym, then you must factor this into your workday as much as possible.

In a lot of cases, I consider my walking time as work time too; well, that's how I justify it to myself. When I go walking, I listen to podcasts that are related to my work, and I also like to listen to audiobooks. My audiobook listening is always in the non-fiction space, so that is where I get my dose of self-help and productivity knowledge. Walking and learning at the same time exercises not only your body, but your mind too. During the coronavirus lockdowns, my walks were the highlight of the day after trying to work from home and run a home school. There are definite mental health benefits to getting outside and into nature as much as possible. Without fail, if I am ever having a bad day, an hour's brisk walk always lifts my mood.

. . .

A healthy work-life balance is something that most people struggle with in their busy professional lives, and I have never been immune to that. When I was younger and working for other companies, I would frequently work in the evening, and was always contactable by email or instant message. I didn't mind working the extra hours, as I considered it the way you try to get ahead in your career. As I got older, got married, and had children, I stopped doing that, especially around the time I started making the online training courses in the evenings. That still isn't a great work-life balance, but at least the work I would do in the evenings on my courses was for me and my family, and not for someone else.

Since quitting my full-time job and working for myself, I have tried to get the balance right between work and home life. I found that difficult to achieve sometimes when working from home, as it was always so tempting to "just finish this one thing...". We have already talked about how I don't enjoy working from home for any length of time, which is why I preferred renting a small office where I could go to work. I find the routine of getting ready for work and leaving the house a good way to start the workday, and the commute home helpful to signify that the workday is over.

Like a lot of entrepreneurs when starting out, I struggled to say no to any work or projects that came my way. I felt that if I said no to anything, opportunities would stop. So, I said yes—and piled on the pressure. Everyone does this when they start out. Sometimes, I did minor projects for people, which paid ok for what they were, but they took my attention from what I should have been doing to build up my business. Since then, I have become much better at identifying what work or opportunities get me to my goals and saying no to anything else. If you don't do this, then you can become burnt out, which is not a pleasant state to be in.

Summary

Running a business can be one of the most rewarding things you do in life. If you are not careful, though, it can start to affect both your physical and mental health if you don't look after yourself. Sitting at your desk all day can hurt your back and overall posture, as well as contribute to you putting on weight. Constant work and long hours can also affect your mental health and lead to both burnout and depression. What's the point of putting in all that great work to build a business if you become too ill and burnt out to enjoy the rewards in the years to come?

By taking a small bit of time each day to get some exercise, even if it is only a short walk, you can boost your mood, get some fresh air and help manage any office-based weight gain. You don't need to strive to become an athlete or a zen meditation expert, but small steps to manage your workload and look after your body will keep you in an excellent condition to tackle any problem that life and your business throws at you.

Workshop Questions

(1) Look at a map of your local area, or go from local knowledge, and work out at least three different walking routes you can do. Aim for walks that will take around 30 minutes, one hour and two hours.

(2) If you are working from home, decide upon an end-of-day ritual you can follow to create a mental separation from the working day. This could include powering down your laptop, putting it away and then shutting the door to your office, or any other activity that you can use as a signal to finish the day.

(3) Take a page of paper and label it the "Worry Chart" and split into three columns. Down the left-hand side of the page, write down anything that is causing you a problem or anxiety.

1. In the middle of the page, try to identify the causes of the problem you just identified.
2. On the right side of the page, try to identify what you could do to reduce that stress or anxiety-causing problem.

16

BEATING PROCRASTINATION AND STAYING FOCUSED

We've all procrastinated before. You look at the clock to discover that it's 6pm. already, four hours after you said you'd be done with your project. Before you know it, 8pm. creeps along, and you still haven't even started. You can distract yourself for a while during the day, but the thought of having to complete the task is always hovering in the back of your mind. In an attempt to ease your guilt, you might seek out other distracting activities. Maybe you take on a new project, only to find you are unable to finish that one, either. Now, you have multiple responsibilities, your mind is overwhelmed, and you are exhausted.

Our struggles with procrastination can be incredibly frustrating, especially when you have other things you need to do *after* the task you're putting off. The weight of these moments of hesitation can tear us apart and keep us from completing a seemingly simple task. Procrastination is an endless cycle. It goes:

- Having to finish a project.
- Putting it off.
- Feeling guilty about not starting.

- Rushing to complete the project.
- Beginning a new project.

This cycle can leave us so overwhelmed that we might not complete the task at all. But the good news is that procrastination is something you can overcome. It's all about shifting your mentality. You can go from wanting to find anything to avoid the task at hand to facing it head-on. In this chapter, we are going to break down why procrastination is such a big problem and what you can do to set yourself up for success.

What is Procrastination?

Procrastination is a self-imposed delay in productivity. Procrastination occurs anytime you postpone something without a real reason for doing so.

We all know what it feels like to procrastinate. Procrastination is often intentional. It's something that we do even though we know we shouldn't. It's an act of avoiding the task at hand. It involves completely disregarding whatever it is that needs our attention and instead, putting that attention toward something else.

Procrastination is different for everyone. Some people will sit right at their desk and actively ignore what they need to do. Others will hunt around their homes, looking everywhere for a new task that can replace the old.

Some people procrastinate large tasks, like getting a job or planning their wedding. Others can procrastinate the simplest things, like sending an email or taking a shower.

When diving deep into procrastination, there are a couple of things to understand: how we procrastinate; and the excuses we make for procrastination.

Methods of procrastination. We all use different methods when procrastinating. The tasks we do will always differ, but these types of delays are the most common among many individuals. The first kind is leaving things to the very last minute. Sometimes it's easy to do this because you trust that you're able to get the task done within the right timeframe. Perhaps you have already completed the task before, so you know that you'll be able to get it done quickly and easily.

The second kind is avoiding the task altogether. Something about it is scary. Maybe you're worried about the workload. Perhaps you're not sure of the best way to complete it. Or perhaps failing is your biggest fear; so, the best way to avoid failure is to avoid the task completely!

The third method of procrastination is using distractions to make it seem like you're not procrastinating. Perhaps you're completing other tasks in order not to have to face the one that needs doing. It's easy to find new tasks to get done when there's one you're trying to avoid.

The justifications of procrastination. To make procrastination feel okay, we often try to justify to ourselves why we're not doing the specific task. These justifications are excuses that can make our procrastination seem better, and as though we're not doing anything wrong at all.

Avoiding something doesn't always mean we're procrastinating. Maybe you had to finish a work assignment, but first, you want to pay your bills. If both tasks need to be done, then it can be better to do something rather than nothing. However, if you have a work assignment due at midnight and you choose to pay your bills when they aren't due until next week, this is likely procrastination.

We often avoid the place where a task needs to be completed, telling ourselves that it's out of our hands, when we had control over whether or not we were there. Maybe you have to go to the doctor's office. You can tell yourself, "Well, they're only open nine to five every day, and that's when I work. So, I can't go!" In reality, you could likely find time to leave work early one day to complete this task.

To aid us in our procrastination, sometimes we trivialise our tasks. Maybe you have a class assignment due, but it's only worth ten points out of the total 3,000 that the class is worth. So, instead of doing it, you convince yourself it isn't important that you do it at all.

We might compare ourselves to those who procrastinate more than we do, to justify our procrastination. Perhaps you have to clean out your closet. You tell yourself, "Well, my sister's closet is way worse than mine. So, I'm fine."

We might blame our external circumstances for our procrastination. Perhaps you blame the construction workers outside for making noise and distracting you from your assignment. However, to overcome this obstacle, you could have put on headphones or gone to the library.

The more excuses we have, the harder it is to overcome procrastination.

Why Do We Procrastinate?

What is it that causes us to procrastinate in the first place? Procrastination is not an accident. It is intentional. Even if you can't figure out why it is that you're putting tasks off for so long, there will be an underlying reason that is driving you to make these choices.

Not all procrastination has to be wrong. Sometimes there is what is referred to as constructive procrastination. You have to look at what you are doing to determine if it's helping you to complete the most important task. A good technique is at the start of every day, look at what you need to accomplish and prioritise that list into a top three. Even with a full to-do list, if you can achieve that top three list, then you have had a good day. Those top three tasks may be based on a deadline, or if you are struggling for mental energy and the deadlines are not as pressing, you may decide to focus on tasks that require less concentration. Either way, prioritising your work at the start of the day into a top three means that if you can complete those tasks, you will feel good about yourself and feel more motivated.

Use some questions to help you know whether or not you are procrastinating.

- When do you tend to procrastinate?
- What do you do instead of the task that needs to get done?
- Does this help or hurt you?

We often put things off because we are waiting for the "right" time. There will never be a right time. We can't wait around and hope that a task will become easier the longer that we wait. There is no better time than 'now' to get things done.

. . .

Fear of failure. When discussing general fears, one of the biggest things people are afraid of is failure. We're scared that we're never going to achieve the dreams that we set out to achieve. We are scared that we will embarrass ourselves if we fail. We're afraid of disappointing our loved ones. We're worried we'll never get the things we want in life.

Fear could be the thing that drives you to get what you want in life; however, fear of failure can unfortunately take away any drive you had to begin with, and this is where procrastination comes in. Procrastination can be the way that we avoid failure. If you never do something, then you never have to be afraid of failing at it. We can take a cue from Frank Herbert's "Litany Against Fear" from his *Dune* series of books, as it very much applies to conquering a fear of failure:

"I must not fear.
Fear is the mind-killer.
Fear is the little-death that brings total obliteration.
I will face my fear.
I will permit it to pass over me and through me.
And when it has gone past, I will turn the inner eye to see its path.
Where the fear has gone there will be nothing.
Only I will remain."

-*Dune*, **Frank Herbert.**

The best way to avoid the disappointment of failing is to avoid doing what you need to do. This idea keeps people trapped in the same mentality. They become fearful over what's going to happen once they begin their task.

Fear over judgment can also be crippling. People don't want to receive negative feedback. Maybe you take a year to finish what should be done in a month because you're worried about criticism.

Those scary voices are getting into your head; they're making you stressed and anxious. They are telling you all of the horrible things that could happen. But this could be the very thing that drives you to work if you learn how to manage your fear correctly and use it to achieve greatness rather than to procrastinate.

By procrastinating, you're letting down the future you. Remember that it's going to be very disappointing if you don't complete your tasks. We often care too much about other people's opinions of us, and not enough about what our future self will think. We should shift our focus instead to working on achieving our goals, regardless of what other people will think. At the end of the day, you will be able to look yourself in the eye in the mirror and have the satisfaction that comes with knowing that you completed your tasks and earned your downtime.

Letting people down. How will the people we love react if we were to fail? We sometimes avoid doing anything because we're afraid of who we will let down if we fail. What if somebody is expecting something from us? What if we don't meet their expectations? You think you might be able to avoid hurting others if you don't attempt the task at all.

You have to remember that you are not responsible for the emotions of other people. The only perspective that you control is your own. You can't put this amount of pressure on yourself. When you make your actions the sole factor in determining somebody else's emotions, it can weigh heavily on you. That immense pressure is going to make you crack. It's the very thing that keeps us from completing the task that needs to get done as fast as possible.

It's okay to let people down. You can't make everybody happy. Even if you were to complete a task correctly, they might still not be satisfied. We can't control how other people will react, so it's best that we focus on ourselves and our own responses.

Being a perfectionist. Perfectionists very often struggle with procrastination. If you are a perfectionist, you procrastinate because you know that you don't want to mess anything up. A perfectionist can avoid any criticism if they simply don't participate in the activity that needs their attention. A perfectionist is going to see all of the negative aspects of their work. They won't just want the overall project to be finished; instead, they will want everything to be perfect along the way.

Imagine that you're doing something such as losing weight. You procrastinate this task because it's not just about the weight that you want to lose. You want to have the perfect gym outfit. You want to take the perfect selfies. Perhaps you want the ideal Instagram stories to make people want to follow your life. You want every step along the way to be perfect. Unfortunately, a journey as difficult as losing weight is going to have a lot of negative aspects to it. It won't always turn out perfectly, so you have to learn to suspend that desire to fulfil those unachievable expectations.

Perfectionists believe that they're either a failure or a success, with no grey area in between. They don't see criticism as constructive, but instead use it to validate their biggest insecurities.

Remind yourself that if you are a perfectionist, you are looking to achieve something that is fundamentally unachievable. There is a famous saying that helps highlight this point, "Perfect is the enemy of done.' If you strive for constant perfection, you will never complete anything, as perfect is an unachievable goal. Focus on your underlying fears and what failure represents to you. Only when you tap into your most significant emotions are you going to be able to understand why you are putting yourself under so much pressure.

Low energy. Sometimes we lack the energy to get a task completed. It might be that you simply don't feel like doing something. You may rather lie on the couch and watch TV than do your work. Who wouldn't want to do this?

What we don't realise when we procrastinate for this reason is that we're making the enjoyable activity *less enjoyable*. You might not have the energy to get a project done, but you need to find it. You need to finish the task at hand so you can enjoy the activities that make you happy.

Rather than lying on the couch and watching TV from 8pm until midnight, and then trying to rush to get your project done after the fact, do your project from 8pm until 10pm. Once you have finished, let yourself lie on the couch and watch TV for the rest of the night. Your energy is only going to deplete as the night goes on, so you have to take advantage of what energy you have as early as possible.

If you are struggling to get something done because of your energy levels, give yourself a 20-minute nap. Alternatively, you might take a break; you can get a coffee, take a walk, or have a cold shower. Do something quick to increase your energy levels. Even if you only have the energy for 15 more minutes, that's still better than not getting any of the task done at all.

Sometimes kids can be draining. They can take the energy right out of us. Don't forget to schedule moments of self-care. It can be easy to feel you need to take care of a child all day long, but don't forget that you should put yourself first. If you have kids, permit yourself to go on a date night (or to do something similarly relaxing) every once in a while. Unhealthy diets can keep energy levels low. We'll discuss proper nutrition a little later on.

Lack of focus. If you have trouble focusing, it might make you unable to complete your tasks. When you lack focus, it's time to change your circumstances, not just your mindset. If you're sitting at your desk and you can't stop staring at the TV or using your phone, change your environment. Changing your environment could be as easy as spending the day or afternoon in your favourite coffee shop with your laptop and a pair of headphones. You could also make use of your local library. A change of focus now and again can-do wonders for increasing your concentration if you get stuck in a rut. If you have been working from home for an extended period, especially if you were forced into it during the 2020-2021 COVID-19 pandemic, then getting out of the house to work might not be an option. Changing the layout of your home office could give you the necessary environmental change that's required. You need to be very careful with this option, though; spending lots of time rearranging your workspace is fine once in a while to change up the environment but remodelling your room often can easily cross over into procrastination territory.

We often expect ourselves to begin to focus on demand. That's not going to happen all by itself. You need to train your brain to focus and then cultivate that ability and put all of your efforts into maintaining a high-level focus.

When you have trained your focus, you will find it is not as challenging to maintain your energy levels and complete your tasks.

. . .

Distraction is easy. Distraction is all around us. When you are procrastinating, it's all too easy to find ways to distract yourself. When you're bored, it's even easier to lose focus and become distracted. Some days, you may be able to work without being distracted by anything. However, on the days when you might be having trouble focusing, every little thing can be a distraction.

That project that you put off for five months suddenly becomes your main focus if you're trying to procrastinate. If you're somebody who hates doing dishes, you might clean the entire house (aside from the kitchen sink) as a form of procrastination. Distractions are going to be everywhere. Rather than letting ourselves give in to those distractions, we need to create the tools necessary to overcome them.

Think of the ways you are constantly being bombarded by Twitter, Facebook, Instagram, etc. These apps and sites can make it difficult for us to pay attention, too. We will soon discuss the importance of overcoming these distractions and maintaining focus.

General unpleasant tasks. Sometimes, the thing we don't want to do is the thing we really have to do. If your task is to go outside when it's snowing and shovel the driveway, that's not very fun. There's nothing exciting about it. If your task is to get up at six in the morning so you can go and work out, that's not fun either.

If you're unhappy with a task, it's rather easy to put it off. For example, paying your bills can be hard when it's the last thing you want to do.

The general unpleasantness of a task can encourage us to procrastinate. When this occurs, it's time to evaluate the situation and discover a way to make it more fun. For example, you might reward yourself for completing the unpleasant task with an activity you enjoy, like 15 minutes of video game time, or calling a friend to catch up over coffee.

Maybe the timing or location is wrong. Perhaps the actual task can be altered or broken down into bite-sized pieces. Sometimes, when you have a big task in front of you that needs to be tackled, it's not about hitting it head-on. You can strategise and look for a way to beat it. At the same time, you can make sure that it doesn't end up overwhelming you. Let's take a look at some of the best ways for you to overcome procrastination.

How to Overcome Procrastination

There are a few simple steps you can take to avoid procrastination. Begin first by noticing what tasks need to be done. Sometimes we feel overwhelmed when we consider all the things that we have to do. Instead, pay attention only to the most important task on your list.

Next, discover how you are procrastinating. What are you distracted by? Are you lost in your thoughts? Are you doing something productive?

Then, ask yourself *why* it is so hard to get the task done. If your answer is, "Because I don't want to do it," that's fine! To dive deeper, examine:

- If you're bored with the task.
- If it makes you uncomfortable.
- If you're afraid of failing.
- If there's something you'd rather do instead.
- If you're feeling overwhelmed.

You will usually discover that one of the reasons listed above is keeping you from completing your task. Once you discover your reason for procrastinating, you can begin to implement the following methods to help you genuinely overcome procrastination.

We are not perfect. To overcome perfectionism, remind yourself that perfection is completely unachievable. No one in all the world is perfect. Nobody has ever completed a task perfectly, either. It can be correct but still not perfect. As humans, we can be extremely self-critical. We can look at the things we've done and only pick out the mistakes. You'll likely never be 100% delighted with what you accomplish.

Rather than continuing to put immense pressure on yourself, focus on making sure you are not seeking perfection. Don't compete with others, either, or compare yourself to them. When you compare yourself to others, you will invariably compare their strengths to your weaknesses. You will notice what they are good at while ignoring what *you* excel in.

Then, when you look at yourself in comparison to others, you will notice what you are bad at instead of what you are good at. Our brains aren't always the best at logically analysing our abilities. You are just as good as your competition because you are unique and dedicated.

There will always be circumstances that separate you from others. Ask yourself when setting goals if you would give your intentions to other people. Would you expect the same from them? Would you criticise others in the same way you criticise yourself? Do you believe they are better or worse because of what they've done? We often judge ourselves much harsher than we would any other person, but that is not fair. You are making unrealistic expectations for yourself. If you would not ask the same of a friend, why is it okay to ask that of yourself?

Failure is not fatal. Sometimes, we might try to avoid failure at all costs. In reality, you should embrace it. Failure is a healthy, natural part of the learning process, and can be your biggest teaching tool. It lets you know what you should and should not do.

Sometimes, the only way to gain perspective is to experience failure. Let yourself make mistakes. Have moments where things could have gone better. Allow yourself to feel those negative emotions associated with failure because that is what will help you grow the most. Give yourself the chance to fail because if you don't, you're also not giving yourself the chance to succeed.

If you're afraid you might fail, you can predict what might go wrong and try to avoid that. It's good to be prepared, to anticipate that you might fail, but not to the point that you develop a debilitating paranoia. You have to realise that the worst-case scenario is usually not as bad as you might expect. Failure shows you how to redirect your life. It's not just about what *not* to do. It helps you understand what you have to do next.

Consider an individual who continues to procrastinate rather than doing their homework. They're too afraid they're going to fail to actually start their assignment. In reality, failing one test is not the end of the world. Instead, you can let yourself fail and realise that it won't feel as bad as you thought it might. Then, the next time you're studying for a test, rather than sitting there and being anxious for two hours because you're scared of failing, you remember that even if you do fail, you'll survive; you'll move on. You can then put all of your attention towards actually healthily completing the task.

When you fail, that's just a reminder that you have a second chance. If you fail over and over again, it shows that you're not using these situations for proper growth. You're not giving your attention where it's needed; you're missing the lesson the failure is showing you. Instead, you are letting yourself be afraid and feeling bad because of these failures.

When you do have a moment where something goes wrong, and you could have made a different choice, really reflect on the mistake. Don't beat yourself up or feel bad. Instead, remind yourself that we all make mistakes, and this is simply an opportunity for you to learn and grow.

Do your best. Perfection is not real. It's an unattainable state that we need to stop chasing. You cannot expect a perfect outcome. As long as you're doing your best at all times, *that* is perfect. Perfection is simply the realisation that things could not be better. When giving your all in a situation, you are the most perfect you can be.

Sometimes, we have these high expectations for ourselves without realising that they are unachievable or impossible. You might expect yourself to make a trillion dollars in a year. In reality, you can't do that because it's impossible. It would help if you focused on doing your best, not on attaining your impossible goals. This is where comparing yourself to others can hurt your productivity. Focus on yourself and what you can do, not on other people.

Be happy with the outcome. When you fail, maybe it was because you waited until the last minute to complete your work. Maybe there was a mistake that you could have avoided. Perhaps you thought to yourself, "I should be doing better," as you were completing the task. You need to take that moment to reflect healthily. You still have to learn to be happy with the result of your work. Furthermore, when you do something well, you need to learn how to be happy with yourself. You shouldn't only reflect on negative results. If you would congratulate a friend on their achievements, giving yourself a little pat on the back for a job well done shouldn't be too difficult.

When raising a child, you don't just punish them for bad behaviour; you reward them for good behaviour as well, because this is how they will learn that these good behaviours have value. We need to reward our inner child in this same way. You need to speak to yourself with kindness.

Remind yourself that you are worthy, you have value and you have done great things. Even though you may not have achieved the best possible result, you still put your effort towards it. Your effort is what matters most. Knowing that you *could* have done better is knowledge of how you can do better next time. Don't only focus on your weaknesses and improving those, but on your strengths and the ways you're flourishing, too.

Think of someone that you look up to. Maybe it's a famous director or writer. Think about that person's first project. It might not have been their best work, but it was still a project that they poured their energy and effort into completing and putting it out into the world. The person you most look up to was able to take the good aspects of their work and build on them over time, eventually creating something even better. They didn't focus solely on their weaknesses; they were able to achieve greatness because they knew their strengths.

Set goals. There are two major steps in reaching all of your goals: Plan, and then Do. Make sure you're prioritising the right tasks. Each day, make a to-do list of the most important tasks and order them by what needs to be done first. Then, give yourself an estimate of how long each task might take to get done. Rather than doing tasks in the order you want to do them, do them in the order of what needs the most urgent attention.

Find someone to hold you accountable. If you tell someone else of your struggles, they can help ensure that you are focusing on doing the right things rather than becoming distracted. We're a little too good at quieting that inner voice that tells us what we should be doing, but it's much harder to shut off when it is coming from another person.

Whenever you set a goal, make sure it's achievable. It's easy to set extremely high goals, but when they're impossible to accomplish, they're only setting you up for disappointment.

Once you achieve a goal, set another. Make sure you are setting smaller goals and positively reinforcing your good behaviours. Not only will it make the larger goals easier to achieve, accomplishing something can boost your self-esteem and keep you productive.

Begin to separate your tasks into smaller ones. Rather than trying to sit there and do everything all at once, try to separate the larger task into several parts. If a task takes you two hours to complete, take it 30 minutes at a time. Once you've managed to complete a task, you can then focus on rewarding yourself.

Give rewards. Giving rewards is a way to encourage yourself positively. Too often, people will punish themselves for not doing their tasks. Don't reprimand yourself. Instead, use positive reinforcement to help encourage good behaviours by rewarding yourself on the successful completion of your work. Be proud of yourself when you act. You could have chosen to continue to procrastinate, but you didn't. That's something to be proud of.

Clean up as you work so that cleaning up doesn't become its own task. If you're working on a project that can get messy, like painting or crafting, clean up after yourself as you go along. This way, you are rewarding yourself by freeing up time it might have taken to clean up.

The harder the task, the greater the reward should be. Similarly, easier tasks should be rewarded in small ways. Don't reward an hour of work by going on a shopping spree or out to dinner. If you work for an hour, give yourself 15 minutes to do something you enjoy. Your rewards should take up less than a quarter of the time it took to complete the initial task.

. . .

Use positive self-talk. Use positive affirmations to remind yourself that you are going to complete a task. Often, we use negative affirmations without even realising it. These are phrases like, "You can't do this," or, "I never do anything right."

Focus on using happy affirmations that remind you of your worth and value. These include sayings like:

- I can do this
- I am worthy
- I am capable
- I have value

Forgive yourself if you have been procrastinating. It's easy to get caught up on ideas like, "I should have done this," or "I could have done that." Instead, pay attention to what you can do going forward. Your mistakes are opportunities to learn and grow.

How to Achieve Better Focus

To rid ourselves of bad habits, we have to work on our ability to focus. We must understand how we focus and how we lose focus. What might it be that is distracting you? What does that distraction offer you?

Maybe you have to finish your work, but the video game in front of you is providing you with more entertainment. One makes you feel good; the other makes you feel bad. How can you turn that around so the task you are completing makes you feel good? Focus on shifting your perspective.

Starting right away. The first thing you can do to help yourself is to start tasks right away. Don't sit around for thirty minutes before getting started. For example, let's say that you have to do the dishes after you get home from work. Don't go home and sit there for thirty minutes. Letting those dishes sit there only makes your free time less relaxing. Even if you don't want to, do the dishes straight away. The sooner you start something, the sooner you get it over with. So, do your best to get the job done from the moment you have the chance to start.

. . .

Multitasking. Many people multitask because they think this is the way to get things done the fastest. In reality, multitasking can make it harder to get a task done. Rather than giving one task at a time 100% of your focus, you're now giving two tasks about 40% of your attention each. That other 20% is spent transitioning from one task to the next.

You might get the two things done faster, but the quality of both may have suffered. Perhaps you get two things done within three hours, even though both tasks would have taken two hours each to do separately. However, a few days later, you get feedback and discover you have to edit your work more than you normally would. You might spend an additional two hours editing. You end up spending more time on the projects than you would have if you had focused on one at a time. Rather than multitasking and going back and forth, carve out time to dedicate yourself entirely to each task individually.

Over-schedule time. It's easy to be hopeful that you'll get tasks done faster than you think. For example, maybe you have three things to do that will take about an hour each. You managed to do one of these things in only half an hour in the past, so you set aside one-and-a-half hours to complete three tasks.

That's your first mistake. You can't schedule yourself based on your peak ability. You might be able to get something done quickly, but you should give yourself some wiggle room. You want to schedule even more time than you need to get things done. Don't give yourself three hours; give yourself four hours. You might get all three done in 30 minutes, and that's great! Then you have all that extra time to do something you enjoy.

It's better to have too much time than not enough. You should always try to avoid procrastination altogether; but in all likelihood, you will still procrastinate. Pencil in some extra time so that procrastination doesn't hurt your productivity.

The Author's Approach

I have had a strange relationship with focus and procrastination over the years. I used to be someone who could get nothing finished. My wife used to jokingly call me "Half-a-Job Haunts", as I would start a project, get bored with it after a while and move onto something else. By the time I was in my early thirties, I had got better at taming procrastination and improving my focus. The way I do it, though, flies in the face of conventional productivity advice.

Earlier in this chapter, I mentioned that multi-tasking can be very inefficient. If you multi-task throughout the day, then this is very much true. However, I multi-task projects all the time, and it is how I ensure I can get things finished.

For example, I will work intensively on a project for a month or two. Eventually I will start getting bored with that project, and I will do something else, intensively, for a few months. When I get bored with that project, I move back to the first project. Because I have had a few months' break from that project, I come back to it with fresh eyes. This technique is known as "slow motion multi-tasking", a phrase coined by Tim Harford in his 2019 TED talk, "A Powerful Way to Unleash Your Natural Creativity".

The cycle of moving through a project like this can go through two or even three iterations before I get to a completed project. For me, I believe this allows me to do my best work, and not having a boss breathing down my neck and nagging me about deadlines really helps.

I am not suggesting working this way will be good for everyone; just that it works for me, after decades of struggling with being unable to finish projects. When I go through this repetitive focus-switching process, I get a few projects close to release at the same time. I have had some friends comment that I seem super-productive because I release a lot so quickly. What they haven't seen is the six to nine months leading up to that point, where I have been working intensively on one project and then switching to another. I worked on this very book in this manner. I honestly don't think I would have ever been able to write a book of over 150,000 words as a one-project sitting. I dovetailed the writing of this book in between many other projects over a two-and-a-half-year period. Also, having a professional editor work on blocks of chapters at a time also helped put a natural break in the process towards the end of the book.

During the first coronavirus lockdown in the UK in 2020, I paused the writing of this book as well, as I didn't have the mental capacity to both write and homeschool my children. That also created a natural break in the project while I worked on something easier.

As I am finishing writing this book in early 2021, I am just near the end of another country-wide lockdown but being so close to the end of the project, I decided not to pause my writing this time.

I appreciate that there may be some productivity purist reading this section and wincing at the prospect of me flitting between projects, which is why I left it to the "Author's Approach" section. My advice is always to do what works for you. Working this way is best for me, now that I am self-employed, but that doesn't mean it will be best for everyone. This technique was most definitely not compatible with my full-time employed career. Companies don't like you stopping a project after a few months to work on something else, so in those cases I just had to push through it, and it was painful sometimes.

When I am working, I always put on noise-cancelling headphones. Whoever invented noise-cancelling headphones should get a Nobel Prize for Productivity (which I just invented), as they are brilliant at helping to drown out background noise. I like to listen to music when I work, but nothing with vocals, as I find them distracting. My personal favourite type of music to listen to when working is film soundtracks, which is essentially modern classical music. I can always zone out with a bit of Hans Zimmer playing. I don't play the music too loud, as it is bad for your hearing, but loud enough to be pleasurable.

For me, the working environment is crucial to getting a lot of productive work done. I have mentioned before in this book that I prefer to work from a rented office. I have the office set up just how I want it; it is comfortable, inviting and a great environment for work and free-thinking. Most importantly, there are no kids there arguing, which makes a big difference. I can work from home in small bursts of a day or two, but I find it very hard to work and live in the same environment. I am probably in the minority there, but I just prefer to keep my home and work life separate if I can. As you can imagine, the lockdowns of 2020 and 2021 made it difficult to be productive.

Summary

We are all going to procrastinate from time to time. Overcoming procrastination doesn't mean avoiding the task, finding a better way not to do it, or hoping that these issues go away with time. Don't wait around for the motivation to come to you. It's a mental process. You have to overcome the obstacle now, not later.

First, identify what it is that you must do. Ask yourself why you are procrastinating and notice the methods you use to avoid the things that need to be done. Dive deep to find the core cause of procrastination. If you do that, overcoming your procrastination will be far easier.

Remind yourself that you cannot drastically change yourself or your behaviours overnight. Lessening the amount of time you spend procrastinating will take time and effort. Do the bare minimum when you are struggling. If there is a daunting task in front of you that causes you to feel overwhelmed, start with the very first step. Take each moment as it comes and keep your brain centred on what is happening now. It's much easier said than done, but you can do it. Doing something is always better than doing nothing at all.

Workshop Questions

(1) For the following statements, mark yourself on a scale of zero to five; zero being "does not describe me at all", and five being "describes me perfectly".

1. I will often fail to meet work deadlines.
2. I am often late to appointments.
3. I very rarely get tasks finished on time.
4. I get overwhelmed by my daily tasks.
5. I delay making decisions.
6. I try to avoid getting started on difficult tasks.
7. I put off daily tasks.
8. I am scared of making the wrong decisions.
9. I try to justify my reasons for delaying getting tasks complete.
10. I am easily distracted.

11. I cannot finish a task unless it is perfect.

(2) Look around your work environment and make a list of anything that you can see as being a distraction, such as a TV, games console, or websites on your computer.

(3) Alongside the distractions, also write down what you can do to mitigate these distractions affecting your work.

17

THE BENEFITS OF STAYING SMALL AS AN ENTREPRENEUR

When starting a business, you will have many different options to adjust the size of your business and plan its future growth. Rather than going the traditional route of finding seed money, getting Venture Capital (VC) funding, and hiring a lot of staff, you can focus on being the sole employee of your company and building it slowly over time. This bootstrapping method of natural expansion instead of growth hacking gives you an opportunity to have more control over your company, feeling the full effects of the benefits yourself. By focusing on the advantages of staying small, you'll be able to excel in these areas, making the most of your small business.

There will always be an element of apprehension in being an entrepreneur. What if my company goes out of business? What if I don't make enough money? What if I lose everything? These are common fears for those who put their money into their own business. Having an investor means that you have other opinions to consider and individuals who can guide you to avoid some of the risk. That in itself can be the reason you might seek out other investors. However, attaching your business to anyone else also means bringing on entirely new risks. Fear can keep us from what we know is best, but when you learn to embrace these fears, they can be the very thing that helps your business thrive.

Falling prey to competitors. Competition is one of the most pressuring aspects for business owners wanting to go bigger. One of the best markets to get into is one that doesn't have any competition. However, in a world where you can find pretty much anything you want online, this market is dwindling.

There will always be competitors out there. Even if you don't have direct competition, mega retail corporations offer customers the lowest possible prices for many products, simply because they can afford to do so.

Though competition can be a scary thing, it can also be what helps us drive our business to the top. Customers are going to be looking for their best options, and that is where you can swoop in.

Don't let the fear of competition make you feel as though you need the advantage of an investor on your side. Instead, remember that being a small business might be the very quality that potential clients are seeking out. They may want that close connection to their products and are looking for legitimate companies that care.

Through your competitors, you can also discover what it is that sets you apart from the rest. You don't have to look at competitors and think, "What do they have that I don't?" Instead, look at them and ask, "What aren't they offering that I can?"

Avoiding failure. When you're playing with your own money, it's understandable to want to avoid failure at all costs. What if you invest in the wrong product? What if your advertising falls flat? What if customers aren't interested in what you have to offer?

The idea of failing can be terrifying, and that fear will often keep us from the exact lessons that can be learned from trial and error. Sometimes people will be afraid to give up. They will continue to push forward even though they should call it a day. Sometimes, instead of continuing with something you know isn't working, it's best to start over. It can feel defeating, but with that failure, you can learn something valuable out of the process.

Once you make a mistake, you know how to never make it again. Maybe your business has already failed, and now you've concluded that finding investment elsewhere is the only way for you to find success. This could be the case, but you might be able to do it on your own. If you worry about making the same failure again, seek out what it was that caused the lack of success in the first place. When you can find the leak in the ship, not only can you repair it, but you can learn how to build an even better ship next time.

Remaining patient. One challenge that entrepreneurs must learn to overcome is impatience. When you are offered a large sum by someone who wishes to invest in your company, it can seem like an answer to your hope of achieving your goals in a short time.

What you must remember is that your goals can be consumed by the hopes and desires of those who are giving you the money in the first place. Patience is one of the essential qualities of entrepreneurs. You want to wait for good things to come, because even though it takes time, when they do come, they will be all yours, and provide you with the solid foundation needed for continued success.

You can't build a house overnight; a baby takes nine months to grow; an acorn won't become a mighty oak tree in an hour. Though these things take time, they stay around for much longer. They provide you with strong foundations for a profitable business. A rapidly growing company can fall just as fast as it can rise if you aren't careful along the way.

The Risks of Growing Too Quickly

When aiming for rapid growth, you would do well to remember that there are risks that can't be overlooked. Getting a $100,000 investment from five different people might sound great—think of how much you could do for your business! Then think about how much they are going to make you do for your business, and how much control you may start losing. The risks might not be as significant for some companies, but when creating yours, you must consider the effects of these investors making potential demands on your business.

Think of someone who is a fast runner. They might be able to sprint quicker than you'd be able to manage, but the faster they run, the harder they will fall. Likewise, in a rapid-growth business, the consequences of a mistake are likely to have a far greater impact.

It is much better to allow your business to grow slowly from the ground up. You will be able to more easily pick yourself back up once you've tripped and stumbled, than you will if you've slammed hard into the ground.

You can also take this slower process as a chance to deeper investigate what it was that caused the downfall. You might have made a mistake or had a moment of failure, and it went by so fast at the time that you weren't able to process what actually happened. You can overlook the minor things that cause a considerable ripple effect if you are too focused on quickly getting over it and starting again.

Lacking innovation. The larger the company you run, the more difficult it can be to adapt to a rapidly changing market. You have to get things approved by several people at once, instead of being able to do things more quickly on your own.

Having more people involved in a company means having more ideas flowing in and out. It also means having more people whom the concept has to get by. You could have a board of ten people for your company, nine of whom support an innovation or initiative. Still, that one dissenting person could keep the idea from becoming a reality.

It can take weeks to approve decisions; and if one investor disagrees, you have to start all over again. You might spend a month coming up with a pitch only to be shot down and have to create an entirely new proposal. If you were to come up with a new idea on your own, you can implement it and see results within the time it would take to go through everyone else.

A company that's all about making money can sometimes play it safe instead of experimenting with new ideas and innovations. When you have investors, you are obligated to serve their interests. Mostly, investors aren't giving you money because they believe in your message or vision; they are investing because they believe in your ability to make them more money. If you don't fulfil that promise, they can pull their funds, and this can often mean taking the safe route and sticking to what you already know makes money, rather than trying out new things and seeking innovation.

Being overly optimistic. Whenever you get involved with investors, you might get a little overly optimistic. You have more financial freedom, which means you have more options for what to bring to your business. You can take more significant risks and invest in more ideas because the money is going to help support that. At the same time, all of this optimism can be rather blinding.

It's easy to hope that you can satisfy all parties, but this isn't always entirely possible. There will always be someone that is frustrated; saying "yes" to one person can mean saying "no" to another.

Getting a large investment from others might make you feel like you will have things more comfortable. Other partners and more financial padding can alleviate many fears. However, running a business will be a challenge no matter its size.

When there is a setback, it can feel hard to deal with, especially when the setback affects others in a larger company. When you're running your own company, it's easier to expect that there will be moments when you make mistakes, but the burden of dealing with those mistakes lies with you alone. While it can be harder to deal with setbacks on your own, the effects are limited to just yourself, which can make dealing with a setback easier.

The Benefits of Staying Small

One of the most important aspects of staying small is the endless freedom you'll have. You are the boss. You are the single person that others will go to when they need help or have a problem. You have the final say, and this is a great benefit, but it can also be your greatest fear.

You are the one that has to pull the plug on ideas. You are the one that has to say, "No." You are the one that will hurt the most when the business takes a fall. The buck stops with you.

While these fears might exist, you can't let them overshadow the advantages of being the one in charge in a small business. You get to do whatever you want, whenever you want. You can decide where to put your money and what products to make or services to provide. That doesn't mean you have to do this alone, either! You can hire others for their expert advice and conduct research to hear what your customers want. Though you are the one that might take the biggest hit, you're also the one that will see the biggest rewards.

Connecting with the customer. As a small business, your most significant advantage will be connecting with your customers at a more personal level. Don't just think of every person that walks through the door as a transaction. Envision them as an investment through an ongoing relationship. By making that connection, you're setting your company up for life. Not only will they give you money at that moment, but they are more likely to be repeat customers.

Earning the trust of your customers can be more easily achieved when you take the time to get to know them. You will be able to discover who they are and why they are seeking you out as a business. Perhaps they like one of your products or services. It could be your overall product design aesthetic that has managed to attract them. Repeat customers are an essential aspect of any growing business. Not only will they return for future transactions, but they will also tell people they know about your company.

Unexpected changes. A small business is going to have a lot more flexibility. Maybe you get to a point where a product isn't working in the marketplace, or perhaps a new trend in the market has emerged that you want to try. These things can take months to implement within a larger corporate structure because of the time the approvals process can take. Everyone has to be on board when making a big change. Even after everyone has agreed, you'll have to take time to train employees and work out any kinks in the idea.

When it's just you, or maybe a small team, you can quickly try out new ideas with minimal risk and bureaucracy. You can swap around merchandise in your store. You can change prices on your website overnight. You can approve decisions rapidly and change up your production levels. You are the one deciding what to do with the money with no one stopping you in between. One small change can have a ripple effect across the entire company. When the pond is small, the ripples won't travel as far.

Taking risks. Even if something fails or doesn't go according to plan, you can bounce back much quicker than a large business. When you're working with investors and a vast team, they're usually focused on growing their initial investment. Of course, we sometimes get money from people close to us, such as long-time partners or even family members. Aside from these outliers, those who give you their money trust that in doing so, you will provide them with a larger return.

They're not doing this as a gamble, and they won't be interested in risking all their cash. Instead, they will make choices based around the guarantees you make. The bigger you are as a company, the larger the crater will be after you fail. Not only might you have to deal with the aftermath of the risk falling through, but you could also lose the trust and faith from your investors after a proposed business plan doesn't work out as expected.

When you take a risk as a small business, and the worst-case-scenario occurs, you only have to clean up the mess for yourself, not a team of angry investors.

Your business, your money. By staying a small company that you gradually build up over time without relying on investors, any profit that you make is yours alone. When you have investors who all have a stake in your company, a portion of those profits will eventually have to be divided between those investors as dividends. Paying out those dividends is how the investors make their return; while their investment helped you to grow the business, you ultimately start to lose control over the money that you make.

The freedom that comes with running a small business by yourself can be one of the most beneficial aspects to staying small. The money you make is yours and yours alone. You choose how much money is used to invest in future ideas, and how much you will take in return from the profits when you have paid your tax bill. You might have less money in a shorter space of time than you could with investors, but you will ensure you have as much control over your money as possible, and that feeling of control can be so fundamental when you are starting in business.

Important Strategies

The benefits of owning your own business without investors are clear. Staying small gives you more freedom, flexibility, and control. You might make more money in the first place in a large business, but it comes with so many inherent risks that it's a gamble that won't always offer a return in the end.

Remember to dedicate yourself to your business consistently—and this doesn't just mean making as much money as possible, as fast as possible. Instead, focus on creating a strong structure and foundation for a long-lasting business. It's better to make a substantial $500,000 in profit over ten years, rather than $500,000 in one year with a company that fails after 15 months because you have too many overheads.

Create a story. Your biggest asset as a small company is the personal story that you associate with the business. Why should people choose you? What is it about your brand and your business that pulls other people in?

When people choose to go to a small business rather than a larger corporation, there is often a more personal reason. If it were about money, they would choose the cheapest option. If it were about quality, they'd still be able to find that elsewhere even if it meant paying more.

People coming to a small business want to find a personal connection to your company, and that's where creating a story will help. Let people get to know you and your brand. Explain what prompted you to start your business and what need you are seeking to fill. Help them become a part of the company, not just a person who gives their money to you. We will be talking more about branding and personal branding later in the book.

Social media engagement. Small businesses have customers who tend to be more willing to buy online. Not only will they seek you out on social media, but they will share it with people that they are close to within their social groups, which allows you gain new customers as well as repeat customers.

If your customers write social media posts about your products or services, make sure you share their posts where they have tagged you or your products. Don't just keep your business on your website. Immerse yourself into the everyday lives of your customers and engage with them on visible public social networks. Frequent social media engagement gives your business a personal touch that will help to set you apart from larger faceless companies. People enjoy being paid attention and tend to be more willing to buy from someone that they can make a connection with online who doesn't look or feel like just another corporate social network robot. Making the effort to make that personal touch and connect with your client base is how you will create a dedicated following that keeps your company thriving.

Taking in feedback. When you're close with each customer that comes through your door or visits your site, you'll be able to take in the feedback they have to provide. When listening to feedback, you can understand their needs better and know what they want from your company in the future.

When you release a new product or services, it will rarely be perfect straight away, and it is this valuable feedback from a customer that helps you develop and refine your products further. You can think of this as a collaborative relationship with your customers. Feedback will not always be friendly, especially online, but even from what feels like hostile and negative feedback, you can pick up on a general theme and use that to help improve your product.

This also highlights the importance of good social media engagement; when someone leaves a review about your product online, you can engage with them and send a reply. You should always thank people for feedback and reviews, whether positive or negative. If someone does leave a negative review, never overreact or have a go at the customer, even if they are horrible to you. Just thank them; if possible, advise them what action you will be taking to rectify the issue for the future (or if it's something you can fix, reach out to them); and then try to learn as much as you can from their feedback. In the end, it will help you create better products or services.

Eventual expansion. You don't have to stop the process of growth with your company just because you're a small business. You can still expand over time and create new products, but you should aim be in control of that growth and do it organically and on your own terms if you can, as opposed to relying on the whims of investors. You can get creative with the ways that you can expand, and in a way, that's exciting for your close customers. You can also make sure that you are offering new products and taking your money and putting it towards innovation. Rather than simply getting bigger, the focus can be on getting better, expanding the money along the way.

The Authors Approach

I have previously mentioned that I did not intend to scale too much, which led to my decision not to hire any full-time staff. While I do want to grow the business over time, I am happy to take a steady approach to this. When I was considering when to leave my full-time job and instead go full time building online courses, I discussed the situation with my wife, and set some targets to hit. While we both agreed that me working for myself was going to work out in the long run, both of us are relatively risk-averse, so the timing had to be right. Fortunately, the business of making online training courses became profitable very early on, so I saved as hard as I could. The trigger for me quitting my job and going full time was having one year's salary saved up as a buffer. I fully appreciate that saving to that level is not what a lot of people would do. I know people who have quit their jobs with only a few months' worth of pay saved up, but that felt like too much of a risk for me personally.

My wife and I also reviewed all of our spending to see where we could optimise. As with a lot of families, it becomes too easy to spend more than you think over time, so we cut back on some things that were not important, and this made financial planning feel better for us.

To make the transition from full-time employment to self-employment feel as normal as possible for my wife, I agreed to pay myself the same salary that I was earning in my previous job. This was made possible because it was getting easier to predict my income from the views of my course, and the fact that I had a large buffer saved up. From my wife's point of view, when I paid myself, it was the same amount of money going into our joint account; the only difference being that the transaction on the bank statement said my name instead of my previous employer's name.

I also decided early on that I was not going to seek any funding for my business. In a traditional start-up situation, it is common for the founders to seek investment from angel investors, seed funds and potentially, venture capitalists. It is also common for founders to take out large loans and spend on credit cards to start their companies. This was never going to be an avenue I explored. I'm not too fond of debt, and by taking investment, you begin to lose control of your business. I wanted to be entirely in control. Successes are my own, and any failures are my fault and my fault alone.

Everyone has a different tolerance and appetite when it comes to growth, debt and financing; mine is to be cautious. I want to grow the business and earn more, but I am happy taking a slow and steady approach to it as long as all my and my family's needs are met.

Summary

While an initial investment offer might seem like a great deal, there are many risks that can actually outweigh the benefits. Give yourself the opportunity to explore the many advantages of remaining the sole owner of your company and staying small.

As an entrepreneur, there will be many hiccups you run into along the way. These include:

- Lacking innovation
- Being too optimistic
- Putting your money all in one place

Instead, discover the benefits of being a sole owner, such as:

- Taking risks that are more easily managed
- Adapting to change
- Flexibility

Your company shouldn't just be about making money. Make something great that continues to provide not just to your customers, but to your future self.

Workshop Questions

(1) With your business and product idea in mind, take two sheets of papers and label one of them, "Staying Small" and the other one "Going Large". Imagine what your business might look like in both circumstances. Think about the following aspects:

1. The advantages of staying small for your circumstances.
2. The disadvantages of staying small for your circumstances.
3. The advantages of growing larger for your circumstances.
4. The disadvantages of growing larger for your circumstances.
5. Does either case make you feel worried or anxious?

(2) If you were going to increase the size of the company, work out some example costs for doing so. Consider the following:

1. How many staff you think you would need, and the relevant market rate? You should consider both freelance/contract rates and full-time employee salaries.
2. Look at your local market for costs of suitable office space.
3. Consider additional costs like insurance, etc.

Now that you have a rough yearly figure, work out how many units of your product, or paying customers for a service, you would need in order to break even and cover your costs.

(3) Repeat the second exercise, but this time apply the costs to keeping your business smaller; such as yourself being the only staff, working from home or utilising a small office/co-working space, etc.

(4) When you have completed parts two and three, you can use these projections to help you decide if you want to keep the business small or increase its size over time.

18

HIRING EMPLOYEES VS FREELANCERS

Whether you're an entrepreneur with too much on your plate or a company owner looking to slash costs, hiring freelancers over employees might seem like a convenient option. But is it? While the number of freelancers worldwide grows year after year, and outsourcing projects to qualified remote workers becomes increasingly attractive, there are also risks involved with trusting someone outside your company with meaningful work.

The possibility of remote work is changing the views on doing business and re-defining work. There is an increase in people choosing to work as freelancers and consultants. Research shows that nearly 34% of the US workforce freelances either full time or part time. Freelance work contributes $715 billion annually to the economy. The increase in US freelance workforce from 53 million, measured in 2014, to over 56 million in 2018 may be explained by the fact that more and more employers are cutting benefits to slash costs, with technology developments enabling and supporting remote work. Also, there's an ever-growing number of freelancers available through platforms like Fiverr, Upwork, etc., not to mention those on LinkedIn and those who check out online job boards for opportunities.

Who Are Freelancers?

Freelancers are individuals who are qualified and experienced in providing project-based services within a specific industry. Whether it's IT, marketing, freelance writing, graphic design, or another field, freelancers represent independent workers who seek clients for short or long-term projects. Most often, freelancers work remotely or online, although it's possible to find those who work directly with clients in their local area.

Unlike company employees, freelancers are entrepreneurs who run their own service-based businesses, and this makes them somewhat similar to company owners; they run their accounting books, have business bank accounts, and pay taxes. Like all entrepreneurs, freelancers seek to grow their business and increase their network of clients using methods like publishing blogs, advertising their websites, and promoting their portfolios, which are the collections that showcase the most prominent pieces of their work.

Freelancers mainly work on projects that can be both short- and long-term, and they most often work with multiple clients and on multiple projects simultaneously to secure their business. However, a freelancer isn't an ordinary employee. Considering that they run their own business, freelancers operate by applying for projects or reaching out to prospective clients directly, undergoing interviews, and giving proposals based on the estimated value of tasks at hand.

While freelancers are often solopreneurs, the nature of their work can often blur the line between an independent contractor and a company employee. This chapter will help you distinguish the two by going into more detail about how to set the two apart and how to decide whether to work with freelancers or to hire employees.

What Distinguishes a Freelancer from an Employee?

Many business owners have suffered the consequences of trying to cut costs by reducing their headcount and hiring freelancers for regular work. Doing so could get you in trouble with the Internal Revenue Service (IRS) and the Department of Labor in the US, or a department like Her Majesty's Revenue & Customs (HMRC) in the UK. Most countries will have an equivalent government tax department. Whether the changes are noticeable in your paperwork or a former contractor with a grudge decides to claim their rights, you could find yourself in legal proceedings for seemingly no reason. This mainly happens if you don't draw a good line between your freelancer and employees (if you choose to have any). Mistakes are easier to make than you think, which is why it's essential to understand what sets freelancers apart from employees in the eyes of your staff, contractors, and the law. Here are a couple of specifics to keep in mind when working with freelancers.

Independence. How much is the individual free to determine their work hours, personal responsibility, and involvement with the work? The more a person can decide on all aspects of the work, the more they are likely to be considered a freelancer. With an employee, you are dictating the majority of the work process, from work hours to payment. However, with a freelancer, you are in a negotiating position. You are not setting the terms on your own, but instead negotiating with the freelancer on all aspects of the job.

Usually, you and the freelancer meet either in person or online to discuss all aspects of the project, from goals to tasks, timetables, and payment. Unlike an employee, who applies for a job by making an argument as to why they think themselves to be the best fit, a freelancer focuses on the project that needs to be done and negotiates their terms for doing the work. Unlike an employee, who agrees on a pay cheque, a freelancer determines the cost of their service based on the intricacies of the project, like size, volume, complexity, duration, and resources that will go into the work. As such, the freelancer is more similar to a supplier than an employee.

No obligation. Full employment is more interdependent than freelance. A freelancer isn't obliged to take up nor finish the work, and they can pull out from the agreement at any time, unlike an employee. Your employee needs to follow company requirements and policies, from work hours to dress code, while the freelancer's only duty is to provide the work laid out in the independent contractor agreement (ICA).

While it may be awkward—and often is, working with someone who is under no obligation to follow through with the contract—you are also without a responsibility to keep paying the freelancer when you no longer see the need for their involvement. Unlike an employee, ending an ICA doesn't require any other conditions aside from paying for the work that's already completed. This means that when it comes to contracts, both you and the freelancer are free to end the collaboration as you see fit.

Possibility of substitution. Does your freelancer have the right to use a substitute, or are they required to work with you personally and directly? Most often, working with freelancers comes with the possibility of them having someone else doing the work for them. An employee, on the other hand, is solely responsible for the job. Pay attention to whether or not the contract contains a substitution clause. If you want to make it clear that your freelancer isn't an employee, add the clause that gives them the option of finding another expert who'll fill in for them in case they're unable to finish the work.

How to prevent misclassification. Hiring freelancers to do the employee's work for the purposes of cutting costs is also known as misclassification, and it is illegal in the US. Misclassification can happen unintentionally if you aren't careful enough to set clear boundaries with the freelancer. The classification of freelancers and contractors can also be a problem in the UK, too, with the IR35 legislation having big tax implications if a freelancer or contractor is being treated as a disguised employee. This partly came about as staff members were resigning as employees and coming back straight away on higher day rates to do the same work. Here are a few tips to avoid being accused of misclassification.

Don't treat the freelancer the same as an employee. Many business owners like to stay on good terms with their freelancers, so they start treating them like employees, especially if they are located close to each other in the same town or city. They offer benefits or additional perks to make them feel like they're a part of the team. However, it's essential to make a distinction between contractor and employee, both internally and externally.

Don't use company resources. Freelancers should use tools that they own, such as laptops, phones and any other devices they need to complete a project. It's expected of them as professionals, and the only exception is if the work requires any specialist equipment, specific to a particular project, that would be out of the ordinary for a freelancer to own. If you're allowing freelancers access into your systems, be sure to limit their access to company tools and information. This means that you should provide the freelancer with the tools that are necessary to do the job but ensure they don't have access or privileges higher than is necessary for them to work.

Don't tie them down. A freelancer shouldn't be obliged to work with a single company. Instead, they should have the freedom to work with multiple clients, independently from your project. While a freelancer can spend time working exclusively on a more extended project, it is important to consider that the longer the freelancer spends working on your project, the more likely they are to be seen as an employee—particularly in terms of the IR35 tax regulations in the UK that we mentioned earlier.

Hiring Freelancers: Advantages and Disadvantages

Let's look deeper into the advantages and disadvantages of working with freelancers in your business. We'll start with some advantages.

Reducing costs. When you account for the total time spent on the project, freelancer agreements can be about 20-30% less expensive than employment agreements; and potentially, you can save even more. With a remote freelance worker, you don't have to pay for office space, supplies, benefits, or anything else. You are paying solely for someone's time to use their expertise to complete a piece of work or a small project. For a small company, this is very important as it lets you manage your money more carefully.

Take this book as an example. Once the chapters have been written, I hand them off to a professional editor to straighten them up for me. I don't employ the editor. We have a freelancer agreement where I am charged a price per block of words, which means it is easy to budget how much it will cost to edit the book. Once the price is agreed, I pay a portion upfront and then settle the rest on delivery. The editor doesn't work exclusively for me; she takes on other clients at the same time. This means my editor can manage her workload, and I can pay for the services that I need. Achieving this level of flexibility is fantastic and cost-effective.

Reducing risk. Depending on where you live, when you fire full-time staff, they have certain rights that they are entitled to—and rightly so, such as sick pay, holidays etc. There are also many employment rules and laws that you, as an employer, have to comply with. If someone goes off sick for a long time, or you make a bad hire and need to replace them, this can be very costly to your business in terms of both money and time. You can also incur a lot of stress in managing a team of people whose livelihoods you are responsible for supporting. While this may make it sound like hiring staff is bad and to be avoided, that isn't the intention.

Hiring full-time staff in certain situations makes sense; but for a lot of tasks that need doing when you run a small business, a freelancer makes more sense as you do not have to incur any of these overheads. If a freelancer has to take time off, you don't cover their sick leave or their holidays. Your only risk is that a freelancer might be late delivering something, but that can be resolved by regularly talking to each other.

As the engager of the freelancer, your risks are reduced. All you have to worry about is the price for the job, the impact of late delivery and how to handle the potential problem of low quality of the final delivery.

. . .

Talent diversity. Screening freelancers gives you more possibilities to detect talent in the exact areas you need. As an employer, you are offering a working position within your company; as a company looking for a freelance worker, you're discussing a project or a specific piece of work. There's a big difference here, as your focus isn't on finding someone to fill in a position, but instead to follow through with the exact demands of the work. With this in mind, you can screen freelancers specifically for the work you need to be done, and for the time they're needed. With an employee, you commit to hiring and paying them for a certain amount of time, even when the work is no longer necessary.

Better performance. Freelancers depend on the quality of their work to get reviews, recommendations, and references. They also run their own businesses, so depend a lot more on the quality of their work and client satisfaction than employees. With freelancers, you can expect more emphasis on quality as they always do the best they can.

Large talent pool. Working with freelancers allows you to reach talent across the globe, which often means getting work done for lower cost. It also minimises risks in case relationships and projects don't work out. Not every freelancer engagement will be successful. If you have issues with a freelancer or the quality of their work, you can simply choose to not hire them again. If the same issue happens with a full-time employee, this can be a much harder problem to deal with, as you would need to either coach them to maximise their potential or consider managing them out of the business.

High speciality. Freelancers usually specialise in a single area, making them highly effective in the type of service they provide. Also, they have broad experience in doing similar projects for other clients, continually building their knowledge and developing skills.

. . .

Available on a project basis. Working with freelancers allows you to hire talent as needed, giving you the flexibility to hire experts in the areas required, strictly during the necessary time frame. It also allows you to hire different experts for different types of projects, all without having to commit to a long-term contractual agreement.

No geographic constraints. Another great benefit of using freelancers is there are no geographic constraints on who you hire. You don't need to hire anyone who lives locally; you can pick and choose from a global talent pool. With our highly connected digital lifestyle, we have all the tools we need to collaborate with and deliver high-quality work from the computers in front of us. As an example, as the author of this book, I live in the United Kingdom. My book editor lives and works in Perth, Western Australia, and the designer of the book cover lives and works in Germany. The physical miles between us all make no difference as we can communicate via email, or if need be, with a video call. If you need to collaborate with the freelancer frequently during the project, then you need to consider time zones, as having someone in a similar time zone is going to be more convenient for you both. Using the editing of this book as an example: my editor and I couldn't live much further apart if we tried. Still, the work we do together doesn't require much real-time collaboration, so if there is half a day between email replies, it is not an issue.

As you can see, there are many advantages to hiring freelance workers. Now let's look at a few disadvantages.

Stretched thin. Freelancers rarely focus on your project with the same level of commitment that an employee does. As they are always looking for new opportunities and new clients while carrying out the work you need completed, they have their own schedules that require coordinating. While an employee works on your terms and to your schedule, a freelancer is an independent contractor who determines their own hours and availability. Adding to that, there is the possibility that they might drop you if your project no longer serves their financial goals, the same way you can back out of the deal; although this is unprofessional, I have had it happen to me before. This can cause trouble if they have a rare set of skills or the project requires a long-term commitment. To prevent risks with freelancers, many companies hire a team of individuals, in case someone becomes unavailable.

Lack of relationship. A relationship with an employee is one of commitment and loyalty; with a freelancer it is one of personal interest. While freelancers generally love having long-term clients, their math is based solely on how your work meets their financial goals. As freelancers can't count on the safety of an employment contract, they need to choose—and drop—clients with the same calm rationality a CEO uses to fire a redundant workforce. This also affects your in-house relationships. If your work requires maintaining relationships with clients or customers, you can't entirely rely on freelancers for that. With employees, you have a mutual goal, which is the growth of the company that fills everyone's bank accounts, pays insurance, and secures retirement.

Absence of monitoring for remote freelancers. Unless the work hours are agreed upon, freelancers choose their own hours that may or may not be compatible with yours, especially if they are remote workers; this can make keeping an eye on their work performance difficult. Employees, on the other hand, work hours dictated by your company and are available to train and supervise as needed. When I work with freelancers, I tend to book them for work where I can set a clear set of requirements and goals up front, and then they can work on them without checking in all the time. If they are working on something that takes a month to deliver, then I might check in once a week or once every two weeks. If it is work that you need to collaborate very closely with them on, a freelance relationship can be very hard unless they are working at the same location as you.

If you specifically need to work on a project with a remote freelancer that does require more frequent collaboration and monitoring, then this is fine. Still, it should be something you plan for, and you discuss and agree on the rules of engagement upfront before starting the work. You should also bear in mind that a freelancer may be working on multiple projects at the same time and not exclusively your project, unless agreed upfront.

The relationship between you and the freelancer is based on trust. You shouldn't need to keep on top of them regularly to get a piece of work delivered. You trust that they will deliver by the time you both agreed. If that trust breaks in either direction, then you can choose not to hire them again, or they can choose not to work with you. This level of flexibility is quite refreshing.

Misaligned goals. There's more goal alignment with employees than there is with freelancers. Remember, freelancers work to establish their name and reputation, while employees share your goal in growing your business, as it simultaneously grows their careers. This means that employees will be more committed to your work than the freelancer, and more motivated to contribute to your company's growth. This particularly goes if there's an opportunity for promotion, where the majority of employees will work hard to upscale their career.

Questionable reliability. When you're working with freelancers, you're working with individuals who have the opportunity to fake or inflate their reviews, portfolio, and claims of expertise. Regardless of their reputation, it's always possible for a freelancer to not deliver the quality promised.

Failing to deliver can happen for numerous reasons: exaggerating their skills to land a project; over-scheduling themselves in order to profit; agreeing to do tasks beyond their abilities; dropping projects due to emergencies; or merely disappearing. While working with a freelancer can potentially save costs and secure the right talent for the job, it can also cost you more if they don't follow through with the agreement. Considering that neither of you is legally obliged to carry out the work, there's very little you can do to compensate for the time lost in case the freelancer abandons the project half-way through.

Hiring Employees: Advantages and Disadvantages

As with hiring freelancers, there are pros and cons to having permanent employees. Let's start with some of the advantages.

Commitment and loyalty. If you have staff already, then your employees' financial security depends on the growth of your company. They understand that the better they do their job, the more likely they are to have long term, stable work. Freelancers don't share the same commitment to your company, as growing their own brand and business is their top priority.

Training. With employees, you can monitor their progress and skills to decide where and when they need an upgrade. By training employees, you are enabling them to work in a manner and with a skill set necessary for your growth. With freelancers, the degree of expertise remains unfamiliar until you see the results of their work. This is also the time when you're obliged to pay, even if the quality isn't as promised and the claims of expertise prove to be exaggerated. Investing in your employees by giving them upskilling opportunities within your company also fosters loyalty to you as an employer, and often sees a return on that investment in your employees' commitment and quality.

In-house knowledge. Having a team of permanent employees helps you create an authentic working climate, and your staff to navigate the work process according to your goals and company values. Employees know and understand your company policies, and they will do a better job of incorporating them into the work. This is important across all areas and project phases, from knowing how to design graphics to understanding what communication style to use when creating content and talking to third parties. Simply put, employees are capable of understanding and representing you better. A freelancer getting to know your brand for the first time risks misinterpreting instructions and losing potential benefits of having the work done in alignment with your brand values and policy.

While we can definitely see there are advantages to hiring full-time staff, let's now look at some of the disadvantages.

Financial obligation. You're obliged to pay employees even when the work is slow, and you're also obliged to pay additional taxes and employee benefits. This can be overwhelming if you're a start-up or an entrepreneur. Depending on the size of your business, supporting full-time employees can prove to be unattainable. This particularly goes for entrepreneurs who can't rely on a constant workflow to support the headcount.

Having full-time employees usually means additional costs, such as office space, utilities, supplies, etc. Freelancers usually work within their own space and use their own resources, saving you the extra cost should you not wish to rent an office space. After the Coronavirus lockdowns of 2020 and 2021, the dynamic of the workplace is changing so that full-time employees are more accustomed to working remotely. At the time of writing, it is unclear how many companies will move back to their original office, go completely full-time off-site, or run a blended model.

Missed talent. Limiting your team to local professionals, if you want them to work in-house, can cost you missed skills and expertise. When hiring remotely, you have the opportunity to screen and interview a larger number of applicants, compare their portfolios, and obtain rarer talents.

How to Decide Whether to Hire an Employee or a Freelancer?

How can you decide between hiring a freelancer and hiring an employee? Here a few things to consider.

. . .

The size and complexity of the project. If your work is project-based and temporary, you could benefit from an independent freelance worker. However, whether you choose a freelancer, agency, or a consulting company depends on the size and the complexity of the project. Keep in mind that freelancers are individuals, and as such, can only tackle a limited workload as they usually work for multiple clients simultaneously, which could impact when you get work delivered and how long it takes.

Dependency and responsibility. While employees may depend on you for training, instructions, and guidance, freelancers work independently. When hiring a freelance workforce, they should already be familiar with your requirements and be able to negotiate the terms. Also, freelancers function as independent businesses, which means that they pay their own taxes and run their own business administration. Essentially, working with a freelancer is a good idea if you're confident that you want to turn the job over to someone else without having to train and monitor them.

Unlike employees, freelancers work on their terms and participate in determining the compensation. While some freelancers dictate their rates, others prefer negotiating the price. Most often, freelancers will have a set of rates depending on the difficulty, complexity, and volume of the project. Still, working with freelancers can be a budget-friendly way for you to add talent, innovation, and competitiveness to your business.

What's particularly important is that freelancers have the so-called breadth versus depth of experience, meaning they probably have experience working on projects similar to yours across multiple companies and different business settings. They have a broader picture of the necessary work for the desired result, unlike employees who might be facing the project for the first time.

Resource and skill availability. If you don't have a necessary skillset in-house, then you're better off with a freelancer. Also, if the project requires resources that you don't possess and aren't required for future projects, then hiring a freelancer or an agency who are equipped with the tools needed to do the work is a better idea. The same goes for training. If training your staff to do the work would be a necessity, it would take up both their time and your resources. On the other hand, investing in a freelancer would mean that you don't have to spend money on training, as it is their responsibility to keep their skills up to date.

Project demands. If your project demands constant monitoring, in-house knowledge and experience, and nurturing relationships with your clientele, then hiring staff members is likely a better choice. However, if the work can be done as a side-project, with less involvement from you and your staff, and can be completed with less monitoring, you're better off with a freelancer.

Another point to think about is whether or not the work is pre-defined with particular deliverables. If not, an employee would be a better choice, as a measurement of achievement is necessary for successful freelance work. If you can't agree on the type of results to expect, it's hard to determine the work process, rates, and deadlines with a freelancer. On the other hand, if the work requires tools and equipment that are specific to your company, an employee is a better choice. Not only are they better trained to use your resources, but it's also less likely that someone will use your ideas to either copy or emulate them into their process and create competition. This is important if you're hiring freelancers within your industry when there's a chance that they can use your project input to profit on their future projects, hence creating competition.

Employees vs. Freelancers Checklist

To help you decide between hiring a freelancer or hiring an employee, here are two short checklists.

You should hire a freelancer if:

1. You're an entrepreneur with inconsistent workflow and no existing employees.
2. The cost of training your current staff justifies outsourcing the project.
3. You don't have the resources that the new project demands.
4. Your project demands talent and skills that your current staff don't have.
5. Your project is temporary or short term.
6. Your project is long term, but a once-off.
7. The project can be done remotely.
8. The work can be outsourced for a lower price.
9. The project doesn't require fixed work hours.
10. The project doesn't demand skills that are specific or unique to your brand/business.
11. The work doesn't demand thorough knowledge of your company's policies, values, or work process.

On the other hand, you should hire an employee if:

1. The work is regular.
2. The project requires familiarity with your clientele, work processes, policies, and company values.
3. The project requires talent that's available in-house.
4. You have the resources required for completing the project.
5. The project doesn't have tangible results or deliverables to measure success.
6. Training your current staff is more feasible compared to outsourcing the work.
7. The volume of the work doesn't interfere with the usual workflow.
8. The project requires regular or constant monitoring.
9. The project requires consistent work hours.

The Authors Approach

From the point that I decided to leave my full-time employment and work for myself full time, I decided that I did not want any employees. The thought of having people working for me, depending on me for their incomes, filled me full of dread. I have been a senior leader for many companies where I have had to make decisions that impact people's livelihoods, but this was not what I wanted for my venture.

If I had gone the route of employing people, then I would have scaled the business faster, as I would have had people to help me produce courses and online content, and to help with the organisation of classroom workshops. I decided early on that massive scale was not important to me. Don't get me wrong—I do want to scale and grow, and in turn, earn more—but I only needed to take my business to a level that provides a comfortable life; one that allows me to work on the projects that are important to me, and to spend more time with my family.

In hindsight, I feel as though I made the right decision in not employing people, as the lockdowns experienced during the 2020-2021 coronavirus and COVID-19 pandemic would have made it very stressful to have people depending on me. As all of my classroom teaching bookings were cancelled, it would have been very hard to justify keeping staff on to help out. Even though they would have been cushioned for a while with the UK's government-supported furlough scheme, eventually I might have had to let people go, and that is a level of stress that I don't need. By keeping myself as the sole staff of my business, I managed to weather the storm without affecting anyone else.

Even though I don't employ anyone, I do need help from time to time. Over the years, I have built up good working relationships with various freelancers who help me with tasks such as graphic design, typesetting, and book editing. All of my freelancers are geographically distant from me, and that is fine. Out of a regular team of seven freelancers, there is only one that I have ever met face to face before, as I used to work with them at another company.

I enjoy working with freelancers. It is a simple transaction. I have something I need done, they give me a quote, I pay half up-front, they do the work, and I then settle the rest of the invoice. It works great for me, and it works great for them as they work with lots of different clients. From a budgeting point of view, I can plan and spread costs appropriately, so I never overstretch myself.

To make budgeting more manageable, with my online business bank account, I have created a freelancers sub-account. When I need to hire people to do some work, I move the money into that sub-account, so there is never an issue with me paying them. I only commission work if I have the money already set aside. This was even more important in the early days as I was growing. It isn't so important to do now, but I still do this out of habit. Then once the work has been delivered, I pay my freelancers straight away. I don't do the usual trick of waiting 30 days or so before paying. I'm not too fond of it when that is done to me, so as a matter of principle, I don't do that with people I hire. Because of all of this, I have built up some excellent working relationships with my freelancers. Even though they don't work for me full time, they do feel like colleagues, which is nice.

Summary

Freelancing can be a win-win situation for both service providers and their employers. While employers save costs on employee benefits, freelancers leverage the opportunity of remote work to add a supplemental income, manage between jobs, or start their own business. There's an added benefit of flexibility in agreements for both freelancers and companies that allows both sides to navigate, change, and update the process as best seen fit.

However, freelancing and working with freelancers is a two-edged sword. On the one hand, commitment and long-term career possibilities remain options available only through a worker-employee relationship. Employment offers stability and benefits (e.g., a retirement fund and health insurance for employees) and the opportunity to grow loyalty and steady working connections from the employer's point of view.

The ultimate decision depends mainly on the size of your business and the nature of the project. While larger and medium-sized companies benefit from growing their employee talent pool, small businesses and entrepreneurs are often better off with freelancers. In case of smaller businesses and start-ups, investing in employees can prove too much to bear, while hiring freelancers gives just the right amount of flexibility regarding schedule and deadlines, with the added benefit of obtaining the specific skills you need.

Workshop Questions

(1) Make a list of your core skills, and also the skills you do not have and would need someone to do for you.

1. For the skills you do not have, think about how often you would need them applied. Would the skills justify a full-time staff member, or would a freelancer suffice?
2. Answer the questions from the following checklist to also help decide if you need a freelancer or staff member.

(2) Run through the following checklist to determine if you should hire a freelancer:

1. You're an entrepreneur with inconsistent workflow and without existing employees.
2. The cost of training your current staff justifies outsourcing the project.
3. You don't have the resources that the new project demands.
4. Your project demands talent and skills that your current staff doesn't have.
5. Your project is temporary or short-term.
6. Your project is long-term, but a once-off.
7. The project can be done remotely.
8. The work can be outsourced for the lower price.
9. The project doesn't require fixed work hours.
10. The project doesn't demand skills that are specific or unique to your brand/business.
11. The work doesn't demand thorough knowledge of your company's policies, values, or work process.

(3) Run through these following questions to see if you should hire an employee:

1. The work is regular.
2. The project requires familiarity with your clientele, work processes, policies, and company values.
3. The project requires talent that's available in-house.
4. You have the resources required for completing the project.
5. The project doesn't have tangible results or deliverables to measure success.
6. Training your current staff is more feasible compared to outsourcing the work.
7. The volume of the work doesn't interfere with the usual workflow.
8. The project requires regular or constant monitoring.
9. The project requires consistent work hours.

19

PRODUCT BRANDING

When you are looking to find your path to freedom, you need to make enough revenue not only to let the business thrive but so you can also live a comfortable life. To be profitable, you need to sell enough of your product or service to cover your costs and make a profit. To entice potential customers to purchase your product or service, you need to stand out from the rest of the products on the market.

Branding is the marketing practice of making a particular design, name, slogan, or picture readily identifiable with a particular product, produced by a specific company. This helps consumers distinguish this company's products from similar products made by other companies.

One of the main reasons why branding is needed is because good branding makes a memorable impression on customers. It allows customers to know exactly what level of quality they can expect from products from a particular company. Once a company becomes established, and the word spreads about the quality of their products, the branding will directly impact how well their products sell.

There are many different name-brand items out in the world today, and many of them are products that customers could find elsewhere with a different name and for much cheaper. But many people are more than willing to pay more money for items from companies that they know that they can trust.

Nike, for example, has made an annual profit of over 30 million dollars for the past five years, with their profit margins climbing steadily. The reason for this amount of profit isn't because there aren't other manufacturers that produce excellent quality products (there are many), but because millions of people around the globe understand that Nike makes products that are high quality. People are willing to pay more for products that they feel will bring them benefits.

The main reason why branding works so well for a business is that it means people can distinguish their products from similar products made by competitors. It separates your company's products from the rest of the competition and lives up to its customers' expectations. This is what you need for the business that you're starting. The products that you are relying on to ultimately make your business successful need to stand out from other competitors. Your product will reflect your business—and you as the owner.

Why Branding Is Important

The branding of your products is one of the most critical aspects of maintaining a successful business. Positive branding will change the way people perceive your product and your company. Just having the right type of branding will increase business and profits, and will grow awareness of your brand, which will lead to more business and financial gain.

People recognise good branding. The most crucial reason why branding is essential is that it brings recognition to the company. When customers are satisfied with a specific brand of a product, word gets out, and positive reviews start to spread. This will lead to more interest in that particular brand of product. As soon as the branding or logo becomes well known to people, they begin to associate those types of brands with the company, and vice versa.

Think of all those words in common usage that were once brand names but became so well associated with that product that the brand name *supplanted* the name of the actual product? Brands like Kleenex and Coke in some parts of the United States are now generic terms for tissues and soft drinks of just about any flavour, respectively. The same is also true for brands like Klaxon, Taser, Google, and Xerox.

The logo is arguably the most important factor of branding because it's the logo that people remember most about a particular product. People remember the raging bull on the Lamborghini badge, just as well as the black stallion on Ferrari. The logo is, in essence, the face of the company. It is why it's a good choice to have a professionally designed logo for your branding. If you've spent years building up the idea of your business and want to make it successful, remember that people will relate the logo of your branding directly to your business. Your logo will be the face of your company, so choose wisely. Alternatively, if you're unsure about the logo, multiple agencies can help you design one, and we will look at this later on in the chapter.

Good Branding Will Increase the Value of Your Business

Branding will establish your business in people's minds and is therefore a key ingredient in generating and maintaining future business. Having good branding for your business and your products will give you more leverage amongst your competitors, and it will make it more likely that people will buy from your business. Once a business is firmly established in the marketplace, and people recognise the brand, they are more inclined to purchase products from the company. This increases the overall profits of the business and maintains its future integrity.

Good branding will attract new customers. When your branding is well designed, people are going to want to purchase the products that your company has to offer. If that good branding on your products is backed up by good performance, then word-of-mouth can do some of your most powerful advertising. A reliable brand will create more and more business just by satisfied customers referring your products to people that they know.

This means that the new customers are more likely to choose to do business with you above other competitors because they recognise your brand and believe it to be reliable based on what others have said. Once a brand becomes well known and established, satisfied customers will become the business' best source of advertising to others.

Good branding will help make employees proud to work for you. Employees that work for well-established companies with positive branding tend to have a higher satisfaction level, as well as pride in the company and in the work they are doing. Working for a company that is reputable and held in high regard by members of the community will make employees feel prouder and more fulfilled in their positions. Any reputable brand will make people proud to work for them. As an example, Formula-1 racing drivers are generally proud of the racing companies that they represent, and they wear their companies' logo as badges of honour.

Even though your company will most likely stay small—even a single-person company—you should bear in mind that you may need to look for freelance employees to fill gaps in your business. Fortunately, most freelancers are just as open to working for reputable companies with strong brands as full-time employees would be. Conversely, if your brand has a bad reputation, then even freelancers, who have don't have any loyalty to one particular company, might not want to work with you.

Good brands are more trustworthy. The marketplace is full of people that are trying to make a quick buck. Even though any business that has a "fly-by-night" mentality may make some money in the beginning, there will be little chance of repeat business later on. Profitable companies that have reliable brands are usually people's first choice when looking for new products. People trust a good brand and are generally willing to pay for it, on the grounds that they would rather buy a product that is double the price of another but lasts much longer.

There is an unconscious acknowledgement that a well-designed brand has obviously had significant money invested into its creation, and therefore the product attached to it is likely to be of a higher quality, as the company would have too much at stake to put shoddy goods out onto the market and risk tanking their brand. This is also why people tend not to trust your basic brand/discount label as much, even though there may be little difference between them than the more widely recognised name-brand products.

Good branding supports advertising. A business needs good advertising to intrigue people enough to purchase their products. Advertising and branding need to work hand-in-hand together to create a trustworthy appeal to different types of customers. Having a good brand will work as a form of advertising in itself, but there is much more that needs to be done. Good branding is only the first step in an ongoing process. You will find that you will attract more customers by having an easily identifiable brand because it acts as a form of advertising.

Develop Your Brand

Knowing the basics of what defines branding is only the beginning of the process. You may have an idea of what type of branding you would like to use for your business, but the real work begins with the development of your brand. This development is broken down into sections, namely the vision and the mission statements.

The vision statement is what you envision for your company to become. It focuses on tomorrow and all of the developments that you want for your company. The mission statement, on the other hand, is directly focused on the present and current developments of the company as a whole. Many people make the mistake of using their vision and mission statement interchangeably, but it's important to have both. Even though these two aren't interchangeable, they do rely heavily on one another because they don't make sense alone. Your business needs to have purpose and meaning, as its development relies heavily on it.

. . .

Develop your mission statement. Your mission statement is what drives your business daily. It's the core of your business, and a representation of what you and the rest of your business do. The mission statement leads to the types of objectives that you want your business to accomplish. It will also help you identify the kind of culture that your company represents. When developing your mission statement, you want to answer questions like:

- What does my business do?
- What types of customers do we serve?
- How do we effectively serve them?

The ripple effect of the business' mission statement makes the company, ultimately, more valuable. A well-written mission statement can motivate a team of employees towards a common goal. But the inverse can be said about a weak mission statement: it can have the opposite effect on the growth and attractiveness of a company, decreasing the company's value in the long run.

If you are aiming for a smaller business, you will likely be working by yourself a lot of the time. This means that you are going to need to act as the content marketer for your business, publishing content aimed at specific target groups for the purpose of marketing. It would be best if you designed a content strategy that supports your company's mission statement and describes how your business operates. You may take some time to establish an online presence, but once you do, all of the content that you create for your business needs to support the mission statement.

Develop your vision statement. The vision statement needs to describe the future of the business, and therefore, it gives the business a specific purpose. When developing your vision statement, you should answer questions like:

- What are your hopes and dreams for the business?

- What problems are we able to solve that will benefit our customers or act towards the greater good?
- What are we striving to change?

Creating a strong vision statement will ensure the steady development of the business, both externally and internally. Having a clear vision for your business will make it more successful, especially if you choose to have people working for you, as it will give them purpose and direction. This often leads to innovation because a purpose-driven business sees its success as a whole.

Ultimately, the lack of a clear vision will harm a business because it has no direction, like a boat on the open sea with no-one at the helm. Even if your company is solely run by you, you still need a strong vision statement. You need to know where your business is going to ensure that it stays on track and has measurable goals.

The content marketing side of the vision statement needs to describe *why* your company does what it does. This helps the business stay on track with everything that it needs to focus on in the long run. It helps the business stay true to its beliefs and to its purpose. All of the content created by your business needs to keep its vision closely in mind. It doesn't matter how small the content for the advertisement is —it can be a tiny segment in the newspaper or a huge billboard—the content still needs to stick closely to the vision statement of the business. Let's take a look at some brands that have good mission and vision statements.

Tesla

> *Mission:* To accelerate the world's transition to sustainable energy.
> *Vision:* To create the most compelling car company of the 21st century by driving the world's transition to electric vehicles.

Elon Musk may be a rather controversial figure to some, but he definitely knows how to successfully brand his business, which is now one of the most renowned electric car manufacturers in the world.

Tesla has kept its mission and vision statements simple and to the point. These statements work because the words have been very carefully selected. They use the word "accelerate" in their mission statement to keep emphasising the type of work that Tesla does; likewise, "driving the world's transition" in their vision. They also make use of bold statements such as "the most compelling car company of the 21st century", which represent the types of goals they want to reach and maintain in the near future.

Amazon

> **Mission:** To serve customers through online and physical stores and focus on selection, price, and convenience.
> **Vision:** To be Earth's most customer-centric company, where customers can find and discover anything they might want to buy online.

Amazon is one of the most lucrative online platforms in the history of the internet. Their mission and vision statements are straightforward and show that they are envisioning great developments for their business. They work because they are to the point about what they offer their customers. Amazon's bold statement that "customers can find and discover anything they might want to buy" is very attractive, and their focus on having a wide selection at competitive prices, with the convenience of local bricks-and-mortar stores in addition to their vast online presence, allows them to appeal to the broadest possible market.

TED Talks

> **Mission:** Spread ideas.
> **Vision:** We believe passionately in the power of ideas to change attitudes, lives and, ultimately, the world.

TED Talks is one of the most influential online streaming sites, hosting speakers on multiple different educational topics. Their mission statement is one of the simplest ever made by any company because it consists of only two words: *Spread ideas.*

Their mission statement may be simple, but it's exactly what TED Talks strives towards. They use the best speakers to spread the best ideas to the general population. This makes them one of the most influential platforms in the world. Their vision—that they believe passionately in the power of ideas to effect change—works because TED Talks' mission is to spread ideas to people all across the globe. Their vision is all about the type of impact that they want to make on the world through the sharing of their curated knowledge.

Brand Guidelines

When it comes to the branding that you want to use for your business, the most important aspect is consistency. The best way to stay consistent regarding your branding is to closely follow a brand style guide. This guide is a sort of rulebook that contains specifications on everything that is part of your brand. It covers things like colour, typography, imagery, and logos. Using a style guide will help you know exactly how to share your brand with customers and, in time, the world.

Depending on your resources, needs, and time, you may decide to design static guidelines that can easily be shared via online platforms as a PDF. Doing this type of design can enable them to be printed or read quickly. Regardless of the type of formatting that you want to use for your brand guidelines, you need to ensure that it's easily accessible to the general public. It's imperative to ensure that these guidelines are easy to read and simple to use, because you may be sharing these guidelines with employees, freelancers, and eventually, many of your customers.

Identify everything that you want to include. Your brand guidelines will essentially be the amalgamation of your brand strategy, which functions as your "business bible". Therefore, your guidelines should include every detail that you believe people would like to know about your brand. Obviously, different brands will have unique contents and information specific to their company, but all brand guidelines should include the same basic items.

Your business' brand heart. This is a higher-level description of your brand's fundamental principles. These principles need to describe the purpose of your business and why it actually exists. They need to explain your vision of your business and what kind of future you want to lead your company toward. They need to detail your business' mission and how you want to create the future you envision. Finally, they need to define the values of your business and the principles that guide your behaviour.

You can also consider adding other details into this section of your brand's guidelines like the history of the business, any milestones it has achieved, and a little more information about the company's background. All of this information is important because it describes the fundamental heart of your brand. It explains who you are, what your business does, and why it all matters.

The vocabulary of your brand. How you speak about your company is very important to its ultimate success. Words have power and using them correctly can greatly benefit a business. Your business' vocabulary needs to include the essence of your **brand**—its personality, voice, and tone. It needs to include the tagline of your business. Finally, it needs to include messaging pillars in the online platforms.

Any other pertinent details regarding communication or similar elements should also be implemented. This can include words and phrases that you don't want to use when talking about your business, which comes in handy when your company is concerned about diplomacy. Use these messaging tips to carefully design the verbal elements of your business and its advertising.

The visual guidelines that you want your branding to follow. One of the greatest attractions to customers is how your branding and products look. If something looks unappealing, then people won't be attracted to your brand, no matter how impressive your products or services are. In the past ten years, companies that took the time and effort to make their branding and products attractive outperformed their "non-visually inclined" competitors by a significant margin.

Your guidelines should focus on making a comprehensive visual identity for your business which includes colours, logos, typography and fonts, illustrations and photography, data visualisation, iconography, web design, and videos. There are other visual factors that can be considered according to the individual needs of the business. This list isn't exhaustive, and you can adapt it according to what you think would help your business most.

Create your brand guidelines and include examples. Everything that you would have done in the first two steps would have contributed towards the outline that you should use to design your actual guidelines. With your outline completed, you can successfully make brand guidelines for your business. They must include the dos and don'ts, how-tos, and real-life examples that can help promote your business.

In the different sections of your guidelines, you want to provide enough information for readers to be fully informed, but not so much that it makes it difficult to read. The readers will lose interest long before they finish, so keep it simple and to the point. Brand guidelines are meant to show, not just tell.

For all messaging guidelines, you should include examples of commonly seen cases like:

- Press releases
- Social copies
- Product descriptions
- Business and marketing emails

These examples are important because they show readers how your brand's messaging guidelines work in practice.

For all of the visual guidelines, you should include personalised aspects that make your business unique and stand out from the competition. This is where you can let your creativity come to light. That said, if you believe that your creative skills leave something to be desired, then you can employ a graphic designer to help you with this process. It is costly to do so, but it's worth it in the long run to make your business branding seem more attractive. Include visual aspects like:

- Different colour palettes
- Strategic logo placements
- Specific typography placement
- Image guidelines like page placements and specific dimensions

After you have worked on the design of your brand guidelines, you need to finalise the design by keeping a few key points in mind. First, you need to keep your design simple. Your guidelines need to be comprehensive enough to educate the reader, but not bore them. Bored readers won't take in half the information that you want them to retain.

Then, you need to watch the language that you use in the design. Keep to simple, non-technical words that your readers will easily understand. If your readers have to pull out a dictionary to get through your guidelines, then the guidelines have missed the point and the overall purpose.

Next, include handy tools and tips to help your readers benefit from your guidelines. These can be personalised according to the type of business that you run. If your business is online, then you should consider including links to additional applications and platforms that can help the reader maximise on certain business functions.

Finally, you should consider incorporating checklists into your guidelines. It's difficult for everything to be passed through the head of the company, and sometimes it becomes hard to stay on top of everything. Checklists can provide the ability for anyone in the business to check the work that they have completed and ensure it's up to the company's specifications. If there are boxes that aren't checked then they know where to start fixing.

One of the primary reasons why people in general ignore brand guidelines is because they're simply not sure where to find them, and then get too scared to ask. If your guidelines aren't readily available online, then people aren't going to follow them. Ensure that they are easily found and that you have an attractive web page. This link can be shared with everyone in the company or with all of your customers if you wish for them to see the guidelines. This website address also needs to be regularly shared with employees so that any new employee knows exactly where to find the guidelines. It's fine to have a hardcopy of your guidelines, but with so much of the world moving to a paperless office, it's much wiser—and environmentally sound—to stick to online content.

Your business and brand will keep growing and expanding. Evolution and development are part of the world that we live in and that extends to your business. As your business develops, your brand guidelines will need to adapt accordingly. If your brand was developed in the 20th century, then you can't expect all of that information to still be valid now in the present. You need to ensure that you spend enough time updating your brand guidelines to keep them current. If you work with a team then speak to them on a monthly basis to ascertain what's working and what isn't. It's the best way to ensure that your guidelines stay up to date.

Logo Design

Your company's logo is the figurehead of your brand and the first thing that visually appeals to your customers. Ergo, it's vitally important to get it right. This has to be one of the most detailed parts of your branding that you spend the most time on. People remember every detail of your logo, whether you want them to or not. Nothing about your logo should be mediocre or substandard.

This is why it's in your business' best interest to ensure that the design choice of the logo is memorable, intentional, and that it specifically conveys the message you want people to remember about your business. It's happened far too regularly that small business owners cheaply or quickly designed a logo for their business which became misleading and confusing. And some logos don't say anything at all about the business itself or what they do. Bad logos have been the downfall of some companies; people didn't shop at the business because subconsciously, they didn't find it attractive.

. . .

The psychology of fonts, shapes, and colour in logo designs. Human psychology has a lot to do with the success of businesses. The psychology of a logo's shape, font, overall composition, and colour are incredibly important because this is one of the deciding factors of whether a customer will purchase your brand or not.

The font style in a logo evokes different emotions in people, so spend time analysing what types of customers to which you want to appeal. A recent study showed that fonts like Arial and Times New Roman are categorised as "mature" and "stable," but are also unimaginative as they are used in so many places. Make sure you spend enough time reading up on the different types of fonts that you could use to appeal to your customers.

Logos come in many different forms, but there are three basic categories that logo shapes can be: organic; geometric; and abstract. Each shape engenders different emotions and will appeal to a different range of people. Once your logo becomes established with your company, it becomes the face of your brand and you won't be able to easily change it, so choose your shape designs wisely.

Organic shapes include things that naturally occur in nature and can range from rocks to streams to jagged edges to mountain ranges. These shapes can be included in a logo to communicate a specific message to the customers. Many camping and fishing businesses use organic shapes in their logos because they accurately portray what their company is about without having to say much.

Geometric shapes are generally man-made things that include straight lines and mathematically precise angles. These shapes communicate a sense of power and strict order. They can be used safely and effectively in many types of logos, and you will be able to use them easily in your business' logo.

Abstract shapes are things that are normally represented as symbols common within some cultures. Many of them have clear meanings and can easily convey a message without saying anything. These shapes include hearts, stars, and arrows.

The colour of a logo is one of the most essential facets of the logo itself because colour has long been recognised as an emotional intensifier. Logos can vary in colours and some can be completely monochromatic, which means the logo can be altered according to the backdrop if you need it to stand out. Logos that include many colours are normally more attractive to children, which is why many logos on plush toys have a rainbow of colours.

Of course, if your company has any important colours that are key to your business, you will want to incorporate those into the logo itself. Spend enough time going through the different colours that you are interested in to see if they complement your logo.

Branded Websites

The main purpose of your website is to both entice and inform your potential customers with your business and your brand. You want to draw them in and then win them over by being the trustworthy business that you claim to be. This will quickly result in paying customers.

That said, your website can also be your business' downfall if you aren't careful with its design. Websites that are chaotic, unhelpful, and difficult to navigate will turn people away very quickly. Potential customers that you could have had will move onto more user-friendly websites without giving your site a second look. Research has found that 79% of potential customers will exit the site within the first 30 seconds if they find the site confusing (most customers spend less time than that if there are other promising sites available). According to an online survey, 81% of people will extensively search for a product online before committing to buy it. Therefore, it is imperative that your site is easy to use and has the pertinent information that the customers are looking for. If you want your website to be successful, it needs to incorporate the following elements.

- Your website must send a strong message to the customer. The message needs to be concise, clear, entertaining, informative, captivating, and closely aligned with your mission and vision strategies.
- Your website must have a consistent design.
- Your website must have all of the pertinent and crucial business information. This includes details like hours of operation, products and services, pricing, product

information, staff bios, company history, contact details and store location(s).

Protecting your brand. Because the business world is now largely digital, many (if not all) aspects of a business need to be placed online. But with this online access comes a certain amount of risk. There are several unscrupulous people in the world that are intelligent enough and skilled enough to wreak havoc on a website and potentially damage a brand of business forever. People will steal your content if you're not careful, especially when the popularity of your business begins to grow. Ignorance is no protection here, and if you want to keep your business and your brand safe, you will have to take steps to protect yourself.

First of all, you want to set up alerts on Google. Google is one of the most popular search engines in the world, and you can use it to your advantage if you know how to navigate the site. Google has spent millions of dollars setting up and designing free programs and software to be more attractive for people to use. All you need to access these free services is to have an active Google account. You can set up a Google Alert to inform you every time there's a problem with your site. If you are uploading content that infringes on someone else's copyrights, the Google Alert will message you so you can fix the problem before it worsens.

If you are determined to create a brand, then you will need to implement the correct intellectual property (IP) protection to safeguard your brand, your business, and your content. It's prudent to seek advice from an attorney that specialises in intellectual property so that they can help you along the path of protecting your business. They will be able to help you with exactly what type of protection your business will need.

Another consideration is for you to create a distinctive trademark for your brand. Trademarks in the United States, and indeed around the world, will receive a varying degree of protection according to how individual they are. If there are elements in the trademark that are very common, then the trademark won't be completely exclusive. "Quiksilver", for example, will receive strong protection because it's unique, but "Wave Rider" will only receive some protection because both of those words are commonly used in logos. Choose your trademarks carefully and make them distinctive to stand out from the rest.

It's important for any business owner that is interested in developing a brand to apply for a trademark with the US Patent and Trademark Office, or the trademark office in your country, relatively early into their business' life. The reason for this is because it takes time to get the ball rolling and there are many forms to fill out and hoops to jump through to register a trademark. It would be wise to employ the help of an attorney with the process, even though you can attempt to register for one online.

If you're in the process of developing something novel and revolutionary, then it's important to look at creating a patent for your work. There are many people that will copy your idea and take the credit and glory if you're not careful. If you believe that your work/product is revolutionary, then protect yourself by patenting it to prevent future problems. Be warned though, if you do decide to go down the patenting route, that it can be very time-consuming and very expensive. You also have to be aware that even with a patent, in the case of an infringement you will need to be able to afford to defend that patent. If you feel you need to go down the patenting route, then you must talk to a qualified patent lawyer and seek their advice.

The Authors Approach

From the early days of running my online training business, my main brand has been a personal brand, which we are covering in the next chapter. Although I was creating my online courses, they are published on a training platform that I do not own. That brand is not mine, even though I am contributing to the promotion of it when I do marketing for my courses.

Since starting my business, I have had the intention of creating my products as books and courses that I publish myself on a platform that I control. The book you are reading here is part of those products, and the brand is "The Path to Freedom", which consists of this book and a series of online workshops that people can take.

Before embarking on *The Path to Freedom* brand, I wanted to explore the publishing process for books so that I could learn as much about it as possible. I did this by writing a series of short books under an umbrella brand called "A Gentle Introduction". For example, I have books called "A Gentle Introduction to Agile Software Development", and "A Gentle Introduction to Beating Procrastination and Getting Focused", to name a couple.

The idea was to publish a series of these books and learn about the publishing and promotion process. If I was going to make any mistakes in this, then it was with this series that I wanted to make them, before I started working on *The Path to Freedom*. Overall, these experiments were quite successful. The books did reasonably well, although none of them were huge sellers. They made a good profit and generated some positive reviews.

One issue I had with this brand was that it was very broad in its appeal. The books covered a vast array of subjects that would appeal to different audiences, and as a single-person company, this makes them quite hard to promote effectively, which I now firmly believe to be a mistake that I made. But I am glad I made this mistake early. With this book and subsequent material, I have homed in on a more specific niche. It is about starting a business, which in itself is quite broad, but I have narrowed the focus to people who are reluctant to start a business due to worrying about the risk. Hopefully, this works out. From what I have learnt and the advice I have been given, when you are working as a small single-person company, picking a niche is essential, and I didn't do this before.

When it comes to promoting the brand of *The Path to Freedom*, I am both trying to leverage its own brand identity, and also my personal brand, as the book is written by me and includes a lot of my thoughts.

When I started out running my business, I did write a mission and vision statement, and they have largely remained unchanged through all this time. They are as follows:

Mission Statement: To help professionals improve.

Vision Statement: Help people succeed in their careers through writing, videos, public speaking, and training.

Everything I do is about helping people succeed, and I feel these statements embody that well. I have not deviated from these statements all the time I have been working for myself.

Summary

Since you are starting out a particular brand of business, you will need to keep a number of aspects in mind before continuing. The brand of your business and product is one of the most important selling points. Branding is important because it will attract customers to your business as they associate trustworthy brands with quality products.

Take the time to accurately set up your mission and vision statements to let others know how and why your business exists. Your logo is the face of your company and it's one of the aspects that people will always remember first when thinking of your brand. Take the time, effort, and expense to design one that is worthwhile and attractive. Colours, fonts, and shapes will all make up integral parts of your logo. Decide which ones will work best for you.

Develop a website for your business so that customers can easily navigate your site and view the products/services that you offer. Don't have a site that's difficult to navigate because potential customers won't stick around long if it's too confusing.

Workshop Questions

(1) When developing the brand image for your business you need to think about many aspects of that brand. Start out by answering the following questions:

1. Who are my customers?
2. What customers do I want to have?
3. Who are my competitors?
4. What is my competitors' brand position?
5. What problem does my company solve? Does anybody care?
6. What is my value proposition? Is it distinctive? Is it relevant to my customers?
7. When people think about my company or product, what are the feelings and associations I want them to have? Are they unique?
8. What are the functional benefits that we deliver to our customers?

9. What are the emotional benefits that only we deliver to our customers?
10. What kind of personality will my brand have?

(2) Have a go at writing example mission and vision statements that represent your brand.

20

PERSONAL BRANDING

Many of the products that you use around your home and your office may have name brands attached to them. These name brands have specific attributes that are positively associated with them because of the type of company they represent, and that's one of the reasons people purchase these products. Just like these products, you too have unique qualities and specific features that people recognise. This is why building your personal brand is one of the most effective marketing tools available to you.

Effective personal branding isn't about showing off or bragging, but if your business is a one-person operation, then it's important to create the necessary perceptions that will attract customers to your business. This is needed because buying and selling in today's markets is becoming more competitive by the day, meaning you need to use the right tactics to stand out from the crowd.

Creating a brand as someone new to the business is just as important as a large company building its brand. No matter the size, small business or corporation, they are trying to sell products to the same consumers. It's crucial to build your branding because people like to hear the story of the struggles and successes behind the founder. It makes them more relatable as real people, making it more likely that the customer will feel inclined to buy.

What is Personal Branding?

Unlike product branding, personal branding is the practice of marketing people and their businesses as brands, instead of goods. This is an ongoing process that continually builds the reputation of the individual or group within a company. This, quintessentially, maintains the image of the company as a whole.

Since you are focusing on making sure your small business survives, you need to keep in mind that your personal brand always needs to promote you. Your personal brand is a combination of experiences, skills, and personality that you share with your customers. It tells your unique story and becomes an extension of you online, and the impression you leave on your potential customers when they browse your profile. It is the measure by which they will judge your business, which is why it's paramount to develop the right type of personal branding.

There are many different celebrities active in the world today and making headlines, but a few of them have gone above and beyond to create and develop a remarkable form of personal brand. These are just a few with the most effective.

Tony Robbins. For some people, Tony Robbins is a name that may not ring a lot of bells when you first hear it, depending on your age. Until you search "Tony" in Google, and before you get to his last name, he's one of the first results that pops up. Once people see his picture, they remember who he is—a world-renowned author and motivational speaker who has made incredible strides with people.

Tony Robbins has spent years developing his digital footprint and has one of the most effective brands of any celebrity. When you go deeper into the search, you are introduced to more information than expected.

With such an incredible online presence, his personal branding is unbelievably effective. Of course, you won't need to have branding as large as Tony Robbins (unless you're aiming at becoming an online celebrity), but you do need to aim for personal branding that is effective enough that people can get to know the real you with a few clicks and keyword entries. Customers are more likely to purchase goods, content, or other saleable products if they are familiar with you and can relate to the type of person you are.

Michelle Obama. Michelle Obama soared into the public eye when her husband, Barack Obama, won his position in the White House. During his two terms, Michelle Obama had an exponentially growing online presence covering who she was and what she believed in and supported. The Obama family already had a strong personal brand because of the celebrity status that was thrust upon them. That didn't stop Michelle Obama from showing the world that she was an incredible woman, an influential thought-leader, and so much more than just the president's wife. She developed her personal brand as an influential fighter for human rights and is globally renowned both for the type of person she is, and the humanitarian work she does.

Richard Branson. Richard Branson is the perfect example of personal branding done the right way. He has multiple social media platforms that allow people to connect with him and better understand the type of person he is. He doesn't hide behind his failings and has openly discussed his multiple bankruptcies, allowing people to see that even with all of that success, he is still human. Because of this, people are inclined to relate to the type of person he is and more likely to use his merchandise or engage with the brands he is affiliated with.

People like to see that successful people are human too. They like to see that they are humorous and fun and enjoy everyday things. People like to relate to others. This is why effective personal branding is one of the most valuable marketing tools that you can have for your business.

Developing Your Personal Brand

Now that you have a more focused idea of what a personal brand is, it's good to know where to start. People get overwhelmed thinking about little hang-ups at the beginning, which leads to lack of a plan, or one that is poorly designed. It's important to have a unique voice and to set yourself apart. To accomplish this, these ten rules need to be followed.

Have a focus. If you are trying to be everything to everybody in the online world, you will fail. This type of idea is unfocused and leads to problematic outcomes along the way. Decide on your key message and stick to it. This is the guidance that Cooper Harris, current CEO and founder of Klickly, offers regarding the type of message you need to aim for.

Harris knows what brands need from personal experience. Her brand has undergone significant and dramatic changes in the past several years. She went from successful actress to tech entrepreneur and handled this shift by focusing on the small bits of information and messages she received from outside sources at the time.

Keeping your branding and messages focused on your target demographic will make it much easier to create a unique personal brand. You will be more easily able to create online content which will define you and make people more interested in your products.

Since you are trying to keep your brand as focused as possible, you need to think of creative ways to keep your brand specific but versatile and always interesting. One of the ways this can be accomplished is by creating a specific niche for your personal brand; you need to have a focused specificity for your brand.

You want to do this because it allows you to keep your content and message consistent. This makes it more memorable to the community that is interested in your business/product. The more specific your brand, the more significant it is to your target consumers.

Be genuine. If you are aiming to stand out in a crowd with a memorable brand, you need to make sure you use genuine content that illustrates who you are as an individual. People are very quick to see who is copying another person. Copycats don't do well in the long run to develop their brands.

People like to engage with people on a personal level—especially those they admire. Celebrities, authors, entrepreneurs, and small business owners alike all find that consumers are more likely to purchase their goods or services if they can individually relate to them as people. People prefer and will lean towards the genuine; this is why content that is personalised goes such a long way. It also makes it much easier to manage content. People that use non-genuine content need to conjure up a lot of information to sound appealing. This takes a lot of time and effort.

Your brand should be something that you can add to daily without taking up too much of your day. You need to portray that you are a master of whatever skill set, advice, or experience you are offering. This will allow the content that you are regularly submitting to reflect who you are. If you are expertly skilled in a specific area, your reputation among those interested will help you create the brand you want.

Tell a story. People are attracted to stories, and if your brand isn't telling a story, then it's probably already lost half of the potential audience that could become your customers. The most effective way to have an attractive personal brand is to tell a true narrative of yourself. No one will care about you advertising your product on social media without understanding the story behind it.

Many successful entrepreneurs spend enough time interacting with their target audiences to ensure that they stay interested in their brands. This interaction can be performed in multiple ways, and just because something seems unorthodox at first, it doesn't mean that it won't work in the long run. Many small business owners wanting to increase awareness of themselves, their products, and their businesses regularly use social media platforms to either release videos or engaging content about their brands. This attracts people to the company and quickly spreads through word-of-mouth recommendations.

Making a regular video to connect with your audience and

prospective clients will create that personal touch that many people are looking for. You can use your smartphone to record yourself spreading the word about your product and thanking the patrons that support you.

Consistency. Having a narrow focus and being consistent are very similar to each other and two of the most integral factors in building a successful personal brand. It's much easier for you and your business to get recognised for an individual topic if you are consistently creating awareness. Your brand is going to make certain promises to customers, and you need to ensure that those promises are kept, both online and offline.

If you demonstrate a certain level of consistency in your business and your brand, then people will know that your products, means of communication, and appearance will be reliable. Tiny discrepancies and problems can lead to the derailment of the effectiveness.

While developing your brand and remembering that you need to have a certain level of consistency, you should also be consistent in something that makes you and your brand unique. People remember the details that make someone stand out, so try and ensure that you can do this for your ideas. Some businesses use mascots, while others have witty catchphrases that pop up after every video. Some companies even use controversial tactics to be remembered. But all of them keep a certain level of consistency to ensure that people associate those consistent forms of unique advertising with their business. Consistency is one of the paramount aspects of a successful brand.

Know that failure is inevitable. It's human nature to avoid failure because let's face it—failure isn't an enjoyable part of life. That said, for your personal brand to be more successful than the rest, you will need to experience failure. Walt Disney was one of the greatest supporters of experiencing failure when one is young, believing it was important because it taught valuable lessons about handling success in the future. Failure makes you aware of what can happen to you during any adventure, journey, or exploit. Walt Disney said that the fear of not trying at all is much worse than anything that can happen when you attempt something.

You'll never achieve the type of successful personal branding that you envision for yourself until you fail a few times during its development. You will quickly realise that you can't have something that stands out from the rest if you stay within your comfort zone. The most accomplished brands only get there by trial and error.

Failures and mistakes are what lead to brands that stand the tests of time. There is no such thing as instant perfection.

Aim to create a positive impact on your audience. It's going to take time to build your brand, and it is best to slowly but surely grow a positive community around your brand.

It's imperative to remember that your brand represents you, no matter what work you are currently doing. You may change your line of work along the way, but it's important to remember that your brand will follow you no matter what you do. The impact you leave on people will follow you because it's how you are remembered. Some believe that it is beneficial to their brand in the beginning to break others down, to attract more followers in people that are interested in controversy. But those types of followers are fleeting and don't do much towards the prosperity of your brand. There are many examples of YouTube pioneers who built their brands on such controversy, and their views and subscription numbers were enormously high—until they took it too far and all of their followers turned on them, leaving them with nothing.

If you want your brand to grow in the long run, always keep a positive and helpful attitude to build a community instead of breaking others down.

Follow successful role models and examples. If you are interested in building your brand, you will need to follow and observe the role models and celebrities you look up to. Many celebrities are excellent at building their brands because their livelihoods depend on it. If you are following in your role models' footsteps, it's a good idea to base your branding in a similar way to theirs. There is no reason for you to reinvent the wheel in this process, and there are many celebrities that have released content on how to build your brand as they did. The internet is a wonderful place filled with all the resources that you could need.

Jason Wong, the CEO of Wonghaus Ventures, is one of the best role models upon whom to base the building of your brand. The reason for this is because several of his content releases have become viral sensations. His brand became associated with everything from Japanese ice cream to inflatable toys, giving him the title of "Meme King".

His ideas became successful because he went about the right way to ensure development. He made it a habit to study the market trends of his interests, making a note of these brands when new releases hit on social media before loading it onto his platforms with changes and twists to make them unique. It's necessary to creatively dissect social trends that allow you to come out with the next big trend. You will need to routinely check on multiple social platform sites to ensure that you are staying ahead of the curve.

This is going to take some work, especially if you are running a business by yourself. It takes time and effort to creatively dissect other releases from impactful individuals. Fortunately, it does become easier with time and practice. Don't give up in the beginning if you feel daunted by the task. This is a necessary aspect of building one's brand.

Live your brand. Building a brand can be difficult if you plan on separating your personal life from your business. Although this is certainly possible to accomplish for some experienced professionals, it's much easier to keep your brand and personal life as integrations into one another.

Your brand should become a part of you, and it should follow you wherever you go. Once your brand becomes a unique and authentic manifestation of who you are, then people will become more interested in you and your message. Your brand needs to amplify what you believe. You shouldn't view it as merely a reflection of your business functions; more an opportunity to showcase the greater ideals that you hold true, like mentorship, charity, and thoughtful leadership.

· · · ·

Let others tell your story. You could spend thousands of dollars on effective advertising, but it will never be as effective as personal reviews that uplift your brand. Word-of-mouth is the best kind of advertising that could happen for your brand. The reason for this is because people trust their peers when they have good recommendations about specific products. Companies can spend exorbitant amounts of money on advertising their products, but the masses may still question whether they should buy it. Many people feel more encouraged to buy a product if someone they know, and trust tells them that it's a good product to buy. Customer reviews are a good way to build trust in a product, but unfortunately, they become harder to trust with people buying fake positive reviews. Websites such as Amazon have strict policies to try and avoid paid positive reviews, but it is a practice that sadly still goes on.

Your branding is the narrative or story that people will talk about you when you're not around. This means that you will have no control over what is said. The truth is spoken in instances like that. If your products and personal brand have impressed people, then they will say so; but in the same light, they will also freely admit if they didn't like what you had to offer. If your brand isn't worthy, people who feel no personal connection to you won't feel inclined to uplift it.

Leonard Maltin, a renowned film critic, said that all that a person has is the reputation and name that is built up over time. If you protect your brand by providing quality products and treating your audience with honesty, then they will likely return the favour with honest recommendations.

Build a legacy that will stand the test of time. Building a personal brand and having a community of supporters behind it is only the beginning step to one's ultimate success later on. Once all of the support has been established, it's vitally important to think about the legacy of your business and brand that you will pass on.

Blake Jamieson, the main artist at Blake Jamieson LLC, said that building a personal brand is much bigger and more difficult than building a business. This is because businesses have multiple exit strategies, where personal brandings only have one: legacies.

A personal brand is something that lasts for much longer than people initially thought. Of course, some fail along the way and are forgotten because they were mishandled. But those who saw their personal branding as lifelong projects that would change, adapt, and evolve knew their brands would become legacies to be remembered.

Creating the right type of personal brand will help you in your chosen field, and it will generate more future business opportunities for you. Your brand will take time to develop and will be an aspect of yourself and your business that you will constantly have to work on. That said, if you do, you will reap the benefits of it.

Common Personal Branding Mistakes

Some aspects and factors can build your brand, so it becomes a legacy one day, but there are also many mistakes that first-timers make while developing theirs. Some of these mistakes can be rectified in a short amount of time; others can destroy your progress. Learning from others' past mistakes can prevent you from making those simple, yet costly errors yourself.

Showing a fake persona. As you are aware by now, you need to have an authentic voice when addressing your target audience. If you don't, you will find that you will lose your audience because of disinterest. This part of branding is vital because people are attracted to what is real. If you have a look at posts on social media, you will quickly see which people have what it takes to make an impression on a broad audience.

Those that make poor impressions on people, or don't live up to what they promised, will inevitably fall by the wayside when their brands are brought into disrepute. It's imperative to be real with your target audience so that they know what type of person you are.

Stealing content from others. Far too many people believe that using common material will increase ratings. This may be the case for a little while, but once a target audience becomes aware that you are using copied content, they will quickly start to feel dissatisfied with your brand.

Many people use the new releases from other business owners to make their brand sound appealing, but this can be a dangerous game. If followers notice that you are using content that is very similar to other people's, then you may put yourself in a position that will gravely damage your image and your brand.

If you're planning on making an impact on your audience, ensure that you use new and exciting content. If you use ideas from other people, you will have to ensure that you put enough of a twist on the material to make it your own. Don't release the same content as someone else because it will hurt your reputation.

Not connecting with your audience. It's imperative to focus on developing your brand, but it's just as important to communicate with people interested in your business. Don't make the mistake of being aloof and not responding to personal messages that customers may send you. Many business owners that have taken the time to connect with potential customers have quickly realised that in doing so, they produce repeat business.

A perfect example of this is Chris Carter, a crime-thriller author who made his name in the market around 2010. He spends a large part of his day responding to fans and curious readers alike, and personally addressing their questions. Readers check his social media profiles for updates as well as consistently buy his books and enjoy any content that he releases.

The personal connection that he has developed with his readers has made his writing invaluable and concreted his legacy in the world of fiction. In the same way, it will be necessary for you to go out of your way to communicate with people that are interested in you and what you have to offer. People respond to the personal touch, so keep that in mind when developing your brand.

Lacking the necessary confidence. One of the most significant problems when building a brand is not having the confidence to pull the trigger. People tend to doubt themselves too much while trying to make their brand, but self-doubt will often lead to failure. If you wish to work in the online market and build a support system that will allow your business to thrive, you will need to have enough confidence within yourself to allow your brand to succeed.

Far too many entrepreneurs have fallen by the wayside because they don't believe that they can make it in the long run. This leads to many of them stopping before they impact their target market. It's true that all work in the online market is competitive, but you won't know how successful your brand can be until you get out there and allow it some time to develop. If you're willing to put the time and effort into your brand, it will be successful, but you need to have the confidence to ensure that it builds with time.

Avoiding video content. Most online users that look for content, information, or advice love to look for easy options for gaining knowledge. It's much easier to watch a video on YouTube than to read through pages and pages of data. Watching the video can be just as informative, it's far quicker, and it allows the customers to actually see what you have to offer. Don't neglect to use video footage to promote yourself or your product because it will negatively impact you in the end.

If you are camera-shy and prefer to be behind the camera than in front of it, you will have to rethink this strategy. Many online users love to see the content that their role models upload, speaking about certain topics of interest. If you want to make an impression that lasts, don't shy away from video content.

Common Promotion Techniques

When you are building the type of business you believe in, you will need to look at certain tactics that will help it thrive. There are many options to choose from when trying to build your brand, and these four will help your branding stand out from the rest.

. . .

Blogging. Blogging is one of the most efficient ways of building your brand online, because it creates a sense of your unique voice that can make an impression on your target audience. That said, it's important to stand out quickly when browsing your uploaded content, as research has shown that most people will only spend around seven seconds on a site and judge it accordingly. If they don't like the content that they see within that seven seconds, they go to another site. It's unfortunately as simple as that.

This means that your first few lines of content need to be remarkably engaging, and that your site needs to be one of the first sites that pop up when someone searches a particular product. People aren't going to wade through multiple pages of a Google search and will typically only visit the first five sites that are listed. This means that you have to be incredibly careful what type of content you put on your website. Using certain keywords in your uploads can help make sure your website or blog is one of the first sites that pop up in specific searches. This is known as Search Engine Optimisation (SEO), which we will look at later in the book.

Blogging is an essential part of building a brand. Online writers can make a full-time career of blogging, and their blog will be the central part of their brand because it comprises the largest aspect of the business as a whole. On the other hand, you might be using a blog as merely a form of advertisement for your business. In that case, your blog needs to be an extension of yourself. Keep your readers interested by building a truthful narrative about yourself; and use specific keywords to increase the likelihood of your blog popping up as one of the first results when searching for businesses or products like the ones you offer.

Keep your blog personal, make sure to add personal touches like videos and pictures, and allow people to get a picture of you. Don't just include the products that your business has to offer, but also show yourself using the products and share how the business has affected your life. People like to experience interesting narratives, and blogging is a platform that allows for precisely that.

. . .

Webinars. Having a personal brand that is noticeable and influential doesn't happen overnight, but one of the ways that a brand can be developed is by hosting webinars. A webinar is a meeting or presentation that is live streamed on the internet. What's great about hosting a webinar is that people can log into the display regardless of where they are in the world, as long as they have a reasonable internet connection and a device that can access the site. This exponentially increases the number of people that can view your presentation, which bolsters your personal brand.

The reason why webinars work so well to boost branding is because of the sheer number of attendees. People attend seminars when they are interested in certain topics, and making your business available on a live, online presentation will increase people's knowledge and understanding of you.

If you are interested in hosting a webinar, then you will need to ensure that people know about it. Advertise on all of your social media platforms to increase awareness of your webinar and send out individual invitations to customers you may have interacted with in the past. A webinar is a brilliant way to boost your brand but remember that you must adequately prepare and create enough awareness before you host one.

Another way for you to ensure that your webinars are successful is to target specific people interested in your topic. This is going to take a little research on your part, but customers will be more likely to watch your other uploads and webinars if they are on subjects they enjoy. If, for example, you are starting a reptile-breeding business, and you regularly handle snakes during your videos, advertise to people that are interested in reptiles. Don't just send invitations to everyone in your contacts because it's likely to be a wasted effort and is classed as spamming. Finding the right people to invite will take some insight; fortunately, it is remarkably easy to find those interested in the subject you are discussing by joining similar groups online and posting in forums related to the subject.

Public speaking. People view public speaking as one of the scariest aspects of increasing awareness about projects they are working on.

Getting up and speaking in front of people is a rather daunting task, the fear of which usually stems from childhood. That said, being able to speak publicly with confidence and authenticity that will make people enjoy listening to you will greatly develop your brand. But delivering a speech that feels rushed, is poorly prepared, or sounds fake will damage your progress.

Practice how efficient you are at public speaking. People are attracted to confident speakers that create a sense of engagement. Crowds enjoy obtaining information that is easy to remember and helpful, and an active public speaker can deliver this to them. Since this is such an efficient marketing tool, it will be advisable for you to practice speaking, one-on-one, to a few people or to larger crowds. If you are nervous about speaking to groups, here are some pointers to develop your self-confidence.

You do need to be knowledgeable about the subject that you are going to be discussing, but this doesn't mean you need to be an expert at everything you speak about. Some of the most popular talks at events and conferences are aimed at a beginner or intermediate level. People respond well to speakers who can speak like they are professionals in the field. This means that you will need enough knowledge on the subject to answer questions that people may ask. Always include humour and interesting stories or anecdotes that revolve around the subject to make it relatable.

You need to rehearse your speech, adjust it, and then rehearse it some more. If you are comfortable discussing a subject, people will take note of your effort and better enjoy listening to you. One of the biggest turn-offs is a speaker that doesn't know the material or topic they're presenting. If you sound like you're reading from cards or reciting from memory, rather than having a conversation with your audience, people will quickly get bored and stop listening. Practice your speeches with a trusted friend or family member and record yourself while doing it so you can play it back later and make any necessary adjustments.

You need to understand what type of audience you're addressing. Customers like a personal touch and they appreciate it if you spend time getting to know them. If you make the effort to get to know your audience, you will understand how best to address them later and include information that they might find interesting.

Familiarise yourself with the venue that you're going to speak in. If you are nervous about making a public speech, then arrive early to look around and familiarise yourself with the place. This will also allow you some extra time to run through your notes.

Finally, remember to smile and breathe. It's going to be stressful when you start making your speech, but once you get started, you will become more comfortable. Your audience will understand that you may be a bit nervous, so remember to smile and breathe. The nerves will pass.

Social media. Sharing content on social media platforms is one of the best ways for people to get to know you and for you to get information about your business out there. If you are only working on one or two social media sites, you may need to consider expanding your reach. There are several social media platforms available, and all of them appeal to a different range of followers. Anyone on social media can ultimately become your next customer, so it's a remarkably convenient advertising tool when used correctly.

When you are building your brand, ensure that you are signed up to multiple social media platforms, and regularly update them. This keeps followers and prospective customers interested in any new uploads that you release. Once you have a growing following, it's important to regularly add new and positive content.

Your brand will take some time to become established but using social media can accelerate this process. Customers and new contacts can easily be formed on these platforms, so ensure you spend enough time there, building your personal brand. Social media platforms are generally free, unless you pay for advertising, so it enables you to have a free form of advertising for your business, and it helps people see you. Your brand can be developed very effectively if social media is used wisely.

Many people may find social media trickier to use than others, or genuinely struggle, either because they are introverted by nature, don't like "wasting time" on these sites, or simply don't know how to use the platforms. If you find yourself disliking social media, keep in mind that you are doing it for your business, not to amuse yourself. Even though you are going to be releasing personal content online to build your brand, you get to choose what information you release, and you can be very specific about this to maintain your privacy. If you are unsure about how to create accounts on Facebook, LinkedIn, Instagram, and Twitter, to name a few, try searching on YouTube to help along the way.

The Authors Approach

Most of what I do in my business is based on my personal brand. The courses I create, the books I write and the talks I give are all from the perspective of my personal brand, which, in effect, makes me the product for the company.

When producing courses, even though they are for other platforms which I don't control, the courses are in my name, and over time I have built up a loyal following of people who watch my content. The same goes for books, blog entries, and even posts on Twitter. Therefore, I try to manage my personal brand very carefully. I rarely court controversy online, I don't discuss politics, and I keep my public image and appearances on topic to what I am trying to convey to an audience. A personal brand can be a fragile thing, and I have seen some people, whose brands I respected, destroy theirs overnight by saying something controversial, and then reacting badly to a public backlash.

With my product brand for *The Path to Freedom*, I am working with two brands. The brand for this book and online workshops, but also my personal brand. As well as trying to give the reader lots of factual information to help them start their own small business, I am sharing a lot of my personal experiences about how I have applied various subjects and techniques in my own professional life. I am hoping that the reader finds them interesting and informative but sharing these is also an extension of my personal brand by giving you some of my insights.

For *The Path to Freedom*, I tell a story in the introduction of this book about how I had a business setback earlier in life, which made me reluctant to start a new business. This story is 100% true, I didn't just make it up; but even though these were life events that I found very stressful and upsetting at the time, they also became a powerful story about why I wrote this book and pursued the whole *Path to Freedom* idea. Humans are social creatures, and part of the way we interact and bond is by telling stories. I hope that sharing the story of why I was scared to run a business helps you relate to me, and therefore bond with the information I present in the book. That is a compelling thing.

I must admit it does feel strange to acknowledge that fact about why I shared this story, but in a chapter about personal branding, it is quite fitting. By carefully thinking about the story of how you came to create your product or service, you are bringing a human and personal feel to your business, which is something larger organisations often lack. That human side of the business is a secret weapon in your arsenal that you can use to try to relate to your audience. Remember though—the story has to be real. Don't try to lie to your audience or potential customers. You will be found out eventually.

Earlier in the book, we talked about the idea of the sales funnel. At the top of the funnel, you have activities that you do to try and encourage customers to listen to you. Then you try to get them to work their way down the funnel to eventually buy a product. Afterwards, they could potentially work their way further down the funnel by purchasing a service or some coaching time. This is precisely the approach I am using.

My ideal scenario is that someone likes what I do enough to buy this book, then hopefully, my online course/workshop. I am not going to necessarily achieve that by continually doing a hard sell against people all the time; spamming people with sales requests will just put people off.

Instead, at the top of my funnel, where I will be spending most of my time, I will be making lots of good, useful and valuable content that I give away for free, with no expectation of making any sales. I will make YouTube factual videos where I tackle different subjects, record business update vlogs (video blogs) and write blog posts. I will create informational posts on Instagram, and also tweet useful information on Twitter. I will hold regular free webinars where I give a valuable 60- to 90-minute talk.

The intention behind doing all this is that if people like my content enough, then they may want to buy the book or watch the course. If they don't, that's fine; they are already really helping me out by reading or watching my content, and hopefully, sharing it with their friends, family and colleagues.

Personal branding isn't all about trying to sell repeatedly. You are trying to get people to bond with you and relate to you enough that they follow what you have to say. If you do that well, then you may be rewarded with sales. Once the book is released and the video course/workshop published, I expect to spend 90% of my time working on personal branding and all the content creation that goes along with it at the top of the sales funnel.

Summary

Your brand is one of the most important aspects of becoming profitable in today's market. People want to see the real you, and once they feel that they have a personal connection with you, they are more likely to buy the products/content you are producing.

In the previous chapter, you discovered how important product branding is, but personal branding is also crucial to becoming successful in the business market. Take the time to build yourself up, so people start recognising you as a brand. Customers want to know the real you, and not just the business that you run.

Be truthful in all of the content you release and allow your brand to tell a story. Aim to positively impact others with your brand and build a supportive community around it. People who demean others to develop their brand will ultimately fail, because they will attract a following of those who aren't usually loyal. Once something goes wrong with you, your site, or your business, many of those followers have been known to disappear instantly. This happens all the time, so don't let it happen to you.

Release content on a regular basis and keep your uploads genuine and authentic. If you use content that comes from others, then ensure that you put a unique twist on the information. Have the confidence to release new content and develop your brand and make it easily accessible to your customers.

Workshop Questions

(1) Write your backstory that shows why you are building your product or service. Think about how your personal story influences the story of your product. This story will become a part of your personal brand.

(2) Make a list of techniques you can use to promote your brand from blogging, podcasting, videos, or public speaking. Think about the content that you can create in each area. Who are the people you want to target the content towards?

21

MARKETING BASICS

Making a success of your business can be difficult and seem overly daunting at times. You may feel that you are doing everything right—your product and personal branding seem good enough, but you may feel that your business, sales, and the interest of customers have become a little stagnant. This is where marketing and sales come into the picture, which are arguably the hardest parts of running a business.

Marketing is the ongoing process of making a product or service attractive enough for customers to want to buy. It involves promoting, selling, researching, and distributing services or products. This process is ongoing because as demand changes, your services or products will need to adapt to stay appealing in the changing market.

It's important to know that marketing is a lot more than merely promoting your business and the products that it has to offer. Promotion and advertising may be the two main components but marketing itself involves several other aspects that need to be considered and developed. To successfully market your business and your brand, you need to view marketing as a thorough implementation of novel and innovative ideas to build your business, which will ultimately lead to the establishment of effective communication and brand development.

Marketing may have many factors that are involved in it, but there is one main purpose of successful marketing: to establish a developing base of supportive and satisfied customers. These customers will provide repeat business and ultimately advertise your business to others through word-of-mouth promotion.

Once you have created and implemented an effective marketing plan, keeping all of your business efforts focused will, inevitably, boost your sales.

The success story of Apple. Most of us know of Steve Jobs and the remarkable technological developments that he made for the company that he helped establish in the 1970s, known as Apple Inc. Although Apple may be a successfully established enterprise today, it started in the same place that many other businesses start—in the back of a garage.

Apple has grown to be one of the largest companies in the world today, competing with massive, multibillion-dollar enterprises like Microsoft and Google. It's considered the largest technology company to date with over 140,000 employees in their service, which profited more than $274 billion dollars in 2020.

Simplicity and beauty became the core characteristics of Apple, and most of their customers soon became aware of these traits after they purchased Apple products. This simple beauty that attracted the customers was backed by a significant amount of reliability and user-friendliness. When positive personal reviews about Apple started to spread, Apple made a marketing strategy that has made them one of the most sought-after digital brands today: they built their success on creating and sustaining loyalty to their brand.

Apple customers are known to be exceptionally loyal to the Apple brand. They will queue for hours, and sometimes days, for the chance to purchase the newest Apple product release. This type of loyalty is not something that is merely bought. Cheap products come and go and offer many freebies on the side to sound attractive. Apple isn't a company that sacrifices quality for quantity, and their customers know that.

The type of marketing that Apple has accomplished is one of the most successful in the world. Not bad for a company started in a garage.

The Four Ps of Successful Marketing

To be successful in whatever business you want to run, you are going to need to have exemplary marketing skills. For a business' marketing strategy to be successful, it needs to identify target markets, and then apply products and services to those target markets. But because so many people have given advice over the years about where to start and how to market, it can be rather confusing. That said, marketing strategies are rooted in customer satisfaction, consumer value, and the quality of the products being provided. Marketing itself can be streamlined into four variables, namely, the Four Ps; Product, Place, Price and Promotion.

Product. The very first action that you will take before considering starting a business is to identify the need for a certain service or product. Whatever you want to deliver to a specific target market needs to be needed or desired. Many small businesses that are still in the developmental phases tend to go through persistent difficulties because they offer products that larger and more established businesses already offer. It's important to remember that customers are inherently going to trust brands that they know. If your business is still developing, and it's offering exactly the same products as a larger competitor, then your business is going to struggle, even if you make your products cheaper. Customers will pay more for brands that they trust.

If you want to start a successful business, then you need to carefully consider what types of products you are going to present to a specific target market. This may seem like the easiest P in the Four Ps, but it can turn out to be the most difficult. Your product needs to be uniquely attractive to the target market. You may be tempted to assume that you will be able to sell any product to a prospective target market, but this will fail unless you have done the right amount of research on the market that you want to sell to.

You need to carefully consider what you want to offer. You want to establish your business as an enterprise that meets the needs and demands of your customers. This takes time, and also means that you need to consider the warranties of your products and the customer support systems that your business has in place. They need to be well stipulated to keep your customers satisfied.

Place. Some businesses thrive because they are placed in the right location. Businesses that are easy to locate and visible from a distance tend to have many customers frequenting them and are more attractive to people than businesses that are off the main roads or hidden in "dangerous neighbourhoods". Deciding on the physical location of your business is important because it will impact the amount of foot traffic that it experiences (if you intend to open a physical location and are not only offering online services).

There are three main aspects that are associated with Place in the Four Ps: the physical location of the business; how the products will be distributed when the business grows; and finally, how the products will be delivered to the customers.

Keep in mind that the location where you decide to put your business needs to paint an attractive picture of how you want people to view your products. The logo is the face of the brand of your products, but your business location and design may become the face of your business itself. Carefully consider why you would want your business to be situated in a particular location and if it would seem attractive to customers.

Price. Choosing the right price that customers should pay for your products can be a little trickier than it seems. There are numerous factors that need to be considered when setting the prices for particular products, like:

- Cash vs credit purchases (some businesses offer discounts on cash purchases to customers)
- Credit collections
- Price vs perception of quality
- Discounts on certain products

These are four of the main aspects that will help you consider what prices you will charge for your products, but you should also research what your competitors are charging for similar products. You need to find a healthy range in the prices that you set, because prices that are set too low may be avoided by customers concerned about being ripped off through "too-good-to-be-true" bargains. Some unethical practices that greedy businesses have attempted in the past have included selling products that are defective or spoiled at a greatly reduced price to recuperate some of the money that they'd lost. This is the type of practice that makes many potential customers wary.

In the online world, setting prices too low for products often causes a race for the bottom where everyone starts setting their prices very low to try and compete, which benefits no-one. Very low-priced products online can have a reputation for being low quality, and this generally holds true. You need to remember that if you have a strong personal brand, you can charge higher prices for a quality product.

On the other hand, you don't want to make your prices too high, as that makes them unaffordable to many people. It may seem tempting to do so, but a reputation for un-affordability will damage your business in the long run.

When you are deciding on the right price for your product, you need to do ample research to find an attractive price when compared to your competitors, and you want to make enough profit to consider the wages, tax, and overhead costs that your business needs to support.

Promotion. Promotion of your business is one of the most effective marketing tools because it communicates the benefits and the values of your products to your customers. People aren't likely to buy products that aren't well promoted because they remain unsure of the products themselves. The four aspects of successful promotion are:

- Self/direct marketing of your products and business
- General advertising
- Sales promotion
- Personally selling your product to customers

If you are ever unsure about whether you should promote your business, try putting yourself in your customers' shoes. This will give you an idea of how they see your business. Successfully advertising and promoting your business will give you a strong chance of staying ahead of your competition. Whenever in doubt about how effective the promotion of your business/products is, then view it from another perspective, or ask someone that can give you their unbiased opinion on whether they believe it's effective or not.

Business to Business vs Business to Consumer

When you're dealing with marketing your business and your products, you need to consider to whom you are marketing. There might be some overlap between the strategies required for the business-to-business (B2B) and business-to-consumer (B2C) models but understanding how these marketing strategies need to differ from one another will determine how successful your business is in the long run.

The primary difference between the two is that B2B is focused on logical marketing, while B2C is focused on emotional marketing. This difference can be further broken down by five distinct characteristics.

How customer relationships are viewed. The most effective way to build B2B relationships is by building personal connections that will produce long-term relationships between businesses. The reason why these types of relationships are so beneficial is because they give you and your business the opportunity to show exactly what types of morals, values, and practices you uphold. This opportunity to connect with your target audience allows you to separate your product and your business from the rest of the possible competitors in the market.

The most effective way to build B2C relationships is by establishing transactional rapport. These relationships encourage consumers to either buy products from your business, or the business of your client. They are established when the customer has a near-perfect experience with your online site or personal interaction with your business. B2C relationships are based on efficiency and the theory that time is money. The marketing strategy here is to not build a personal connection with the customer, because it's not necessary. Because the customer is happy about the time they have saved and the product they have purchased, they will experience higher levels of satisfaction, creating a transactional connection to your business. The basis for this relationship is still an emotional one, even though there are little or no personal connections made.

How branding is viewed. The main branding focus in the B2B market is on relationships. Product and personal branding are developed in the B2B market when your business is consistent, including consistency in what your business values and how your products and services are delivered. Allow the personality of your business to shine through so that customers will be more likely to want to enter into a mutually beneficial relationship with you. Always keep a close eye on the other personalities within the market to ensure that your brand stays uniquely identifiable. Having the opportunity to adjust your branding's vision towards your target audience will help increase your brand's recognition among customers.

The main branding focus in the B2C market is to prioritise your message. Branding is the most important priority and most effective tool in the B2C marketing model. The reason for this is because there is a lack of direct connection between the customers and the business, which means that all the customer has to really judge your products on is the brand that they fall under. Branding allows for precise messaging towards customers. This will establish credibility with the customer, and they will feel a more established form of loyalty towards the brand. Even though a personal connection is absent, customers can still feel like part of the business when the messages are prioritised towards them and their needs. Once again, your focus should be on establishing an emotional connection with the customer through your message.

. . .

How the decision-making process changes between B2B and B2C. Since a personal connection needs to be established in the B2B market, decision-making processes can become strenuous when both businesses aren't on the same page or don't agree upon the same values. This is why an open means of communication is paramount for the success of a B2B relationship, as it allows both businesses to ascertain whether or not the relationship between the businesses will work.

For the decision-making process to be successful in the B2C market, the process needs to be simplified. The consumers are fully aware of the type of product that they want to buy, which makes them more amenable when looking at buying certain products than the customers in B2B, because they have a clear understanding of what they want. If the decision-making process is simplified for the customers in the B2C market, then they will be more inclined to buy your product.

How the targeting of the audience changes between B2B and B2C. The relationships in the B2B model thrive in a niche market. This is why it's important to find your niche so that you can specifically and successfully target certain demographics. By actively using both quantitative and qualitative data in order to find the correct demographic, you will discover which businesses have the same values as you and can form a successful relationship with you.

Unlike B2B, B2C businesses work in much larger markets, so their targets aren't as specific as finding a particular niche. When dealing with a B2C market, it's imperative to follow the marketing funnel when trying to attract new customers. When a successful marketer aims their advertisements that are skewed towards emotion at the top of the marketing funnel, it can result in potential customer leads in the process. Understanding that there are much larger demographics in this market, and emotional advertisements need to be aimed at larger target groups, may possibly lead to successful outcomes later on.

. . .

How advertising content is viewed. B2B businesses are exponentially more likely to work with people that know the terminology, decisions, and business processes that make them successful. If you want to make a mark in a specific B2B sector, then you will need to learn their lingo. To reach the right target audience, you will need to speak a language that they respond to. If you are required to write content for your business' online site or advertisements, you will need to write that content in such a way that it removes the emotion from the decision, and rather, builds confidence in the business that you are trying to appeal to.

B2C, on the other hand, needs content that does target your customers' emotions. B2C advertising content must be written in the type of language that compels the customer to click on the site or read the rest of the advertisement. Copywriting for B2C needs to evoke emotion in the readers for it to be effective. Strategically placing emotional content in these types of advertisements will increase the probability of customers buying products from your business.

Digital Marketing vs Traditional Marketing

It's imperative to have a certain amount of money set aside for you to successfully market your brand, but you also need to know how to use that money to make the marketing successful. Many business owners don't know whether they should carry on using the traditional marketing method to bring awareness to their brand, or if they should switch over to digital marketing styles. Most businesses struggle to make this decision, and even though both methods can bring about certain levels of success, they do produce very different results.

Ensuring that your business stays successful has less to do with how to choose the right target market and quality of the products available, and more to do with leveraging the right kinds of marketing techniques to attract potential customers. If you are serious about increasing your company's profit margins, then you will need to consider reviewing your marketing budget and exactly how you spend the money to advertise your brand.

Traditional marketing is any type of marketing that isn't done online and is the oldest and most researched form of marketing. It includes marketing avenues like billboards, printed advertisements, direct mail, and radio broadcasts. Many marketers and business owners that are set in their ways tend to prefer this type of marketing method because it's successfully tried and tested. Traditional marketing is effective at reaching local and older audiences. There are some additional benefits to traditional marketing. For example, printed adverts can be read repeatedly as long as they're in print.

Digital marketing, on the other hand, is marketing that stays purely on digital platforms. Because of the digital revolution that has occurred over the last two decades with the rapid evolution of technology, it made sense for more and more businesses to move onto online platforms to advertise their brands and their products. Digital marketing companies focus on releasing content in emails, on websites, and in pop-up adverts. This strategy works out to be more cost effective, and it's able to connect to a global market.

Is digital marketing better than traditional marketing? There is an ongoing debate about whether or not digital marketing is better than traditional marketing, and even though there are still many benefits to the traditional method, digital marketing does prove to be far more effective. It's very difficult for traditional marketing to effectively interact with the audience. Businesses using traditional marketing methods need to wait for customers to get in touch with them if they are interested in a product, whereas digital marketing businesses can connect with prospective customers in real time because of social media connections, emails, and instant messages. These direct interactions between brands and their customers allow for discussions to start and any questions to be answered before the customers make their decision on the product. Traditional marketing practices tend to work better with well established brands and products. Digital marketing does work well for established brands too, but it also works well for new products onto the market.

This means that any brand that uses digital marketing as its primary method of marketing has a much better presence with its target audience than brands that rely on traditional marketing only. Digital marketing increases the likelihood of customer satisfaction, repeat business, and brand loyalty.

It's almost impossible to measure how successful certain traditional marketing methods are because there is no knowing how many of the target audience actually read the advertisements in the brochures, newspapers, or billboards. Relying on customers to contact you means that your brand always has to respond from a passive, reactive stance. Digital marketing methods, however, allow you to proactively reach out to customers that have come across your site or advertisement *at that moment,* and you can then follow up with advice for the customer.

All of the traffic on a website can be monitored and analysed to help you understand how effectively the marketing technique worked. There are multiple online tools that you can download to help you track the visits on your sites and follow up with customers. There are versions that you can pay for, but Google produced a free version of this tool called Google Analytics. If you are planning on relying solely on digital marketing methods, then you need to ensure that you use these tools to your advantage.

Digital marketing methods are instantly shareable, and that makes it possible for your business to reach far more customers than any traditional marketing method ever could. Traditional methods take time to print and distribute, whereas digital marketing can have content written, published, and accessible in the space of a few hours. That said, it's important not to rush content that has been written for any digital marketing method, because customers do pick up on typos, incorrect information, and poor grammar. Even though content can be made instantly accessible, it doesn't mean it shouldn't be double-checked and polished before its release.

Finally, digital marketing is much cheaper than traditional advertising. The reason for this is because printing costs will take up a huge amount of your marketing budget. If you are planning on reaching a large audience then you will have to spend more money. Digital marketing, on the other hand, doesn't have the same costs involved as actually printing advertisements. There will be some costs involved to release the adverts on different platforms, but those adverts will become accessible to everyone that visits the platform. This means that digital marketing is able to reach far more people at a fraction of the usual marketing costs.

. . .

The benefits of traditional marketing in the digital age. The previous section may have made it sound like there was little to no advantage in using traditional marketing methods, but this isn't the case. Even though digital marketing is superior to traditional, there are still several benefits that can be realised by using traditional methods.

When you are specifically targeting a smaller group of local consumers, it's definitely helpful to use a traditional marketing method instead of a digital one. For example, the local cattle farmer on the outskirts of a small town is going to benefit far more from printing adverts about his milk being for sale in the local stores than he would from trying to digitally market his product.

Any promotional materials that are used in the advertising process can be reused and eventually recycled. Even though the internet has made a global impact, there are still several smaller communities that rely more on the traditional way of doing things. Brochures are able to be reread from time to time even when there is no internet connection. These types of printed adverts can stay in circulation until they are eventually recycled.

Traditional marketing methods keep a simple sense of familiarity that's easy for people to understand. When they pick up a brochure and read the first few lines, people will know immediately what the business or brand is all about. Digital platforms can be slightly more difficult for older people to navigate, especially if they're still unsure and uncomfortable with the use of the internet.

Finally, traditional marketing methods have proven high success rates. With everything in the world moving towards digital options, it's strange to see that traditional marketing methods still exist at all. But the real reason why traditional marketing will never become redundant is that it's tried and tested. It was the only successful way of advertising before the digital revolution, and it still remains successful today because people are familiar with it. Even though traditional marketing methods aren't as frequently used as they used to be, they will still be around for years to come.

Traditional marketing techniques. One of the most effective traditional marketing methods is using billboards to advertise certain brands. Billboards may be expensive to use, and once your advertisement is up there, it can't be changed for an extended period of time, but using a billboard is a quick way to grab a commuter's attention and make them ponder about a certain product on their way to or from work. Billboards use the effect of pictures on your emotions. The carefully chosen picture evokes enough thought and emotion within a person that they consider buying a certain brand of product. Billboards are remarkable advertising and marketing tools.

Direct mail is making a comeback. Because of all the spam that people get in their inboxes today, they often don't read any of them before discarding the entire bunch. If your brand email or advertisement is considered spam, then it will never make an impact on your target audience. It has been found that actually mailing someone an advert or query letter increases the potential of them actually reading it and remembering your brand.

If you walk around in a mall or other type of shopping centre, you may encounter people handing out flyers and brochures to advertise their businesses inside the centres. This is great to attract people to certain events that are happening in their immediate vicinity. This personal touch to a marketing method does increase the chances of people coming to see what the business is like for themselves because they're close enough to it to let their curiosity win over.

Finally, printing advertisements isn't a marketing tactic that is going to ever disappear, it's merely going to evolve. Newspapers and magazines may be en route to becoming digital, but that doesn't mean that their page layouts are going to be any different than if they were printed on paper. This means that advertisements can still be effectively printed in newspapers and magazines where enough people will see them.

It's important to know that good marketing is needed to sell a good product. There are benefits to both traditional and digital marketing methods, and you need to choose which one is going to work the best for your business.

Popular Internet Marketing Platforms

Since there are so many online sites available to help you successfully market your brand, it can become daunting to know where to go. This section is going to discuss four different platforms that can help you sell your brand or your products.

Google AdWords. Since Google is one of the most frequently used search engines, it's easy to see why using one of their marketing platforms would be beneficial to your brand. When anyone searches for something on Google, the search engine looks through its AdWords platform to determine if there will be an auction amongst the competitors with the same product. Specific keywords are important in determining how effective a page will be and where it will appear when those keywords are searched. If two or more marketers are interested in the same keywords, then a Google auction is activated.

Marketers identify keywords that they want to bid on, and they regulate how much they are willing to spend on specific keywords. Google then creates groupings of these specific keywords that are associated with the advertisements. Next, Google enters the keyword into your account that it deems relevant to the searches that are taking place. Google then takes the maximum bid that you have placed for a certain keyword into account and places your advertisement in the sequential order of other similar advertisements. If your maximum bid was more than your competitors, then your advertisement will pop up above those of your competitors.

Advantages. One of the greatest advantages of AdWords is that it works faster than search engine optimisation (SEO). Both AdWords and SEO are optimisation strategies designed to lead more customers towards your site or advertisements if keywords are specifically searched. As efficient as SEO is, AdWords can work much more quickly and efficiently for several reasons: it can focus on multiple keywords at a time; you have complete control over your campaign; and your adverts get immediate visibility on the top of site pages. We will look at SEO later in this book.

AdWords can increase the awareness of your brand by not only increasing traffic towards your site and adverts, but also by creating an efficient way to communicate to people what your brand is all about. Google AdWords and Notifications can alert you and your customers about potential interest to open up a channel of communication.

AdWords is further able to reach more potential customers through integrated promotions that appear in their Gmail inboxes. By targeting users that frequently search specific keywords, Google AdWords is better able to open a potential link between buyer and seller. An additional benefit here is that you can easily use Google Ads to promote your brand if you are worried about your budget. Google Ads are relatively cheap, and since they work through AdWords, it can still connect you to the right types of prospective customers.

Google AdWords also gives you the opportunity to reconnect with potential customers. Some people are unsure about what they want, and only browse some sites for the sake of interest. But if you believe that there may be a few individuals that could become customers, then you can set your Google AdWords account to track activity on your site that allows you to re-invite the potential customer to your business.

AdWords allows you to consistently measure your performance. It tracks all your site activity, so you're able to see who viewed your site and clicked on your advert, how much overall traffic you had to your site, how many leads were developed and how much each of those will cost you. This data helps marketers understand what successfully worked and what didn't, which allows them to tailor their site or adverts accordingly.

Disadvantages. AdWords seems to have too many keywords that make their searches too broad for the customers. This can mean that you fail to attract the right type of target audience. Additionally, customers have to scroll through a lot of sites until they find what they want, and by the time that they do come to your site, they may feel exasperated and even close your page without reading it. This would make your visitors feel like they had a bad experience, and possibly prevent them returning to your site. This problem is amplified because you would have paid for the AdWords service that ended up disadvantaging you in the long run. It's important to note that although it doesn't always happen when browsers have too many keywords, there is a risk of it occurring.

You are forced to wait for customers to come to you with AdWords, and you may feel like you aren't actively helping people find your site. Having people visit your site can take a long time and you won't be able to constructively analyse the data until your site has had at least 200 views. This wait can be frustrating and even demoralising at times.

To successfully use AdWords, you may need some professional help. Setting up your account is simple enough but understanding how to set up your keywords for your site may take some professional guidance. These are primarily paid services, although there are some out there that provide free assistance.

Twitter Ads. Twitter is one of the most active social media platforms, allowing people to "tweet" short messages of up to 280 characters. Because of the increasing traffic on the platform and an ever-changing algorithm that alters the way messages are uploaded, marketing on Twitter can get completely lost because people simply don't see it. To combat this, Twitter has developed a way for businesses to successfully advertise on their platform in such a way that all users will come across them.

As Twitter is aware of the fact that different businesses will require different approaches, they have designed a range of adverts that can be employed across their platform so that multiple businesses can benefit from them.

Their first type of advert is known as a Promoted Tweet. Promoted tweets look similar to regular tweets, but what makes them different is that a marketer is paying the platform to release that tweet to Twitter users who aren't following them. This allows Twitter users to quickly view the advert before moving on to their other tweets.

The second type of advert available is known as a Promoted Account. Users are able to pay Twitter to advertise their entire account, instead of just a specified tweet that they post. This advert also targets people that don't already follow the business and gives them the option to follow the account from the promotional video.

The third type of advert is known as a Promoted Trend. Trends are the most viewed and commented-on media on social platforms and releasing promoted trends here will expose customers to new trends on the platform. If your business or brand is unique enough, it may fall into the Promoted Trend category.

Advantages. You will quickly notice that you are going to be up against a lot of competition while you are trying to market your brand online, and this is true for most online platforms. Fortunately, there is currently much less competition in Twitter Ads, which increases your probability of being noticed by potential customers. One of the reasons why Twitter Ads isn't as flooded as other sites is because it does have a smaller user base than other social media platforms.

Twitter has around 200 million active users at the time of writing this, and even though that number is large, it's still significantly less than Facebook. It is generally assumed that sites that don't feature as much traffic as other sites may not be as useful, but this isn't the case for Twitter. Several businesses don't bother advertising on Twitter because they feel it is a waste of their time and money—which puts many smaller businesses in a perfect place to make advantageous decisions while both saving money and spreading the word about their brands. Additionally, advertising on Twitter is considerably cheaper than on other sites because of the lower marketing traffic.

If you choose to advertise on Twitter, you are also increasing the chances of introducing your brand to a different audience. Research has found that Twitter audiences are better educated and slightly younger than audiences from other social media platforms. Opening the door to your brand to younger demographics with more money to spend is a great business choice.

Unlike other platforms, Twitter Ads allows you to easily control how broad or narrow you would like your potential customer audience to be. You can control the settings of your adverts to only pop up to a few individuals, or you can set it to pop up to others after a few keywords are entered on their Twitter pages. The choice is entirely up to you who you want to attract and how much money you want to spend on leads.

Twitter Ads is also considerably more linear than other social media adverts. This means that you will be able to focus on what types of leads you get on a daily basis because of keywords that were entered by the audience. If the leads come back at $20 on one day, you will have similar search results the next day, and if you pay the $20 you will be able to advertise to those leads. Other social media sites fluctuate terribly from a few pennies on one day to $100 on the next. This makes it exceedingly difficult to budget, but Twitter has avoided this, making it much easier for marketers.

Finally, research has found that users on Twitter are more likely to read detailed content on adverts versus users on other platforms. Users on Twitter have been more open and receptive to pop-up adverts from marketers as well, especially if the adverts are humorous or entertaining.

Disadvantages. Twitter doesn't monitor data nearly as closely as other platforms, and this can drive certain marketers crazy because data analysis is an important way to stay ahead of the curve. Data analysis allows for careful tracking of target audiences and how they responded to your site or advert. If you aren't able to adequately analyse data, then you are, in a way, going in blind with your marketing and hoping for the best.

Twitter can spend your overall budget very quickly if you're not closely monitoring how your tweets are being spread. If you're not careful, your $1,000 budget can be obliterated in an hour, because other marketers started too high with their bidding and all the money got used before more traffic had the opportunity to see the advert. This is why it's imperative to start out small and then increase the bids as the traffic increases to an amount that you're happy with.

Twitter Ads are not user-friendly for the most part. Many internet platforms made their advert capabilities much easier to use when the competition started growing; unfortunately, Twitter didn't get the memo about making their adverts easier to use.

Facebook Ads. Facebook is the largest and the most renowned social media sites, with more than 2.8 billion active subscribers at the end of 2020. Because of the vast number of different audiences that are available on the site, it's clear that it can easily be one of the best platforms on which to market your brand. If you are familiar with Twitter Ads, then you will find setting up an account to release Facebook Ads significantly easier.

The adverts that you design will pop up in the newsfeeds of users that don't know you. This will increase awareness of your brand. Advert content is often paired with news and video uploads, but user information is never released or sold to marketers. There are privacy policies in place on practically all social media sites to prevent privacy breaches from occurring. Even though you won't physically have your customers' information, your adverts can still appear to them when the Facebook settings pick up specific keyword entries from certain demographics.

Advantages. Apart from Google Search, Facebook is the most visited website in the world, which means that when you choose to use Facebook Ads, your adverts will be viewed by many people. It's practically guaranteed that some of those people will be your target audience, which will greatly help grow your business.

While using Facebook Ads, you can determine how specific you want your target audience to be. Because Facebook is a globally recognised platform, you can decide how far you want your adverts to reach. Some large businesses want global exposure, while others prefer to keep their exposure local. This is all dependent on the types of products or services that are being sold, and global exposure will cost more, so choose carefully how much exposure you want at the beginning of your marketing journey.

Facebook Ads can increase the chances that readers retain the information that they take in from the adverts that they read, by increasing incentives for readers to spread the word about your advert. Facebook also tracks who "liked" your advert and will be able to use them like a lead later on, for further interest or for different adverts from your business.

Finally, Facebook Ads is a very affordable service. Because of the sheer volume of traffic that frequents Facebook, uploading an advert can work out to be relatively cheap but still remarkably effective in attracting customers.

Disadvantages. Because Facebook has such a high volume of users, there is a lower number of views per advert released. There will be some traffic when your brand grows, but this can take time in the beginning. This is one of the main reasons why using multiple platforms in the beginning stages of marketing is imperative to increase brand awareness.

Facebook Ads are effective in data analysis, but again, because of the sheer number of users that the platform has, analysing the data of all of the adverts can take time. This effect is further worsened by people intentionally blocking ads from popping up on their feed. This greatly affects the accuracy of the data released to the marketers and can create a tedious process for them to establish which customers are getting their adverts and which aren't.

Instagram Ads. Instagram has over one billion followers, and also offers a way for marketers to advertise to their target audiences. If you are interested in launching an advert on Instagram, you will first need a registered Facebook Ads account.

Instagram Ads are similar to other social media promotions, but they don't work in exactly the same way. Because Instagram is almost solely dedicated to video and picture uploads, their advert services work in the same format. There are three types of adverts that can be used on Instagram Ads: adverts with pictures, adverts with videos; and sequential adverts, that consist of many images in a sequence that can be swiped through to tell a story.

Advantages. Since Instagram is now owned by Facebook, it's easy to see how some of the same advantages and disadvantages appear on both platforms. Instagram is, however, a unique platform because of the types of content on which it focuses. One of the main advantages of using Instagram is that a marketer is able to target specific demographics with ease. You are able to target your audience by their interests, behaviours, and even locations, making Instagram Ads one of the most focused platforms when it comes to target audiences.

Instagram Ads are very visually appealing because they rely on pictures and videos to convey the message of the advert. The simplicity behind pictures as adverts can work as effectively as a billboard. The additional benefit here is that extra expenses aren't needed to employ a professional photographer, and with the latest technology, it's easy to upload adverts that look professionally done. And really, you save a lot of money by doing them yourself.

Marketers are able to potentially sell more products when they use Instagram Ads, because Instagram has the ability to create shopping posts which can be linked directly to the marketing adverts.

Disadvantages. Instagram has, unfortunately, a somewhat limited audience; even though Facebook has 2.8 billion subscribers, Instagram only has around one billion. This does seem like a lot, but that doesn't mean that many people will see your marketing adverts.

Instagram doesn't handle a large volume of text well, so if you have a lot of content in your adverts, it's not going to look very appealing on this platform. It's prudent to carefully design your adverts for Instagram Ads to have a strictly limited word count.

Because Instagram is so visually oriented, it requires one to change the adverts frequently to prevent people from getting bored of seeing the same ones, which is known as advert fatigue.

Finally, Instagram Ads are remarkably time-consuming. Like all adverts on social media, Instagram Ads take a significant portion of your day to update and manage. Potential customers have the capability to interact and comment on adverts, and that takes daily monitoring, especially if you are planning on keeping interested customers from disregarding your site in the future.

The Authors Approach

I will readily admit that out of everything I have ever done in my career, marketing and sales have to be the most challenging tasks. I expect most small business owners will agree with this. No matter whether you are a software developer, a video editor, a jewellery designer or make vases and pots for your business, selling your products is hard. As small business founders (or potential founders) we all have a core set of skills, and it is these skills that we want to turn into products or services. Unless you have had a career in sales and marketing, then this will likely be the most challenging task for you to accomplish. It is why I have dedicated a large part of this book to get you started on marketing and branding.

For my own business, my marketing falls into two areas: the online pre-recorded courses that I release; and the books that I have self-published. The way I had to tackle both types of product offering had to be treated differently. Let's break them down into the Four Ps, starting with my online courses.

. . .

Product. The courses I produce are made for two companies—a massive online training provider, Pluralsight, who specialise in selling to large corporate enterprises; and a training site called Skillshare. In this relationship, I create the content, and then those platforms distribute it. I do not own or control anything about these platforms; I merely produced the content which they then publish.

Place. These courses live purely online, and people watch them via the platforms' websites or via their phone and tablet applications. My main client with these courses is Pluralsight, and they have been excellent at selling licences to the platform, not only to individual subscribers but also to companies for teams to use. The growth over the years has been incredible as they onboard more customers. Their proposition is desirable to companies as they can use the platform to design training plans for their staff. Even though I don't own or control the platform, I am comfortable in the knowledge that their sales teams are doing an excellent job at expanding the reach of my courses.

Price. The way I earn money from my courses is a little complicated. The end customer doesn't pay a fee per course to watch them, for either Pluralsight or Skillshare. Those customers pay a monthly or yearly licence fee to use the platform, and then they can consume as much content as they want from their libraries, similar to streaming services like Netflix or Amazon Prime Video. You pay a fee and watch what you like. My earnings are calculated based on the number of minutes watched, a negotiated royalty percentage which then equates to a share of a fund that is assigned each month to authors on the platforms. This means I have no control over how much I charge for my content. On the one hand, this is bad, as I don't have that level of power, but on the other hand, I don't have to worry about pricing, which is a hard thing to get right. I leave this in the hands of the expert sales teams who own the platforms.

. . .

Promotion. Promotion of my courses is handled from two sides. First, the platform owners are continually pushing the platform to individual subscribers and companies. Sometimes my courses get explicitly promoted, but in general, they are extending the reach of the platform, which benefits me in the long run. I also do specific promotion of my courses across social media platforms like Instagram, Twitter, and LinkedIn. The majority of the people that follow me are there because they have seen one of my courses, so they are a perfect group to promote to. I regularly tweet about my courses, and I also write blog posts on similar subjects as my courses to help promote them. In these blog posts, I try to offer some value, and not just make it a promotional post. I have also done the same with YouTube, where I will create small videos on a similar subject but also mention I have a more comprehensive course on the same topic and provide links in the video's description.

As part of my promotional efforts, I also do a lot of public speaking at large conferences and smaller meet-up groups. The purpose of this is to spread my brand by offering value through speaking. As part of this, I also mention the relevant courses that I have produced. The conferences I speak at are filled with people who have a subscription to the training platforms I teach on. It is hard to measure the direct effect of talking about my courses on stage, as I never see an immediate uplift in numbers. Still, I wouldn't expect to see a natural rise, since those people are at the conference, and not watching online training courses. The main benefit I get here is by speaking my brand so that if they see me on the training platform, or come across me on Twitter, they will know who I am and hopefully watch some of my content.

Another area of my business that I have been experimenting with is publishing books. Before writing this book, I wrote some shorter books in a series called "A Gentle Introduction To". If you think back to the chapter on product-launching strategies, I talked about creating a minimal viable product with which to test the market. This is what I did with these books; I used that book series as a way to test the publishing process and learn how to market books. I intend for this book, *The Path to Freedom*, to be part of a broader product offering centred around helping people create small side businesses. I want to do this with books, online courses, and classroom workshops. Before launching this business, I tried to make all the mistakes of publishing books first so I could publish this book with confidence. Let's look again at the Four Ps with book publishing in mind.

Product. My intention with the "A Gentle Introduction Series", was to publish the books myself through my own company, instead of going through a traditional publisher. This means using a platform like Amazon's Kindle Direct Publishing (KDP). Their platform lets you upload your book manuscript and publish it both for Kindle e-readers and as a print-on-demand paperback book. The intention was that after Amazon takes their cut on the platform, you are left with a much higher profit margin per book than you would get from a traditional publisher. Therefore, by applying effective marketing practices, the overall profit margin would be increased, and the level of control you have over the books would be much greater. In the traditionally published world, if you want to make an update to a book, you have to wait until there is either a second printing or a new edition has been commissioned. By controlling the publishing process myself, if I want to make an update, I can reload the changes and have it ready to download or print as a paperback book within a day.

Place. The principal place I sell books is on the internet through Amazon. I intend to try and get my books stocked in more stores, or at least be able to be ordered by physical retail, but this will require publishing through some other platforms too, such as Ingram Spark, which gives you a better route through to retail. When I was looking at platforms through which to sell books, I found that especially for very popular e-books, Amazon was the best place to do it, as other platforms are just a small drop in the ocean of potential sales compared to them. If you sell your e-books exclusively through Amazon, you get a preferential royalty rate of 70% as opposed to 35%, which is crucial if you are trying to get as high a sales margin as you can.

· · ·

Price. Pricing can be tricky with books, especially the shorter e-books. The initial series I developed to test the publishing process were all small books of around 25-30,000 words, at about 100 printed pages. When you look at similar books on Amazon, they do not sell for much, perhaps $3.99. It can be tempting to try and undercut other books, thinking that this will lead to more sales. I thought this in the beginning, and I found that this is not a good tactic. When everyone does that, you end up in a race to the bottom when it comes to pricing. If the margins are too low, then quality can start to suffer as people won't get an outstanding return for their effort. I tried lowering my price several times, and on all occasions, it did not lead to increased sales. If anything, they decreased. The best tactic is to look at your competitors, and price your books accordingly, but make sure you charge a price that reflects the level of quality and value people will get from your work. If the book is of high quality and helps people, then they will be willing to pay for the book. I achieved a more sustained level of sales when I priced these short e-books around $4.99 and paperbacks (short 100-page guides) around $7.99.

Promotion. When I first started releasing some short guides on Amazon, I made the classic mistake of just releasing the book, and then firing out a couple of tweets and LinkedIn posts declaring, "TADA! I have released a book." I had a few sales upfront which was a fantastic feeling, but they quickly died down. Unless you have a massive following of fans who will buy anything you release, this strategy doesn't work. You should be thinking more in terms of the sales funnel that we discussed earlier in the book. You want to draw people to your products, but just saying, "Buy my stuff!" isn't very useful—and in fact, if you say that too often, it just puts people off. A better approach is to think about the entry point to your sales funnel, where you produce a lot of content around your chosen topic that gives value to your followers. I started doing this, and I got much better results. I started making short YouTube videos, Instagram posts, blog posts etc. This was not sales content, but actual useful content designed to help the reader or viewer. At the end of a post or video, I would mention that I have a book, but not be pushy with it. Over time, I started getting more sustained sales.

The same principle holds with this book. I produce YouTube videos, podcasts, Instagram and Twitter posts to help people who are thinking of starting businesses or side-hustles. All this content is free. If someone doesn't want to buy the book, that is fine; they still get a lot of value from the other content. If they want to go deeper into the subject, the book is there if they want to buy it. If they want to go further still, there will be an online workshop course.

I have had marginal success with Instagram and Twitter paid adverts before. Still, because my previous books were on a range of subjects, it was harder to advertise them to specific groups consistently. I am hoping that it will be easier to target *The Path to Freedom* towards particular groups of people because it is in a more specific niche.

One marketing platform that I have had massive success with is Amazon's Marketing Services. Even though people see Amazon as a shopping site, at the end of the day, it is just a vast search engine—but instead of serving up webpages like Google, it serves up products. Amazon Marketing Services (AMS) allows you to target your products to people who search for particular products. Like with Google AdWords, you can bid on specific keywords to get your book to show up at the top of listings. AMS requires a bit of experimentation but their analytics are excellent, so you can see how you are spending compared to how many sales you make, and quickly identify if a marketing campaign is profitable or not.

When I started working with AMS, I set small budgets of around $150 each to run different experiments with, to try and identify what campaign would be most effective. This is an excellent technique to use with Instagram, Twitter and Facebook advertising, too.

I made a lot of mistakes when I first started publishing short guides on Amazon, but that's ok, as these products were a learning experiment to understand the process before I invested the time in writing and releasing the book you are reading now. Testing and experimenting with the market is such a valuable tool so that you can learn what works and what doesn't. It's also fun running the experiments. (Well, I enjoyed the process!)

Summary

Marketing is an ongoing process that involves promoting, selling, researching, and distributing services or products. This process is ongoing because as the market changes, your services or products will need to adapt as well in order to stay appealing.

For a business' marketing strategy to be successful, it needs to identify target markets, and then apply products and services for those target markets. But because so many people have given advice over the years about where to start and how to market, it can be rather confusing. Remember that marketing strategies are rooted in customer satisfaction, consumer value, and the quality of the products being provided. Marketing can be streamlined into four variables, namely the Four Ps: product, place, price, and promotion. Focusing on these four variables will help make your business successful.

There might be some overlap with the types of marketing that are needed for the business-to-business (B2B) marketing and business-to-consumer (B2C) marketing methods but understanding how these marketing strategies need to differ from one another will determine how successful your business is in the long run. You will need to know which type of marketing you want to pursue because despite the minor overlaps, they are vastly different. B2B marketing requires developing personal relationships, whereas B2C marketing requires more transactional relationships that are based on emotion.

Traditional marketing is any type of marketing that isn't done online. This includes aspects like billboards, printed advertisements, direct mail, and radio broadcasts. Traditional marketing is the oldest and most researched form of marketing. Many marketers and business owners that are set in their ways tend to prefer this type of marketing method because it's successfully tried and tested. Traditional marketing is effective at reaching local and older audiences while providing additional benefits, such as that printed adverts can be read repeatedly as long as they're in print.

Digital marketing companies focus on releasing content in emails, on websites, and through pop-up adverts. Because of the technological evolution of the world, it made sense to move onto digital platforms to continue with marketing strategies. Digital marketing works out to be more cost-effective, and it's able to connect to a global market.

Although digital marketing is superior to traditional marketing, there is still an opportunity to make a success of the traditional marketing method. It's necessary to know what type of target audience you are looking to attract before deciding on a marketing method.

There are four different internet marketing platforms that were mentioned in this chapter to help increase the awareness surrounding your brand: Google AdWords; Twitter Ads; Facebook Ads; and Instagram Ads. All of these platforms have advantages and disadvantages, but any of them will be able to successfully bring awareness to your brand. Plan the adverts carefully to make them fit in comfortably on each platform and have the desired effect on your potential customers.

Workshop Questions

(1) Think about how you will price your product and service to make it competitive in the market.

(2) Write down where you will market your product or service. Will this be online, or will you use traditional marketing techniques like print, radio etc?

(3) Look at your competitors and reverse engineer their marketing and advertising process. Do they use traditional marketing or are they internet based? What media do they use? What is their social media presence like?

(4) Really deep dive into your competitors' social media accounts, like Twitter, Instagram and Facebook. What level of interaction do they have with these platforms? Do they give away a lot of content to help their potential customers, or are they pure sales channels?

22

EMAIL MARKETING

Digital marketing is the backbone of the advertising industry today, but it all started with email as the primary marketing tool used by companies and brands all over the world. Prior to that, it was still the principal tool used for communication purposes, especially in business. With the changing of the tides over the past two decades, one could be forgiven for thinking that email marketing had died due to—well, everything else. Technology has boomed over the years, and the way people communicate and market their business to existing or potential customers has evolved with it.

Social media has largely taken over the playing field. Even though there seems nothing professional about sending a direct message on Facebook or Instagram to someone a brand wants to attract professionally, the tide has turned us towards a range of informalities that was never thought possible. However, people still use email marketing now more than ever before to market their brand, because although it may no longer seem like the most effective or on-trend way to do business, the truth is the exact opposite. Almost every company in the world still relies on the traditional email system, complete with mailing lists that make it easy to boost a brand and simultaneously reach more people than direct messaging or using various forms of advertising ever could. There are still a few marketing fields in which email may not be as effective as social media marketing, but when it comes to generating sales leads, email as a marketing tool is alive and well. All it takes is a company using it to their advantage.

To get email marketing right is a process. There are a number of boxes to check before a company puts itself out there, and even if you have previously attempted email marketing and failed, there is space to restore your business' email presence. Email is a unique relationship-building tool that allows one to create and sustain an ongoing connection with consumers. It can be used to build new or revive existing relationships with your subscribers in a subtle way that doesn't simply scream, "Buy this product here!"

Apart from not being overbearing, which is code for losing customers, proper email marketing also makes consumers feel connected to your brand. It is a positive way to build a list of your most loyal subscribers and includes those that will not only open the emails but take action when they do. Your company's marketing emails are solely about your customers; they shouldn't be approached with the intention to make money or any other fast goal. First and foremost, it allows your business to create a dimension of trust with the customers, which is most important if you want your business to sustainably thrive. When a company or brand manages to establish trust, it receives loyalty in return, and that's when it really begins to flourish.

Now that it has been established that email marketing is alive and well and forms a big part of digital marketing, it's necessary to learn how to market your brand effectively by using emails to connect with your customers. There is a right and a wrong way of doing email marketing. To avoid getting it wrong, you must be inclined to do the following:

- Build an email list that includes targeted customers.
- Optimise emails to get the best possible open and click-through rates (CTR).

- Automate the email process to generate leads and keep customers.

It is important to recognise at the start that email marketing is the top way to communicate with both existing and potential customers, which means that it is your company's best chance to build a customer network that will push your business forward. Since a company owns its email list and if it is built successfully, it will give you an advantage over your competitors. Many businesses don't pay enough attention to email marketing because they think it's not useful; yet it successfully converts potential shoppers to loyal customers, as 99% of people check their email daily. Those who purchase products that are marketed through this method will spend up to 138% more than online users that do not receive any offers by email.

It's as simple as building a mailing list and choosing an email service provider that suits your business best. Setting up an email service provider is easy because there are so many to choose from, and with the entire internet a booming, fast-paced online business game, anybody can do it. You should choose one that is relative to your business' goals.

Getting Started with an Email Campaign

On average, most customers receive on average over 100 emails daily. What are the chances that a customer would open all of them? If they received an email with content that is rushed or doesn't seem very compelling, would they archive it, delete it, or take a chance and read it? Once an email is opened, what would a customer like to see from a company or brand before purchasing from them?

These are the things to keep in mind. Without a sound strategy in place, a customer's answers to these questions cannot be predicted to help your company in the long run. Again, email marketing is all about the customers, and should cater to them.

The first step is identifying your audience. When sending emails, they must have a purpose. A business can't just send repetitive or useless content to their customers to tick the task off at the end of the day or week. As with everything else in marketing, it has to be impactful and relevant, with content that will set your business apart from every other brand. To do this, you need to have an established buyer persona in mind for your company or brand, and tailor your email campaigns according to that. Because emails are for the customers, your business needs to identify who they are so that it can fulfil their needs.

The next step is about gaining clarity about your goals. When a company or brand is clear about their goals, it makes it more customer-centric, which allows it to improve its marketing strategy. Before your business can create a campaign, you need to think about the goals you want to achieve. This is only possible to do if a business knows who its customers are. When you know who they are and have specific goals in sight, it's easier to go about the rest. It requires research about email statistics specific to your business' industry, which can be used as goal benchmarks. Consider the following statistics.

Business-to-Business (B2B) Email Marketing: When you send emails on which customers can take action, they perform three times better than drip campaigns or nurture emails. 86% of people in business prefer email as the main communication channel, while 60% of marketing professionals believe that email generates a positive return on investment. Clickthrough rates are also 47% higher for emails in B2B than they are for B2C, and subject lines containing an emoji account for a 56% increase in open rate.

Business-to-Consumer (B2C) Email Marketing: While 99% of all consumers check their email inbox daily, 78% of consumers will unsubscribe from an email list because they are receiving too many emails from it. For B2C, email subscribers can help expand a brand as they are more likely to share social media content from that email than from any other source.

E-commerce Email Marketing: For e-commerce marketing, email is considered the best because 86% of customers want to receive promotional emails. Potential customers subscribe to at least one mailing list a month that involves online retail. Emails that are segmented to different target customer groups can generate up to 58% of a company's annual revenue.

Real Estate Email Marketing: For the real estate industry, email is the foundation of communication, and 53% of all real estate businesses get their subscribers directly from their website. Since blogging is usually marketed through email, blogs can help businesses gain twice the amount of traffic by email. Forty percent of companies in the real estate market also use list segmentation to achieve the best results.

Another important step to follow is to ask users specifically to sign up. One may think it's very forward to ask a new visitor to your site to sign up to your email list but think about it—online users visit a website to gain information about its products, services, or a specific brand in which they are already interested. The best thing your business can do to increase the probability of your customers signing up to your email list is to create an easy way for them to do so. People want everything to be fast and effective. If it's going to take more than a couple of seconds to sign up to an email list, most people won't bother. A business must consider this, among many other things, as a vital part of an effective overall strategy.

To make email marketing work, a business needs an email campaign. It doesn't make sense to send out random, unconnected emails that don't complement each other in some way. A sound email campaign strategy is the best way to boost your company's growth by spreading the word and connecting with as many people as it possibly can. You should start by sending one newsletter a week that focuses on the latest news of the brand that is relevant to the customers. If it doesn't directly impact them, it should not be shared. Making it exciting and to the point is the goal. Nobody wants to read a short story when they open an email, they want to see a deal or what a company is offering them upfront. Depending on your company type and goal, you can choose what is relevant to add to a newsletter or even to create an entirely different campaign; for example, a limited-time offer on products. It's also helpful to create different email lists to receive specific marketing emails.

When you decide on your email campaign per email list (if there is more than one), the next thing to do is schedule emails upfront, but also inform the subscribers about the frequency of the emails that will be being sent. It's always important for a business to hear from its customers, so it is a good idea to incorporate a link to a short survey that asks a few questions about your newsletters, based on the content and frequency thereof. Providing content that the subscribers would like to see and keeping a consistent email schedule helps to establish trust, which makes subscribers more inclined to purchase from or recommend a certain brand.

A strategy should be measured in some way after a while because you need to see whether or not it is effective. If it doesn't look like it's working or generating the results you want for your business, it must be tweaked or replaced. The more specific a business is about what its customers want, the better the results will be. Monitoring key performance indicators (KPIs) is a good way to check whether a business' strategy is working or not. KPIs can include a bigger open rate, an increase in the number of website visitors, and more sales.

Building Email Lists

Everything a company does and how it does it is significant when it comes to marketing, especially online. Just placing a tab with a form in the corner of your website is unlikely to help your business gain subscribers. Creating an email list must be done proactively and with care, and there are two parts to this process.

The first part is to attract users with a lead magnet, which is a technique used to give something away for free in exchange for the user's email address. The second part is to create an irresistible opt-in form, which is used to get an online user's information that allows them to successfully be added to an email list. If a business can accomplish these two parts together, it can generate near-unlimited leads.

The ultimate goal of any business choosing to market in this way is to have this process run more or less on autopilot, generating enough sales leads to sustain the business.

To be the most effective tool for your business, a lead magnet should be free and can include anything, such as a PDF, MP3 file, or a video for the purpose of getting an email address from the online user. The lead magnets don't have to cost too much, either, although you will need to invest some time and cost in creating them. You can use an e-book, webinar, white papers, free trial, a free quote, self-assessment, or the one recognised as the most popular—a coupon, because everybody likes a discount. Businesses can get very creative with their lead magnets and often add a personal or unique touch to them.

When your website, online store, or social media page is set up, it will be necessary for you to incorporate marketing techniques into its content to generate traffic to the point of a sale. Once traffic is generated and there are visitors to the website or social media page, a lead magnet is then used to lock in potential customers.

For a lead magnet to be attractive to online users, it has to be simple and easy to consume; it needs to be effective, so that users are drawn to it; it must be useful information or a tool that your potential customers can apply; and above all, it should be actionable. If a lead magnet works effectively, customers will be more inclined to purchase a product or service from the same brand or company.

Staying relevant and striving for continuous improvement will aid in your business' journey to maintain attention. The lead magnet you choose must be useful and suit the customer type and their goals. If it doesn't provide value, it's not worth having. Making it available immediately is a big plus on the business' part. Everybody wants instant gratification, so if the content is given to them immediately after they've subscribed to your mailing list, there's no doubt that they will feel inclined to support your brand.

Creating an Effective Opt-In Form. The headline text on the opt-in form is the first thing online users see after the subject line, and so it's important that it be just as attractive and captivating. The headline must explain the main benefit of the lead magnet and should be an offer that the website's users can't resist.

Online users know that companies want their contact information. Your intention with your company's opt-in form shouldn't be to deceive users or to make a list of promises you probably can't keep. All that it should represent is honesty. If people see that a business is real and up-front, they'll take the offer and subscribe to the email list.

Since an opt-in form combined with a lead magnet is the first interaction your business will have with a potential customer, it should only ask for basic contact details, which includes their first name and email address. Nothing else is necessary, especially not a contact number or postal address at the very start.

Set the opt-in form to include a double confirmation. Although it may seem unnecessary, it is important to verify a customer's email address to prove they own that address.

Testing everything before going live with it, whether it's a business' entire website or just a single feature, is crucial. Think about when you have visited a website and had a bad experience, where something seemed ineffective or didn't work properly. You probably weren't inclined to visit it again—and the same thing applies for your potential customers. Ensuring that everything works in sync is important so that customers won't hesitate to subscribe.

The subscribe button should be kept simple and made a different colour from the rest of the opt-in form, so that it clearly stands out and easily grabs the attention of the user.

Sending Marketing Emails

Email marketing can get out of control if a business isn't careful because it has the potential to go from a few daily emails to hundreds. You will have to manage queries, create emails that need to be sent out to your subscribers list, and keep coming up with new content strategies, as well as managing the daily running of the company itself. To make your business efficient, you should choose an email marketing service that can help fine-tune your strategy. Various Google integrations and marketing tools exist that can easily help create, personalise, adjust, and boost marketing emails to relay the correct message to customers. You can also analyse the success of your marketing emails and teach the techniques you learn to your entire team. In this way, you can become more effective in all aspects of marketing your brand.

When looking for an email management system (EMS), you should consider if it has a customer relationship management (CRM) platform combined with segmentation abilities, automation, built-in analytics, a good relationship with internet service providers, easy-to-build forms, calls to action (CTAs), landing pages, access to downloadable reports, and a simplified process to comply with email rules and regulations.

If you are running a brand, you can't afford to slack with your marketing because you will need to generate results online. Since you won't be relying on the almost-guaranteed results of traditional advertising techniques, an understanding of the different elements needed to deliver effective marketing online is crucial. You will need to consider not only the content that you put into your marketing emails and the links therein that take subscribers to the landing page, but also the timing of the emails. As with social media platforms, people are more inclined to open their emails—or have time to click on the links in those emails—at a certain time of day. Your business' goal in sending emails is to generate more leads, which can be accomplished with the help of the following components.

The first component is content. The content in the body of a marketing email is referred to as "copy". It should be unique, creative, and consistent with what your business wants to portray to customers. Sticking to one topic per email is best, otherwise you risk shifting your readers' attention away from your main message. An email on a single topic is also more compelling to subscribers. If they open your email and see too much going on, they are not as likely to read much of the email copy or take action on it. A topic important enough for its own email, on the other hand, can be much more intriguing.

The next component to consider is imagery. A black-and-white setup for the body of the emails is fine, but unless it's intended to be "classic" or aligns with the concept of the brand, it's not going to get your business very far. When people browse the internet, they almost always find images more attractive to the eye than a piece of content that they have to take the time to read, so your brand or company should choose images that are relevant and suit both the theme and the message that you are trying to convey. It is also smart to pick images that are optimised for any device.

You next need to think about your timing of the email. The best time to read an email is most definitely not Monday morning or late afternoon on Friday. The good time to start with is a Tuesday morning between ten and eleven o'clock—it is usually during business hours; most people would have already sifted through their work emails that had piled up over the weekend; and they have had two or three hours to check their Tuesday work mailbox.

The next element to consider is the call-to-action (CTA). Everything should be relevant when sending an email to subscribers. While the content and images added to the body of the email are intended to target the audience and draw them in, the CTA link must take subscribers directly to an offer of interest, whether it's a sale or an interesting blog post. The CTA should stand out from the content in the body of the email.

A brand is all about persona and what sets it apart from everything else, including competitors and ideas. Don't shy away from sharing innovative ideas and content with your subscribers. There is an advantage to addressing readers with a welcoming and familiar tone. By giving your emails a personal touch, you will make it easier for your customers to relate to your brand and your business, and therefore, make it more likely that your emails will generate leads.

Today, around 55% more emails are opened on mobile phones than they are on the screen of a computer. The body of your email should be optimised for computer, mobile phone, and many other devices—as should your website and online store, both of which can often be thrown out of proportion on the view of a mobile phone.

When a reader receives your email, the first thing they see will be the subject line in their email application. As one of the most important elements to capture the attention of subscribers, a subject line must be clear, concise, and actionable. It also needs to be personalised so that it is aligned with the brand and the content in the body of the email or the message that your business wants to convey.

Segmentation is a tool used in email marketing to break up a big email into various subcategories that are relevant to the preferences and interests of different subscribers. It is always better to steer away from generic emails and deliver a unique take on what to send to subscribers depending on who they are and what their individual interests are. If a business gets this wrong, it may cost them a lot of subscribers that aren't interested in certain topics.

Segmented emails can generate 58% of a brand's entire revenue. Your email lists can be broken up according to geographical location, industry, language, lifecycle stage in the sales process, awareness, previous engagement with the brand, and job titles. You can then personalise your emails based on what's important to your subscribers. It doesn't matter how many subscribers your business has; you can make a few categories that they can potentially fit into and automate your emails to specific groups of people accordingly.

To personalise emails, you can add multiple elements, such as a first name of a subscriber in the subject line. It can be combined with a brief greeting. An email can contain region-specific information where it is appropriate, or content based on the previous engagement history that leads have had with the brand. The more relatable your business is, the more likely subscribers will open the next email or support in other ways. Adding a personal signature at the end of your emails that includes an employee's name also adds a personal touch to it. Additionally, you can implement a call to action for offers that subscribers may find useful.

Once you have made use of email segmentation, you can put the generated segmented lists to use. With the different subgroups, sending highly targeted emails that are automated to improve the efficiency of your marketing efforts is extremely important. This can be done with tools like autoresponders and workflows.

Autoresponders are emails that are sent automatically when triggered by an action, such as when a user clicks on a "subscribe" button after typing in an email address or clicking on a button to download an e-book. The autoresponder sends a direct email to the user, providing them with information based on their activity and the actions they took on a website, or with any other material they used related to the brand and its email system. Setting up an autoresponder is a very helpful way to ensure a response to users or customers without you having to deal with the associated administration work every day. Automating as much of the administration work as possible, especially when it comes to marketing and sales, is a major step toward achieving optimal efficiency. Once your autoresponder is set, it no longer has to be thought about. It does all the work for the business, allowing you to focus on more important things.

If you really want to go next level with automation, you should look at implementing workflows as the next logical step. Where autoresponders simply react to a single cue with a single response, a workflow is more complex, executing a list of actions as a result of the optimisations that you predetermine. It begins with an action that allows the business to qualify a user for workflow, referred to as "enrolment criteria", and a goal—that of the action that allows the business to remove a user from the workflow. It contains tools that recognise if users open emails or perform any action like downloading an offer. It uses this data to set and adjust a group of actions based on the users' behaviour. In comparison to autoresponders, workflows are considered to be smarter, as they can alter the direction of an automated email series based on what is relevant to individual users. These tools are crucial for operating a business successfully because they are reliable. The last thing you want is to send an email to the wrong user or at the wrong time. That will make your company lose credibility and potentially even trust.

You should have someone on the team—or hire a professional—who can design or develop an email template that works for your business. It's not good to seem like you haven't put any thought into it. Apart from the content, the way the email looks must be clean and suit your brand's aesthetic. A designer or developer will present you with a couple of templates, and you can choose one that is high quality and reputable. Once you've selected your designer, you can work with them to customise the format, background, and font until you have a professional-looking template that fits your brand and your business.

When crafting your email template, you must also remain aware of email regulations. It must be compliant with the CAN-SPAM law, which means it should include the brand's company name, address, and contact details. It should also have a visible "unsubscribe" link at the bottom of each email, have a real email address, and a subject line that suits the body of each email. Emails must also be General Data Protection Regulation (GDPR) compliant, which allows customers residing in the European Union (EU) the opportunity and right to choose the type of emails they receive from a business, including the type of products advertised.

When your business sends emails, it is vital that both the subject line and body avoid words commonly filtered out by spam filters, because that will negatively affect deliverability rates and make it likely that your subscribers will miss emails. Preventing getting whitelisted; paying attention to the copy to avoid spam-trigger words; implementing a double opt-in; and using a reliable email service provider are all elements that will help your business sustain long-term relationships with users and potential customers.

Striving for High-Quality Content

Once you have permission from online users to send them content by email, you have a massive advantage because you've created a direct communication channel from the company to the consumer. Proper understanding of how email marketing works and gaining access to online users' email addresses will help your business so you can focus on building a bigger email list. With all the elements set in place, focusing on the quality of the content being put out is also a must. Once your business establishes credibility with its subscribers, it will be easier to send them a range of different emails, as they will become more interested in hearing from the brand or receiving updates about the latest news and products.

If you run a small business that doesn't have a marketing expert who is good with words on the team, investing in copywriting is the best possible thing that you can do to seal in all the work being put into email marketing. Without proper content, your business can't intrigue people or maintain their attention, so it is worth the investment.

When users that visit a website subscribe to newsletters or general emails, they have certain expectations. The copy must be strong and consistent. Keeping it as positive as possible is always helpful to maintain attention. The same goes for keeping promises. If you have said that your company will only send one email a week, then that is all it should send. Just because your business has email subscribers, doesn't mean that they will be there forever. If they are not happy with what they are seeing or the frequency thereof, they will be likely to unsubscribe from the email list. The more your business keeps to its promises and provides content that is beneficial to potential customers, the more loyal they will be to the brand.

Emails should include product advertising to allow customers to engage and make sales accordingly. Pitching products, therefore, should be carefully thought through. To run successful email campaigns, you should pitch a product to your subscribers at least every once in a while. If you pitch products frequently, you ought to consider how you would feel in your customer's shoes. The pitch shouldn't be overbearing, but it should be interesting enough for them to think about whether they want to purchase something from your business or not. Email marketing is also more than just pitching products. A good newsletter that grabs the attention of subscribers is also important. It should be tailored to the type of person the email is being sent to. That is also why segmentation for email lists is so important. With the right tools set in place, your business can deliver stellar copy, keep your readers engaged, and boost your product or service's sales as well as your brand's credibility.

The Authors Approach

I started experimenting with email lists when I self-published my initial book series, "A Gentle Introduction To", on Amazon. In both the paperback and the e-book, I had a link that the user could type in or click that went to a sign-up page. If the user signed up and verified their email address, I sent them a free e-book that I had put together especially for email list subscribers. That e-book was a link magnet that I offered them in return for their email address. The early books I published were part of an experiment to test the book publishing process; building this email list was also part of that experiment to see if people would sign up. Thankfully, this experiment was successful. By simply asking the reader to sign up, and offering them something of value in return, they were willing to part with their email address.

To build my list, I used an email list provider called aWeber. There are many on the market, and Google will give you a list of them, but I chose this one and it was reasonably easy to set up. Even though these e-books were a publishing experiment before the work began on this book you are reading, I didn't utilise the email list as best as I could. Although I sent out the odd mailshot to the subscribers, I eventually let the list go cold, which is a mistake I regret. Tools like aWeber let you set up email schedules where once your subscribers have signed up, you can send out pre-written content to them. This means you can keep providing useful content which will hopefully lead to them buying from you. For people that sign up to my list from now on, after reading this book or from the book's website, I will be regularly providing them with useful content. This content won't be trying to sell to them frequently, but it will provide helpful information and, over time, build up trust between them and me.

Although it seems like people drown in email these days, a well-maintained email list with high-quality content is still a fantastic way to engage with your current and potential customers. You need to treat the list very carefully and not come across as a spammer. Frequently offer them something useful, and every now and again, give them a call to action to visit a site or buy from you. Some will, some won't; but as an overall part of your marketing plan, email lists are highly effective.

Summary

Whilst email marketing is an older technique of engaging with potential end customers, it is still beneficial if you use it carefully. To entice someone to sign up for an email, you need to offer them something of value in return. This could be a report, a book, or a series of videos; but what you give them has to provide them with enough value for them to offer you their email address. Once they are signed up to your email service, you can send them frequent emails to stay engaged. The majority of these emails should also provide value. Most of your email content will be giving them some valuable information; only a tiny percentage of your correspondence should be direct sales content, enticing them to buy something. People are wary of being pitched too frequently, so if you try and sell too hard, too quickly, they will unsubscribe from your email list.

Sending out useful and purposeful content to your mailing list is a part of what is called content marketing. This is where you are producing content, either written or video, that can be consumed by other people, with the ultimate goal of promoting your products and brands. We will be discussing content marketing and its close cousin, search engine optimisation, in the next chapter.

Workshop Questions

(1) Investigate some email list service providers, such as aWeber, Drip, etc. Do they integrate with the service you use for managing your website? Does the service allow double opt-in for new signatories? Can you schedule content to be sent to the subscriber on a predetermined timeline after they subscribe?

(2) Think about a schedule of emails you can send to the subscriber each week, or every two weeks. Think about a series of informational emails designed to give the subscriber value, as opposed to being purely sales related.

(3) Think about who you are targeting with your emails. Is it B2B or B2C? This makes a big difference to the tone of the content that you will distribute via email. With B2C, you can be more personal and less formal; whereas with B2B, you might be more formal and offer more sales-based, white-paper content.

23

SEARCH ENGINE OPTIMISATION AND CONTENT MARKETING

The concept of content marketing has existed for a long time, but it has only just obtained widespread consideration since 2007 (Linn, 2017). Even though content marketing has been around for such a long time, people who are new to marketing still have little idea how to successfully implement content marketing into their branding.

Content marketing is a technique that creates and distributes consistent, relevant, and valuable content to attract a specific target audience. When releasing a product, a business needs to ensure that the product is appealing to their target audience. Content marketing attracts "leads" and those can become customers when they are attracted to a certain product.

Content marketing is a valuable form of advertising and is remarkably different from other marketing methods. People choose content that gets their attention based on its appeal, either because of the content itself, or the manner in which it's written. It is these characteristics that are the main focus of content marketing.

Whenever someone says that they have a career in content marketing, people generally have no idea what it is; even when described to them, they still give rather quizzical looks. It doesn't completely make sense to them.

The best example comes from Michelle Linn, a content marketer and professional blogger. She said that her husband didn't really understand what content marketing was until he told her that he subscribed to a newsletter about the stock market. He was very excited about the newsletter because it contained a lot of pertinent information that would help him make prudent investment choices in the future, even though it had nothing to do with the stocks and shares themselves. She leaned over to him and said, "That's exactly what content marketing is."

Content marketing is valuable and educational but has nothing to do with the actual products that a business sells. Because customers are offered reliable information, they're more likely to become loyal to the brand because of the information offered, and not just because of the products/services that the business offers.

In the previous chapters of this book, it was detailed how to promote and market your brand and your products, but content marketing can improve your brand by making people more interested in the other details of your business. Relying on indirect details to boost your brand takes wit, time, and considerable effort.

The American Girl Example. American Girl is a line of dolls that portray eight- to twelve-year-old girls with a large variety of ethnicities and styles. These dolls were first released in 1986 and became hugely popular with pre-adolescent girls. Although these dolls themselves were hugely popular, the firm behind the creation of the dolls, Pleasant Company, made an enormously profitable decision to focus on the content marketing surrounding the dolls and their business.

They wanted to design content experiences that were not only attractive to the girls who owned the dolls, but also their parents. They designed "in-person" experiences and events for their customers. These events included fireworks displays, painting, coffee dates, and even hotel packages that included the doll and the little girl. In more recent years, they also introduced videos, games, apps, quizzes, and movies, to keep their product "alive" for their young customers.

Their printed publications were enormously entertaining and sought after. Pleasant Company released a book called *The Care and Keeping of You* about girls growing up. Even though it was released by Pleasant Company, it had nothing to do with dolls. But the book became a form of content marketing for the company because people loved the content of the book itself. It became the 76th most popular book on Amazon, which also increased sales of their American Girl dolls.

American Girl's content marketing strategy was focused on how a little girl and her doll can share a wonderful experience together. The advertising campaigns that Pleasant Company orchestrated had little to do with the dolls themselves. But the content that they produced solidified the American Girl line's future, even after Pleasant Company's acquisition by Mattel in 1998, because of the brand loyalty that they created.

Content Marketing for Marketers. The most important part about content marketing is that it needs to focus on your audience, not your brand or products. Your audience is the most important aspect here, and you need to consider what they care about. Your audience wants to know how your business can provide something that they want or need that no one else is able to. In finding a way to do this, you will boost your brand to something that people embrace. It will no longer be merely a commodity.

Content marketing is obviously different from traditional products and personal marketing, and it includes aspects like entertainment, videos, e-books, and webinars. These aspects can be used to answer specific questions that potential customers may have and provide them with insight that they wouldn't be able to find elsewhere. Using creative ways to market content gives you an opportunity to turn your brand into something that stands out, no matter how common the brand may be.

By becoming an authoritative and credible resource on topics that matter to people, your business becomes more likely to be discovered by a specific target audience. By giving people what they want when they need it, your business will start to earn their trust and loyalty. This leads to brand strengthening as customer relationships grow, catalysing an increase in the active customer base and profits for your business.

It seems like an obvious thing to do to benefit your business, but there is a word of caution that needs mentioning. Many individuals involved in content marketing strongly suggest that it isn't a marketing tool that should be used by all business owners. The reason is because this is an indirect marketing method that takes a lot of time, effort, and energy for it to work effectively.

However, it can be one of the greatest tools that you can use for your business and brand if the work is put in to support it. This approach provides a better experience for customers and gives them a positive perception of your brand and business.

Reasons Why Marketers Put Effort into Content Marketing. Using content marketing allows your business to be found by the type of people being targeted. People use search engines like Google to gain the necessary information that they need. Using content marketing and Search Engine Optimisation (or SEO, which will be discussed later), relevant content to your business can be some of the first results that pop up during a content search. Since people are more likely to read the first page, it's useful to be in the top five results.

Content needs to answer questions that people have. These questions can be addressed through written publications, videos, and even webinars. If your content is the information that people want, then they will want to use your business in the future.

Content is only as valuable as its functional ability to attract specific people. If your content isn't attracting an audience, then it's redundant. Releasing content to build an engaged and interested audience is paramount to success. Once a following is engaged, then your content undertaking efforts will increase sales. Once an audience is established, it will be self-evident who your most loyal supporters are. Loyalty can be further deepened by making them advocates for your brand in the future.

Successful content marketing will help you acquire new attention and land new customers. The goal for your business is to generate more revenue as time carries on. Content marketing can be a powerful driving force to make this a reality. When you build an audience that trusts what you say, they're more likely to buy products.

Content marketing can help save money. This is because both traditional and digital marketing can cost a fair amount, whereas content marketing can be done on sites that are free. Many platforms allow people to release their content as regularly as they want, without paying a subscription. The only problem is that there is a lot of other content that you will need to contend with before your audience starts to grow. While producing lots of content doesn't have to have any direct financial cost, especially if being produced in-house, it's important to bear in mind the amount of time it will cost to produce the content.

Search Engine Optimisation (SEO)

Search engine optimisation (SEO) is the action of increasing the quality and the quantity of online search traffic to specific content or a website. SEO works with organic search results and can greatly improve your business.

The concept of SEO can seem rather confusing, but once it's broken down into its basic elements it becomes easier to understand. There are three main parts that build the core of SEO: the quantity of the online search traffic; the quality of the online search traffic; and the organic search results that pop up when an online search is performed.

- The quantity of the search traffic is the number of people that visit a site when searched. They will scroll through the search engine results pages (SERPs) until they find one that interests them.
- The quality of the search traffic is the type of people that visit your site. Traffic to a site benefits neither the business or the prospective customer, if what they search for is a Python coder, and they are instead directed to a python breeder! The right people should be directed to the right site because those people may become paying customers.
- Organic searches are the final large component of SEO. Adverts make up a large percentage of any online search,

but search traffic that you haven't had to pay for is known as organic results.

How SEO Works. Any type of search engine will give you certain results when you type certain keywords into the search bar. But this list isn't arbitrary or random; it would not be useful for a search result to be generated that is unconnected to the terms that you searched for. Search engines give fairly accurate results when keywords are searched because they use algorithms known as "crawlers".

Crawlers search the billions of possible results, and look for similar matches to the keywords that are entered in the search bar. Once the crawlers have found suitable matches for the keywords, the results are fed back into one larger algorithm. This algorithm then organises them according to keyword matches of the search. All the results are collated and returned incredibly quickly—an average search usually takes no more time than half a second—but there are several factors used to determine which sites will be ranked higher on the list of results.

The most influential factors are domain-level features, page-level link features, keyword matches, and page-level content features. There are several other factors that can come into play in how a search engine ranks its results, but there are ways that you can write content that will make the search engine algorithms rank your site higher than others.

Initially, website builders would type content for their sites and hope for the best. There was no way to be certain that their site would ever be found. This is how optimisation was introduced. Optimisation has many aspects, but the most valuable ways to ensure that search engines rank your site higher than others is by manipulating three areas inside your page:

- Meta title tags are the elements of the HTML (hypertext mark-up language) title of a webpage. The title tags are the clickable options displayed when a search is performed online. The right types of title tags can influence how important a search engine will deem the site to be.
- Meta descriptions are HTMLs that provide a brief summary of the page. Content writers type specific keywords into their meta descriptions (the same keywords that searchers will

most likely use) to increase the probability of their page being ranked higher than others.
- Internal links increase the probability of being ranked higher by a search engine algorithm. Specifically, creating hyperlinks to other pages and sites will make your site seem more valuable because the information and content obtained from the hyperlinks are also taken into account by the algorithm. It's important, therefore, to only hyperlink to pages/sites that will raise the value of your site.

Learning About SEO. The current paradigm of the internet is orientated closely to the online market. It is therefore necessary to build an SEO-friendly site. There are three ways to develop your site to maintain an SEO page: acquiring an advantageous domain name; using helpful internal links; and using several keywords that are commonly associated with the subject. A site including those factors has a higher probability of being successful.

Thinking up a site is only the beginning. Building a successful site with the necessary relevant content that will attract compatible traffic is a skill that requires practice. If you are still trying to develop this skill set, it may be to your advantage to hire someone to help you write successful content for your site.

Using SEO for Marketing. People conduct trillions of online searches on an annual basis, so using the internet as a marketing tool is one of the best ways to help your business thrive. Understanding how SEO can be used to successfully market a brand is a fundamental part of overall marketing. Online searching is the primary source of digital traffic to complement a brand's other marketing channels. Vendors that rely on digital marketing need to ensure that enough potential customers frequent their sites in order to turn a large enough profit.

Successfully employing SEO methods will make your site more visible to online traffic and could potentially rank you higher than your competition. SEO methods were refined several years ago because people started understanding how to use those methods to promote their sales. But as technology started evolving, so did the internet. As a result, many sites now offer users direct answers to their questions, which increases the probability of users staying on one site instead of going to others. This works well for the site the users are currently on, but it does reduce traffic for other sites. This means SEO principles have also had to evolve over the years. Methods previously used are no longer as effective as they once were. Some marketers religiously stick to well-used methods like:

- Distributing hundreds of personalised emails every week to potential customers in the hopes that they would click the links in the email and give the site a moment of their time.
- Writing more than 2,500 words of seemingly invaluable and in-depth content for their site or other uploads.
- Ensuring that their site's load speed was fast enough to prevent people from leaving and going elsewhere.
- Ensuring all the technical problems on their site were fixed and the entire system was running smoothly.
- Double-checking every post to ensure it was error-free and had all the links required for the post.

Although these points are important and still need to be focused on today, there are other methods to making more effective SEOs. Relying on these points alone won't significantly increase your site's overall traffic. The issue here is that many marketers don't know what else to do, so they stick to these principles and hope for the best.

Here are a few considerations to increase your search rankings and traffic for a website that already has a lot of content.

Implementing a detailed content audit on all uploads. When watching and analysing data on your uploads, it's important to only keep the ones that people actually read. Get rid of the rest. By removing content that isn't useful, you will streamline the remainder, and people will appreciate the content that is published. Remember that with SEO, quality is far superior to quantity.

If you are unsure about what should be removed, optimise and revamp the content and then republish it. Using this method can release the hidden potential of certain content. Fixing up the words in the post may be all that's needed to make it more attractive.

Keep in mind that you may be biased towards the work that you have written; have someone trustworthy audit what's already published to give you an unbiased opinion.

Linking to other sites to increase traffic. Adding high-quality links to your site will make it more likely to be grouped into other organic search results. There are numerous methods for improving conversion rates, from using pre-written templates to offering free courses to people who use specific links in their content. Opinions vary as to their effectiveness, but the best method that people have found to create links is to write outstanding content. Once this content has been written it's far easier to link up with other producers of similar content to create equally beneficial conversion rates.

Creating successful SEO-driven content is an ongoing process. Creating new links and updating SEO-driven content semi-regularly is a necessary requirement. SEO-driven content is based on specific keyword opportunities in a particular niche. Far too many writers produce content and then find a keyword to optimize the content after the fact. But this is working backward and can negatively impact the site. Writing in this way is like picking keywords out of a hat and hoping for the best, and this can lead to keyword conflicts within the page. More than likely, this method for choosing your keywords will be unsuccessful.

Before creating new content for your site, you should perform an in-depth search of the keywords that will provide your site with the optimal results. Be selective in choosing; concise and insightful keyword choices will be more likely to get your site a higher ranking.

It's important to look for several keywords to use in your content to optimise your site. Using only one won't work. Marketers that use several keywords that target specific groups of data will make your site much more successful. The trick to producing a successful SEO-driven site has nothing to do with how much content you upload and how often you publish it. The truth is that content that's valuable and optimised will get your site much further, even if you're only uploading content once every other month.

Implement an internal linking strategy. People underestimate how effective a simple task such as adding a single hyperlink into a site can increase the traffic to that site. Your SEO will be enhanced when hyperlinks to other sites are added that will corroborate the information on your site. That said, many inexperienced content writers make the mistake of adding links into their content that don't improve the site in any way. Using hyperlinks for the sake of it isn't worth it and can negatively affect the site in the long run. Careful planning is needed before links are created.

A simple strategy can be used to identify what types of links should be used in any SEO-driven site. These three criteria are:

- The link needs to target keywords in other posts.
- The link needs to be a synonym or variation of the other keywords.
- The link needs to be a long-tail, secondary keyword.

Long-tail keywords are more detailed keywords that return more relevant search results. For example, a keyword might be "laptop pc", whereas long-tail keywords are things like "core i7 7th gen Alienware"; or for "leather lounge", long-tail keywords could be "modular home-theatre recliner". People can get fairly specific when searching for something they know they want, and your keyword choices should reflect this.

Your SEO Strategy Will Increase Traffic to Your Site if Done Correctly

In the beginning stages of releasing online content, you may notice the amount of traffic to your site is less than satisfactory. You may feel that you're doing everything right but all your efforts seem ineffective. Troubleshooting begins by ensuring that you are not doing the following things:

- Regularly distributing generic templates and content that doesn't offer any value.
- Using content that's redundant, boring, or not unique.
- Being concerned about regularly releasing content without being aware of its quality.
- Doing keyword searches after writing an article instead of before.

These tactics aren't necessarily wrong, but because they are implemented in the wrong way, they will remain ineffective. In order for your site to stand out from the rest you need to release content that's unique and valuable. If you have a third party writing your content for you, working with them will ensure the right type of content is produced. Even though releasing incredible content is valuable, it's not the factor that will make your site SEO-friendly.

SEO strategies and content marketing will feel overwhelming at first. Whereas other forms of marketing are straightforward and easily performed by people with some experience, content marketing and SEO principles require lateral and unconventional thinking. Content marketing and SEO are designed to promote the published content, and don't necessarily focus on your business or branding. If implemented well, the content is going to be viewed regularly and build a sense of loyalty to and trust in your brand or business.

Keep in mind that many online users become lazy and don't want to search for information that is easily accessible to them. If you offer content that's exceptional and what they're looking for, they will be more willing to purchase products or services, regardless of what you're selling. This is why quality is always more important than quantity. Don't focus on releasing a blog every month if they're not being viewed. Keep the posts simple, entertaining, educational, and unique. This will inspire readers to keep reading.

Finally, educate yourself on different SEO principles so that you can increase the ranking of your site when it's searched. Employing a copywriter to help with your SEO-driven content may be to your advantage if you aren't a strong writer, or don't have a strong writer on your staff. Many copywriters are well-trained in SEO, and they will be able to help build your site in the beginning stages of your business, as well as assist you with quality content every time you upload new information. This may be a useful expense to budget for. If you prefer to manage this work yourself, ensure that you double-check the writing and perform keyword searches before your content is written. Working backward is time-consuming and ineffective.

The Authors Approach

I have been running my blog since 2012. My main blog at (www.stephenhaunts.com) is a general blog about subjects that interest me. The website for this book is focused on the subject of starting and running a business. When I write a post on either of the blogs, I like to use the Google keyword analysis tools to find a series of popular keywords that people are using. By including those keywords in my posts, and any associated metadata and image ALT tags, it helps my blog rank higher in Google searches. For example, if I were writing about "Dealing with Criticism", I might use keywords like *criticism, critique, how do you handle criticism,* or *coping with criticism.* These are alternatives that I found with the Google Keyword Planner tool. By including them in the blog post, I increase my chances of the post ranking well with Google.

When I have released training courses in the past, I have written blog posts about the new releases. In those posts, I try to add relevant keywords to increase the chances of someone finding the post and then discovering my courses.

The same techniques also apply to selling books on Amazon. When you set up your book on the Kindle Direct Publishing (KDP) platform, you have to write a book description; for this, you can select seven specific keywords. Specifying the right keywords here is crucial to good discoverability. Amazon is a search engine, just like Google, so you need to apply SEO. When finding keywords for Amazon books, I use a tool called KDP Spy. KDP Spy is similar in principle to the Google Keyword Planner, in that you specify a search term and it will suggest alternatives that people have searched for on Amazon and what the competition is for those keywords.

Optimising for search is fundamental to discoverability on any platform where you can search, so you need to spend some time planning your keywords. Even sites like Instagram, Twitter and YouTube need to be optimised. One way to help with discoverability on those platforms is using specific hashtags that people sometimes subscribe to; if you include that tag in your post, they will be more likely to see it and discover the message you are trying to convey. When setting up advertising campaigns on Twitter, you can use hashtags when you are specifying the audience you want to target. For example, you might target people who subscribe to the #sidehustle tag.

SEO takes a lot of experimentation. It effectively comes down to good keyword research, and if you are writing blogs and content that people can land on from a search engine, having other sites link to your content helps raise your chances of appearing high up in search results.

Summary

Content marketing is a technique that creates and distributes consistent, relevant, and valuable content to attract a specific target audience. Whenever a person/marketer decides to release a product, they will need to make sure that product appeals to their target audience. Content marketing attracts leads, and those can become customers when they feel drawn to your product.

Content marketing is valuable and educational, but it has nothing to do with the actual products that a business sells. Offering readers valuable information means they are more likely to become loyal to the brand because of that information offered to them rather than the products/services that the business offers.

It does seem like an obvious thing to do to help grow your business, but keep in mind that many individuals involved in content marketing strongly suggest that it's not for everyone. It's an indirect method that takes a lot of time, effort, and energy for it to work effectively.

However, if you're willing to put the work in, it can be one of the greatest tools that you can use. This approach provides a better overall experience for your customers and gives them a positive perception of your brand and your business.

Search engine optimisation (SEO) works with organic search results to drive traffic to your site by using specific keywords and relevant links to improve your site's ranking.

Successfully employing SEO methods will make your site more visible and could potentially rank you higher than your competition. SEO methods were refined years ago because people started understanding how to use those methods to promote their sales. But as the internet evolved with the technology, many sites began offering users direct answers to their questions, to increase the probability of users staying on one site instead of going to others, which reduces the traffic for other sites accordingly. This means SEO principles have also had to evolve over the years.

Your marketing strategies are entirely up to you, and you can decide how you want to market your product, business, brand, and content. Using methods like content marketing and SEO will greatly benefit your business and will increase online traffic to your site. This will increase the number of customers that you have, and it will increase your profit margins.

Educate yourself on SEO principles and consider the help of a copywriter to get your content up and running.

Workshop Questions

(1) Use a tool like the Google Keyword Planner to test keywords for your content. This tool allows you to see how popular different keywords are when searched. Be as thorough as you can with different keywords that are relevant to your product or service.

(2) When you have a list of keywords, plan a series of content for your website or blog that incorporates those keywords. By including keyword-rich content on your site, you will improve your organic results through search engines.

FINAL THOUGHTS

We have now come to the end of this book. My goal was to offer a helping hand to anyone that likes the idea of starting a business, but is worried, scared, or reluctant to get started. Starting a business can be highly rewarding, but I can understand why people might be nervous about doing it. I know because I myself was terrified of starting a business.

When you venture into business for the first time, you can start as small as you are comfortable with by running the business on the side of your main employment. In fact, the only actual difference between a side-hustle and a full-time business venture is the time you dedicate to it. You can start off gradually, building up products and customers, and stay that way for as long as you are comfortable. If after a few years you have enough money saved and enough repeat business that you can go full time without taking on too much personal risk, then you have the option to do so.

Starting off on the side was exactly what I did when I began creating online training courses. I was perfectly happy working this way until I was happy that by going full time, I was not taking on too much risk.

In the modern internet age, there are many services available to you that enable you to set up a business with minimum expense and technical skill. It used to be that to get a website and online shop open, and to accept payments from debit or credit cards, you had to be a reasonably proficient software developer, or pay someone to build your site for you. These days, this is not the case. You can build a good-sized, profitable and professional-looking business without ever having to type a line of code.

Services like Shopify or Squarespace allow you to set up a good-looking website and sell your physical or digital goods. They handle payments, inventory management, and customer account processing. You can be up and running quickly. Amazon offers many services to allow you to flourish as a business owner. If you are selling physical goods, you can make use of their marketplace, and offer your products against other sellers.

Amazon will even let you send your stock to them so they can dispatch items for you, meaning customers can take advantage of their Amazon Prime delivery benefits. Naturally, doing something like this will affect the overall profit margin with Amazon's fees; but what you lose in overall margin, you can hopefully make up in volume.

If you are creating physically printed books or e-books, you can also have Amazon sell them for you. Their Kindle e-book platform is the most popular and successful e-book platform in existence. If you sell e-books exclusively through Amazon, you can take advantage of their 70% royalty rate. If you wish to produce paperback books, Amazon will even print the books on demand as customers order them, which means you no longer need to print lots of copies upfront with the risk of not being able to sell them. This has really been a revolution in publishing, and something I have taken advantage of myself to significant effect.

If you are in the business of creating training courses, then there are many platforms you can upload content to and make money from, such as Skillshare, Udemy, Teachable, and many more.

The barrier to entry for creating a business online has never been lower, and the demand for online products and services is growing every year. During the global coronavirus pandemic, many people changed their shopping habits and switched to online shopping—not always because they wanted to, but because they had to. Once you have changed a habit and experienced the convenience of shopping online, or using an online service, it is hard to switch back.

Lots of companies that previously had a physical bricks-and-mortar presence have started offering their products and services online. They had to adapt just to stay in business while they could not be physically open. Demand for online products and services will always be there, and the tools to create these businesses get better every year.

I hope this book has helped to inspire you to take action. I really understand the fear of getting started, but once you do, it feels liberating. When you make the first sale of a product, or get your first service subscriber, you will feel as though you have achieved the impossible. If you can make one sale, you can make a second. Before long, with a fair wind behind you, you can scale a business to what you need to survive.

Some people create a side-hustle business and never go full time, as they enjoy it being a profitable hobby. This is also perfectly ok. There are no rules that state you have to create a full-time business. There are also no rules that you have to seek investment, hire lots of staff, or occupy a vast set of offices. For my business, I never intend to hire anyone full time. I like the fact that it is just me. If I need help with anything, I hire a freelancer to help me out. The freelancer gig economy is booming, and there are lots of people all over the world with the skills to assist you.

All you need is an idea, some motivation, and an internet connection and you can get started.

I wish you all the best and I hope you too can create a business that helps you realise your dreams.

VISIT US AT YOUTUBE

If you like the contents of this book, then please visit me over at YouTube where I talk about running small businesses and give updates on my own business.

http://bit.ly/PathToFreedomBook

SIDE HUSTLE SUCCESS PODCAST

Alongside this book, I also run a podcast called the Side Hustle Success Podcast, where I talk about various aspects of running small businesses.

The show is available on most podcast platforms such as iTunes, Spotify, Stitcher and many more.

https://www.sidehustlesuccesspodcast.com

THANK YOU!

Thank you for buying and reading this book. If you enjoyed what you read, then I would be grateful if you could leave a review on Amazon, Goodreads, or the store that you bought the book from.

www.ingramcontent.com/pod-product-compliance
Lightning Source LLC
Chambersburg PA
CBHW071553080526
44588CB00010B/897